Practical Domain-Driven Design in Enterprise Java

Using Jakarta EE, Eclipse MicroProfile, Spring Boot, and the Axon Framework

Vijay Nair

Apress®

Practical Domain-Driven Design in Enterprise Java: Using Jakarta EE, Eclipse MicroProfile, Spring Boot, and the Axon Framework

Vijay Nair
Mountain View, CA, USA

ISBN-13 (pbk): 978-1-4842-4542-2
https://doi.org/10.1007/978-1-4842-4543-9

ISBN-13 (electronic): 978-1-4842-4543-9

Managing Director, Apress Media LLC: Welmoed Spahr
Acquisitions Editor: Steve Anglin
Development Editor: Matthew Moodie
Coordinating Editor: Mark Powers

Cover designed by eStudioCalamar

Cover image designed by Freepik (www.freepik.com)

Distributed to the book trade worldwide by Springer Science+Business Media New York, 233 Spring Street, 6th Floor, New York, NY 10013. Phone 1-800-SPRINGER, fax (201) 348-4505, e-mail orders-ny@springer-sbm.com, or visit www.springeronline.com. Apress Media, LLC is a California LLC and the sole member (owner) is Springer Science + Business Media Finance Inc (SSBM Finance Inc). SSBM Finance Inc is a **Delaware** corporation.

For information on translations, please e-mail editorial@apress.com; for reprint, paperback, or audio rights, please email bookpermissions@springernature.com.

Apress titles may be purchased in bulk for academic, corporate, or promotional use. eBook versions and licenses are also available for most titles. For more information, reference our Print and eBook Bulk Sales web page at http://www.apress.com/bulk-sales.

Any source code or other supplementary material referenced by the author in this book is available to readers on GitHub via the book's product page, located at www.apress.com/9781484245422. For more detailed information, please visit http://www.apress.com/source-code.

Printed on acid-free paper

To Tina and Maya

Table of Contents

About the Author

Vijay Nair is currently Director of Platform Engineering for Oracle's Banking SaaS applications. A Domain Driven Design (DDD) and distributed systems enthusiast, he has around 18 years of experience in architecting, building, and implementing mission-critical applications for the financial services industry around the world. He can be reached at his personal web site `www.practicalddd.com` or via Twitter at `@FusionVJ`. He lives in Mountain View, CA with his wife and daughter.

About the Technical Reviewer

Manuel Jordan Elera is an autodidactic developer and researcher who enjoys learning new technologies for his own experiments and creating new integrations. Manuel won the Springy Award – Community Champion and Spring Champion 2013. In his little free time, he reads the Bible and composes music on his guitar. Manuel is known as dr_pompeii. He has tech-reviewed numerous books for Apress, including *Pro Spring, Fourth Edition* (2014); *Practical Spring LDAP* (2013); *Pro JPA 2, Second Edition* (2013); and *Pro Spring Security* (2013). Read his 13 detailed tutorials about many Spring technologies, contact him through his blog site at www.manueljordanelera.blogspot.com, and follow him on his Twitter account, @dr_pompeii.

Acknowledgments

The first person I would like to wholeheartedly thank for making this book possible is Jakarta EE (Enterprise Edition) guru Reza Rahman. While at Oracle, he kick-started the Cargo Tracker initiative as a blueprint for Java EE Patterns based on DDD. The opportunity that he gave me to participate in the project is something that I will always be grateful for.

Thanks to fellow DDD and Axon Framework enthusiast Swapnil Surve, an architect based out of Phoenix, for the content review and suggestions for Chapters 5 and 6. A special thanks to Allard Buijze (Creator of the Axon Framework) for the content review for Chapter 6.

Thanks to all the folks at Oracle who helped support the writing of the book, my senior management (Vikram, Ticks, Chet), and my own team who educate me every day (Sourabh, Shripad, Hari, Pawan, Dasharath, and Mahendran).

To the City of Mountain View, CA, thank you for providing the sanctuary of a fabulous library where many an hour has been spent writing this book.

Writing a book with a newborn is something sane people do not do. The support provided by my family has been immense during this entire journey, and I am eternally grateful for that.

Thanks to my brothers, Gautam, Rohit, Sumit, and Sachin; to my sister, Vinitha, and her husband, Madhu; to my other babies, Varun and Arya; and finally to my parents and my wife's parents for sacrificing their time to be with us and helping us out.

Last but not the least, to my wife, Tina. Juggling work, taking care of the kid, and ensuring I got my writing time required a superhuman effort with a lot of personal sacrifice. This book is as much yours as it is mine. Thank you!

Introduction

Domain Driven Design has never been more relevant than in today's world of software development. DDD concepts and patterns help build well-designed enterprise applications, be it traditional monoliths or new age microservices-based applications.

This book aims to demystify the concepts of Domain Driven Design by providing a practical approach to its implementation for traditional monolithic applications as well as for new age microservices applications. Using a reference application – Cargo Tracker – the book walks through detailed implementations of the various DDD patterns for both styles of applications utilizing various tools and frameworks from the Enterprise Java Space (Jakarta EE, Eclipse MicroProfile, Spring Boot, and the Axon Framework). This gives a complete rounded view to the reader of the book intending to use any of these frameworks for their DDD journey.

Enjoy reading!

CHAPTER 1

Domain Driven Design

Domain Driven Design offers a solid, systematic, and comprehensive approach to software design and development. It provides a set of tools and techniques which helps break down business complexity while keeping the core business model as the centerpiece of the approach.

DDD has been a preferred approach for traditional (read monolithic) projects for a long time, and with the advent of the microservices architecture, DDD concepts are being increasingly applied even to this new architecture paradigm.

The book is split into two broad parts.

Modeling of DDD Concepts

Implementing DDD starts with a modeling process to identify artifacts (sub-domains, bounded contexts, domain model, domain rules) that map to DDD concepts. The book spends the first couple of chapters giving a high-level overview of DDD concepts and then outlines a complete modeling process to identify and document the related artifacts walking through the use cases of our reference application.

Implementation of DDD Concepts

The book then deep dives into the implementations of these concepts. Using Enterprise Java as the fundamental platform, it walks through three different implementations:

- The first implementation details the implementation of the DDD concepts based on a monolithic architecture using the Java EE/Jakarta EE platform.

- The second implementation details the implementation of the DDD concepts based on a microservices architecture on the MicroProfile platform.

- Finally, the third implementation details the implementation of the DDD concepts based on a microservices architecture on the Spring platform.

© Vijay Nair 2019
V. Nair, *Practical Domain-Driven Design in Enterprise Java*, https://doi.org/10.1007/978-1-4842-4543-9_1

The implementations cover the three main dominant platforms that are prevalent in the Enterprise Java space and provide complete details on implementation of the DDD patterns.

DDD Concepts

With the intent of the book clear, let us step into the DDD journey by going through a quick tour of its concepts.

Problem Space/Business Domain

The first main concept of DDD that we would need to familiarize ourselves with is the identification of the "Problem Space" or the "Business Domain." The Problem Space/ Business Domain is the starting point of the DDD journey, and it identifies the main business problem that you intend to solve using DDD.

Let us elaborate on this concept using some practical examples.

The first example takes a case from the auto finance industry as illustrated in Figure 1-1. If you are in the auto finance business, you are in the business of managing auto loans and leases, that is, you as an auto finance provider need to grant loans/ leases to consumers, service them, and finally if problems arise collect them back or terminate them. The *problem space* in this case can be classified as Auto Loans/Lease Management which can also be termed as your *core business domain* and a *business problem* that you would like to solve using Domain Driven Design.

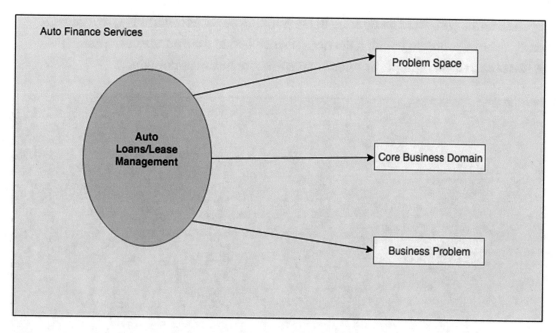

Figure 1-1. *The Auto Finance Services Problem Space*

The second example takes a case from the banking industry. Unlike the first example, in this case there are not one but multiple problem spaces that need to be solved using Domain Driven Design (Figure 1-2).

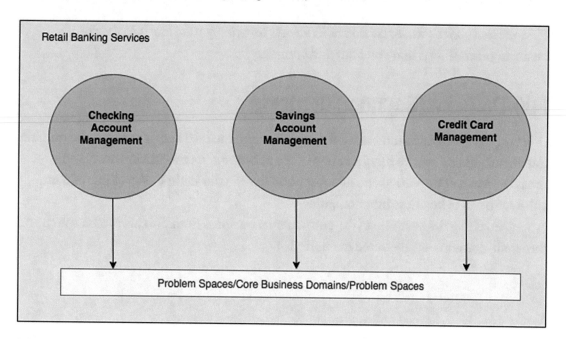

Figure 1-2. *Business Domains within a Retail Banking Service*

As a bank, you could be offering Retail Banking Services (Figure 1-2) to a general customer or Corporate Banking Services (Figure 1-3) to a corporate customer. These services each have multiple problem spaces or core business domains.

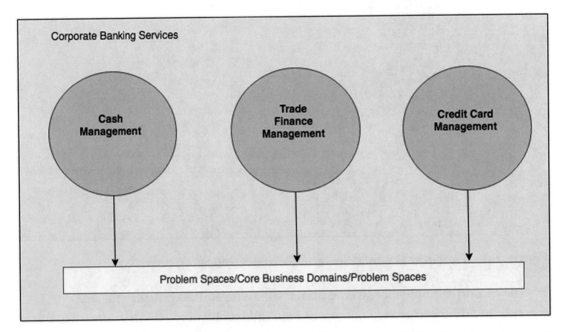

Figure 1-3. *Core Business Domains within a Corporate Banking Service*

Problem spaces/business domains always invariably translate into the core business propositions that you offer as a company.

Sub-Domains/Bounded Contexts

Once we have identified the main Business Domain, the next step is to break the domain into its sub-domains. The identification of the sub-domains essentially involves the breaking down of the various business capabilities of your main business domain into cohesive units of business functionalities.

Again, citing the example of the auto finance business domain, this can be split into three sub-domains as illustrated in Figure 1-4.

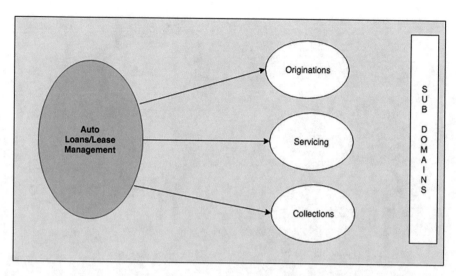

Figure 1-4. *Sub-Domains within the Auto Finance Business Domain*

- ***Originations Sub-Domain*** – This sub-domain takes care of the business capability of issuing new auto loans/leases to customers.

- ***Servicing Sub-Domain*** – This sub-domain takes care of the business capability of servicing (e.g., monthly billing/payments) these auto loans/leases.

- ***Collections Sub-Domain*** – This sub-domain takes care of the business capability of managing these auto loans/leases if something goes wrong (e.g., customer defaults on payment).

As is evident, the sub-domains are determined in terms of business capabilities of your main business that are used on a day-to-day basis.

Shown in Figure 1-5 is another example of determining the sub-domains for one of our Retail Banking Business Domains – Credit Card Management Business Domain.

5

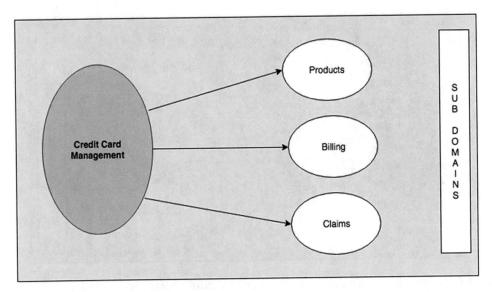

Figure 1-5. *Sub-Domains within the Credit Card Management Business Domain*

- ***Products Sub-Domain*** – This sub-domain takes care of the business capability of managing all types of credit card products.

- ***Billing Sub-Domain*** – This sub-domain takes care of the business capability of billing for a customer's credit card.

- ***Claims Sub-Domain*** – This sub-domain takes care of the business capability of managing any kinds of claims for a customer's credit card.

Again, emphasizing on the actual business capabilities helps in cleanly identifying the sub-domains.

So what are Bounded Contexts?

To recap, we started on our journey by identifying our Business Domains. We further elaborated on our Business Domains by breaking them into various capabilities to identify our Sub-Domains which mapped out to different capabilities within the business.

We need to start creating solutions for the corresponding domains/sub-domains identified earlier, that is, we need to move from the *Problem Space* area to the *Solution Space* area, and that's where Bounded Contexts play a central role.

Simply put, Bounded Contexts are design solutions to our identified Business Domains/Sub-Domains.

The identification of Bounded Contexts is governed primarily by the cohesiveness that you need within the business domain and between your sub-domains.

Going back to our first example of the Auto Finance Business Domain, we could choose to have a single solution for the entire domain, that is, a single bounded context for all the sub-domains; or we could choose to have a bounded context mapped to a single sub-domain / multiple sub-domains.

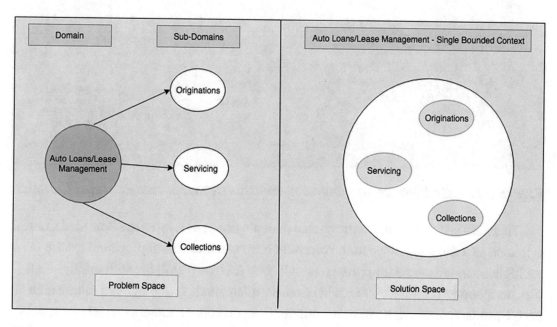

Figure 1-6. *Auto Finance Sub-Domains solutioned as a single Bounded Context*

The solution in Figure 1-6 for the Auto Loans/Lease Management problem space is a single bounded context for all the sub-domains.

Another approach is to solution the different sub-domains within the Auto Finance Domain as separate Bounded Contexts. Figure 1-7 demonstrates that.

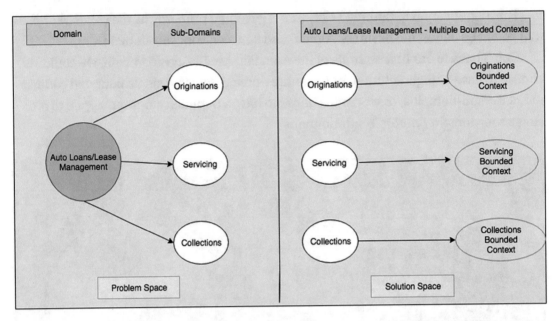

Figure 1-7. *Auto Finance Sub-Domains solutioned as separate Bounded Contexts*

There are no restrictions to the choice of deployment as long as the Bounded Context is treated as a single cohesive unit. You could have a monolithic deployment for the multiple bounded contexts approach (single Web Archive [WAR] file with multiple JAR files per Bounded context), you could choose a microservices deployment model with each bounded context as a separate container, or you could choose a serverless model with each bounded context deployed as a function.

As part of our implementations in the subsequent chapters, we will examine every kind of deployment model available.

The Domain Model

We are now in the most important and critical part of our domain solutioning process, the establishment of the Bounded Context's Domain Model. In short, the Domain Model is the implementation of the core business logic within a specific Bounded Context.

In business language, this involves identifying

- Business Entities

- Business Rules

- Business Flows

- Business Operations

- Business Events

In technical language within the DDD world, this translates into identifying

- Aggregates/Entities/Value Objects

- Domain Rules

- Sagas

- Commands/Queries

- Events

This is illustrated in Figure 1-8. As depicted, the business language constructs are mapped to their corresponding DDD technical language constructs.

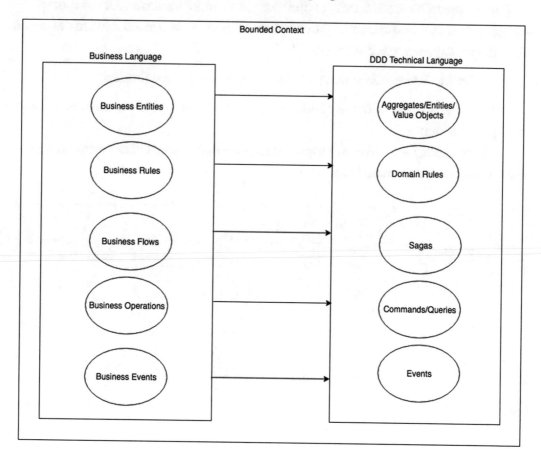

Figure 1-8. *The Domain Model of a Bounded Context in terms of a business language and its corresponding technical language within the DDD paradigm*

While we will be elaborating in detail about these various concepts in the subsequent chapters, let us talk about them briefly here. If it does not make a lot of sense right now, do not worry. The subsequent chapters will ensure that you get a good grounding of these concepts.

Aggregates/Entity Objects/Value Objects

The Aggregate (also known as the root aggregate) is the central business object within your Bounded Context and defines the scope of consistency within that Bounded context. Every aspect of your Bounded Context begins and ends within your root aggregate.

Aggregate = Principal identifier of your Bounded Context

Entity Objects have an identity of their own but cannot exist without the root aggregate, that is, they are created when the root aggregate is created and are destroyed when the root aggregate is destroyed.

Entity Objects = Secondary identifiers of your Bounded Context

Value Objects have no identity and are easily replaceable within an instance of a root aggregate or an entity.

As an example, let us take the Originations Bounded Context of our Auto Loans/ Lease Management Domain (Figure 1-9).

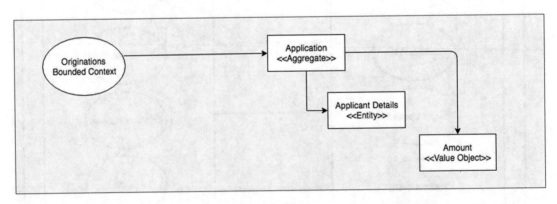

Figure 1-9. *Aggregates/Entities/Value Objects within the Originations Bounded Context*

The Loan Application Aggregate is the root aggregate within the Originations Bounded Context. Without a loan application, nothing exists within this bounded context, hence no principal identifier within this Bounded Context or the root aggregate.

The Loan Applicant Details Entity Object captures the applicant details for the loan application (demographics, address, etc.). It has an identifier of its own (Applicant ID) but cannot exist without the Loan Application, that is, when the loan application is created, the loan applicant details are created; likewise, when the loan application is cancelled, the loan applicant details are removed.

The Loan Amount Value Object denotes the loan amount for the loan application. It has no identity of its own and can be replaced in a Loan Application Aggregate instance.

Our reference application in the next chapter goes through all of these concepts in more detail, so if it does not make much sense now, do not worry. Just note that we need to identify Aggregates/Entities and Value Objects.

Domain Rules

Domain Rules are pure business rule definitions. Modeled as Objects too, they assist the Aggregate for any kind of business logic execution within the scope of a Bounded Context.

Within our Originations Bounded Context, a good example of a Domain Rule is a "State Applicant Compliance Validation" Business Rule. The rule basically states that depending upon the "state" of the Loan Application (e.g., CA, NY), additional validation checks could be applicable to the loan applicant.

The State Applicant Compliance Validation Domain Rule works with the Loan Aggregate to validate the Loan Application on the basis of the state where the Loan Application is created as illustrated in Figure 1-10.

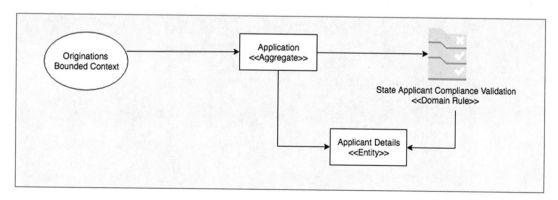

Figure 1-10. *Domain Rules within the Originations Bounded Context*

Commands/Queries

Commands and Queries represent any kind of operations within the Bounded Context which either affect the state of the aggregate/entity or query the state of the aggregate/ entity.

As illustrated in Figure 1-11, some examples of Commands within the Originations Bounded Context include "Open a Loan Account" and "Modify Loan Applicant Details," while examples of queries include "View Loan Account Details" and "View Loan Applicant Details."

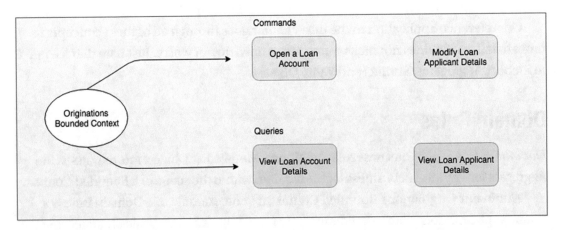

Figure 1-11. *Commands/Queries within the Originations Bounded Context*

Events

Events capture any kind of state change either with an aggregate or an entity within the Bounded Context. This is illustrated in Figure 1-12.

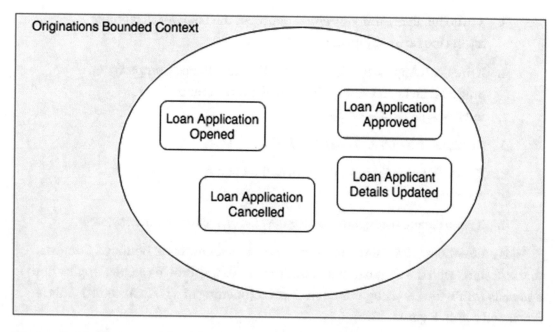

Figure 1-12. Events within the Originations Bounded Context

Sagas

The final aspect of the DDD model is to flush out any kind of business processes/ workflows within your Business Domain. In the DDD terminology, these are termed as sagas. As stated, sagas are the only artifact that is not restricted to a single Bounded Context and may span across multiple Bounded Contexts, and in most of the cases it will span across Bounded Contexts.

The Bounded Context or specifically the aggregate within a Bounded Context acts as a Saga participant. Sagas react to multiple business events across Bounded Contexts and *"orchestrate the business process"* by coordinating interactions among these Bounded Contexts.

Let us look at an example of a Saga within our Auto Finance Business Domain – opening a Loan Account.

If we lay out the business process for the opening of a Loan Account

1.   Customer puts in a ***Loan Application*** to X Auto Finance Company to purchase a new auto.

2.   X Auto Finance Company validates the Loan Application details to determine the best Loan Product for the customer.

3. X Auto Finance Company either approves the Loan Application or rejects the Loan Application.

4. If the Loan Application is approved, X Auto Finance Company presents the Loan Product Terms to the customer including interest rate, tenure, and so on.

5. Customer accepts the Loan Product Terms.

6. X Auto Finance Company approves the Loan Application post acceptance.

7. X Auto Finance Company opens a new *Loan Account* for the customer.

It is quite evident that this business process involves multiple Bounded Contexts, that is, it starts with the Originations Bounded Context (approving a Loan Application) and ends within the Servicing Bounded Context (opening of a Loan Account). This is illustrated within Figure 1-13.

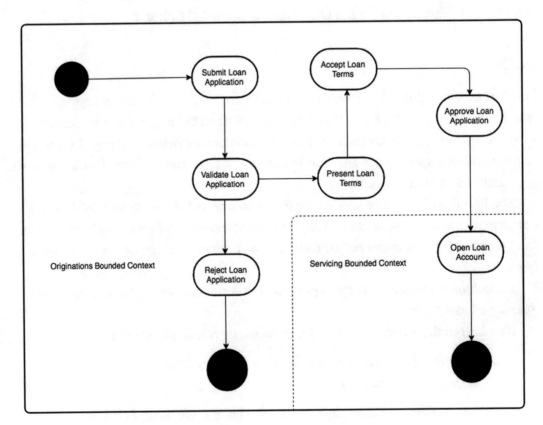

Figure 1-13. *Loan Account Opening Saga*

We now have established a Domain model for our Business Domain and are ready for implementing it.

Summary

Summarizing our chapter

- We started by establishing the main problem space or the business problem that we intended to solve using DDD.

- Once that was established, we split the problem space into multiple business capabilities or sub-domains. We then started moving into the solution space by determining Bounded Contexts.

- The final part was a deep dive into the solution space by establishing the Domain Model for the Bounded Context. This involved identification of Aggregates/Operations/Process Flows within each Bounded Context.

CHAPTER 2

Cargo Tracker

The Cargo Tracker project will serve as the primary reference application for this book. It has been around the DDD world as a reference for DDD techniques for a long time, and during the course of this book, we will implement it utilizing the tools/techniques and capabilities offered by various Enterprise Java platforms.

The Cargo Tracker application is used by enterprises which are in the cargo business. It provides capabilities to manage the entire lifecycle of cargos including Booking, Routing, Tracking, and Handling. The application is intended to be used by the business operators, customers, and port handlers.

We will lay down the groundwork for our subsequent DDD implementations in this chapter by first establishing *a DDD-specific Domain Modeling process*. The intent of the modeling process is to capture a set of *high-level and low-level DDD artifacts*. The high-level artifacts have a low degree of implementation required, that is, these are more design concepts with minimal physical artifacts required. On the other hand, the low-level artifacts have a high degree of implementation, that is, they will be the actual physical artifacts of our implementation.

This Domain Modeling process is applicable whether we are embarking on an architecture based on Monoliths or Microservices.

Core Domain

To begin with in true DDD spirit, the first thing we state is that our Core Domain/Problem Space is Cargo Tracking and the Cargo Tracker Reference application addresses this Core Domain/Problem Space.

© Vijay Nair 2019
V. Nair, *Practical Domain-Driven Design in Enterprise Java*, https://doi.org/10.1007/978-1-4842-4543-9_2

With the core domain identified, we then establish the DDD artifacts of the Core Domain. As part of this process, we identify four main artifacts:

- Sub-Domains/Bounded Contexts of our core domain

- Domain Model

- Domain Sagas

- Domain Model Services

Figure 2-1 illustrates the Domain Modeling process.

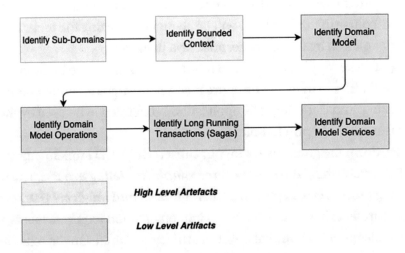

Figure 2-1. *Aggregates within our Bounded Context*

Cargo Tracker: Sub-Domains/Bounded Contexts

To identify the various sub-domains within the Cargo Core Domain/Problem Space, we split the domain into various business areas with ***each business area classified as a Sub-Domain.***

In the Cargo Tracker Domain, we have four main business areas:

- ***Booking*** – This area covers all aspects of Cargo Booking including the following:

  - Booking of cargos

  - Assigning of routes to cargos

- Modification of cargos (e.g., change of destination of a booked cargo)

- Cancellation of cargos

- *Routing* – This area covers all aspects of Cargo Itinerary including the following:

  - Optimal Itinerary allocation for cargos based on their Route Specification

  - Voyage Maintenance for the carriers that will carry cargos (e.g., addition of new routes)

- *Handling* – As the cargo progresses along its assigned route, it will need to be inspected/handled at the various ports of transit. This area covers all operations related to the Handling activity of cargos.

- *Tracking* – Customers need comprehensive, detailed, and up-to-date information of their booked cargos. The Tracking business area provides this capability.

Each of these Business Areas can be classified as Sub-Domain(s) within the DDD paradigm. While identifying Sub-Domains is part of the problem space identification, we need solutions for them too. As we have seen in the previous chapter, we use the concept of Bounded Contexts. Bounded Contexts are design solutions to our main problem space, and each Bounded Context could have a single sub-domain or multiple sub-domains mapped to it.

For all our implementations, we assume that each Bounded Context is mapped to a single Sub-Domain.

The need to capture sub-domains is irrespective of the architectural style that you intend to follow while building out your application, be it a monolithic or a microservices-based application. The idea of capturing the sub-domains is to ensure that at the end of the exercise, we have clearly separated our core domain into different business areas which are independent and can have their own business language recognizable within that specific business area/sub-domain.

Figure 2-2 illustrates the various sub-domains of our Cargo Tracker Core Domain as modules within a monolith, that is, the Bounded contexts are solutioned as modules.

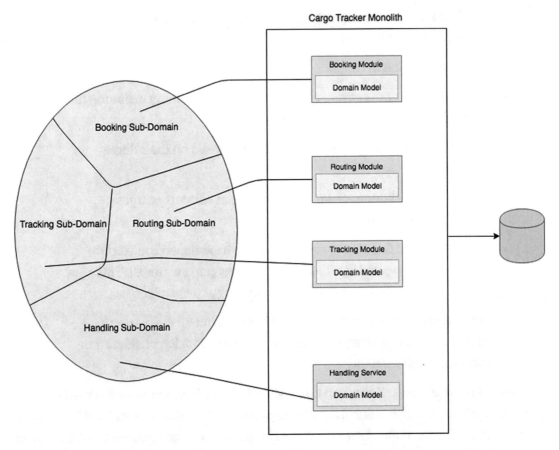

Figure 2-2. *The sub-domains of the Cargo Tracker application as separate modules within a monolith*

Figure 2-3 illustrates the various sub-domains of our Cargo Tracker Core Domain as separate microservices, that is, the Bounded Contexts are solutioned as microservices.

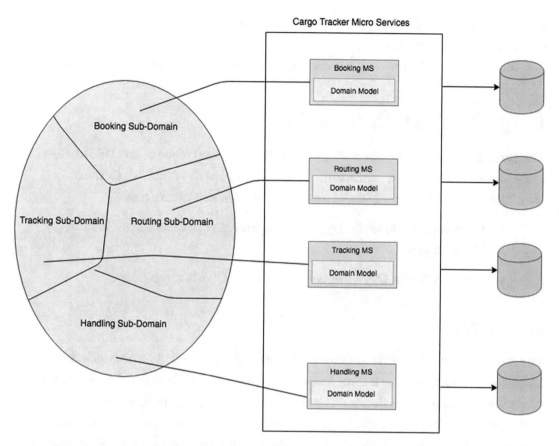

Figure 2-3. *The sub-domains of the Cargo Tracker application as separate microservices*

The design solution of these sub-domains is done via **Bounded Contexts** deployed either as **modules within a monolithic architecture** or as **separate microservices in our microservices-based architecture.**

To summarize this section, using the concept of **Business Areas**, we **partitioned our core domain** into multiple sub-domains and **identified Bounded Contexts as the solution** for them. Bounded Contexts are designed differently depending on the type of solution we are developing. In the context of a monolithic architecture, they are **implemented as Modules,** while in the context of a Microservices architecture, they are **implemented as separate microservices.** A point to note here is the design implementation of our Bounded Contexts is based on our original decision to map a Bounded Context per sub-domain. It is quite common and necessary in certain cases to solution multiple modules within the same Bounded Context in the case of a monolithic architecture and to solution multiple microservices within the same

Bounded Context in the case of a microservices based architecture. The Bounded Context is the final solution.

The next step is now to *capture the Domain Model for each Bounded Context.*

Cargo Tracker: Domain Model

The Bounded Context's Domain Model is the foundational piece of any DDD-based architecture and is used to express the Business Intent of the Bounded Context. Identification of the Domain Model involves two main sets of artifacts:

- *Core Domain Model* – Aggregates, Aggregate Identifiers, Entities, and Value Objects

- *Domain Model Operations* – Commands, Queries, and Events

Aggregates

The most fundamental and important aspect of designing the domain model is the identification of *Aggregates within a Bounded Context*. The aggregate defines the scope of consistency within your Bounded Context, that is, the aggregate consists of a root entity and a set of entity/value objects. You can consider the aggregate as a single unit wherein any operation updates the state of the aggregate as a whole. Aggregates are responsible for *capturing all State and Business Rules* associated with the Bounded Context.

Figure 2-4 illustrates the Aggregates within the Cargo Tracker's Bounded Contexts.

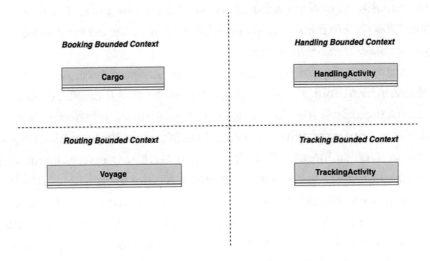

Figure 2-4. *Aggregates within the Cargo Tracker's Bounded Contexts*

Identification of aggregates helps establish the scope of each Bounded Context. Let us identify the Aggregate Identifiers for each of our Aggregates.

Aggregate Identifiers

Each Aggregate needs to be uniquely identified using an ***Aggregate Identifier***. The Aggregate Identifier is implemented using a Business key. For the Cargo Tracker implementation, Figure 2-5 illustrates the business keys for our Aggregates.

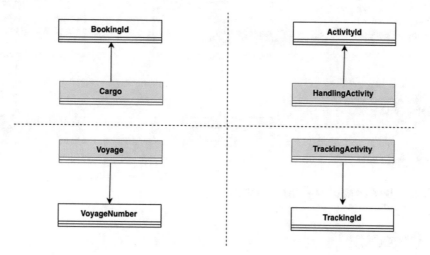

Figure 2-5. *Aggregate Identifiers for our Aggregates using Business Keys*

Each Bounded Context expresses its Domain Logic through a set of ***associations on the Aggregate implemented via Entities and Value Objects***. Let us identify those within the Cargo Tracker application.

Entities

Entities within a Bounded Context have an identity of their own but cannot exist without the Aggregate. In addition to that, Entities within an Aggregate cannot be replaced. Let us look at an example to help define the rules to identify Entities.

Within the Cargo Aggregate (Booking Bounded Context), as part of the Booking process, the booking clerk needs to specify the origin of the cargo. This is mapped as an Entity object, that is, Location which clearly has an identity of its own but also cannot exist on its own without the Cargo Aggregate.

Figure 2-6 illustrates the Entity objects within our Bounded Contexts. The thumb rule to identify Entities is to ensure that they have an identity of their own and that they cannot be replaced within the Aggregate.

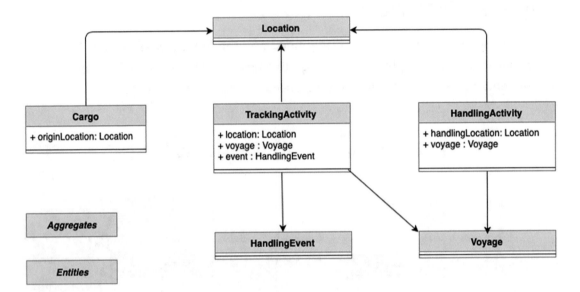

Figure 2-6. *An example of our Entities*

Value Objects

Value Objects within a Bounded Context have no identity of their own and are replaceable in any instance of an aggregate.

Let us look at an example to help define the rules to identify Value Objects.
The Cargo Aggregate has the following Value Objects:

- ***Booking Amount*** of the cargo.

- ***Route specification*** (Origin Location, Destination Location, Destination Arrival Deadline).

- ***Itinerary*** that the cargo is assigned to based on the Route Specification. The Itinerary consists of multiple ***Legs*** that the cargo might be routed through to get to the destination.

- *Delivery Progress* of the cargo against its Route Specification and Itinerary assigned to it. The Delivery Progress provides details on the *Routing Status, Transport Status, Current Voyage of the cargo, Last Known Location of the cargo, Next Expected Activity, and the Last Activity that occurred on the cargo.*

Let us walk through the scenarios and the rationale why we have these as value objects and not as entities because it is an *important domain modeling decision*:

- When a new cargo is booked, we will have *a new Route Specification, an empty Cargo Itinerary,* and *no delivery progress*.

- As the cargo is assigned an itinerary, the *empty Cargo Itinerary* is replaced by an *allocated Cargo Itinerary.*

- As the cargo progresses through multiple ports as part of its itinerary, the *Delivery* progress is updated and replaced within the Cargo Aggregate.

- Finally, if the customer chooses to change the delivery location of the cargo or the deadline for delivery, the *Route Specification changes,* a *new Cargo Itinerary* will be assigned, the *Delivery is recalculated,* and the *Booking Amount changes.*

They have *no identity of their own,* and they are *replaceable within the Cargo Aggregate and thus modeled as Value Objects.* That is the *thumb rule for identifying Value Objects.*

Figure 2-7 illustrates the complete class diagram for the Cargo Aggregate after addition of the Value Objects.

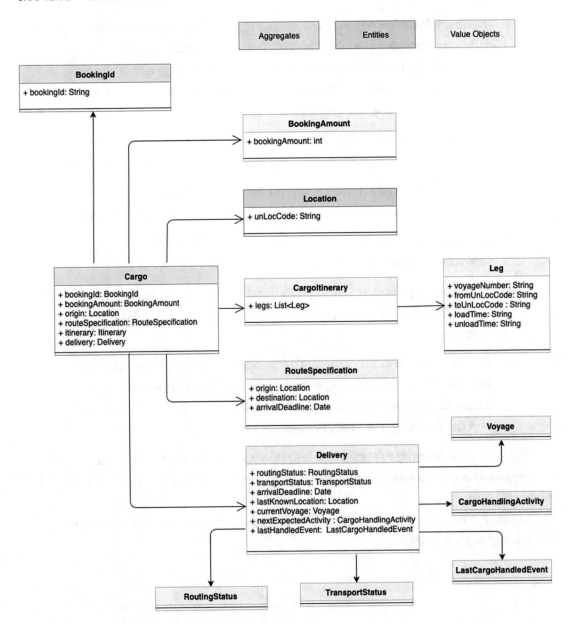

Figure 2-7. *Cargo Aggregate Class Diagram*

Let us look at abbreviated class diagrams for the other Aggregates, starting with HandlingActivity (Figure 2-8).

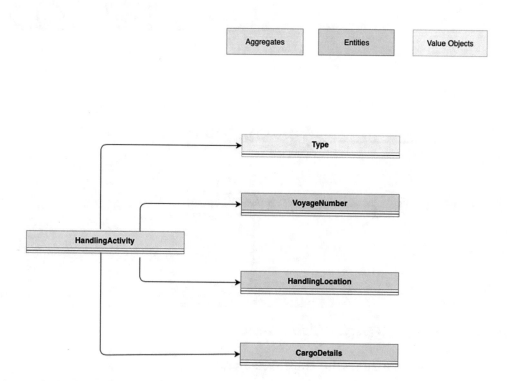

Figure 2-8. *Handling Activity Class Diagram*

Figure 2-9 shows the Voyage aggregate.

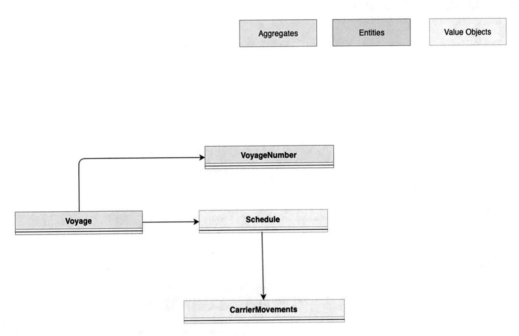

Figure 2-9. *Voyage Aggregate Class Diagram*

Finally, Figure 2-10 shows the Tracking activity.

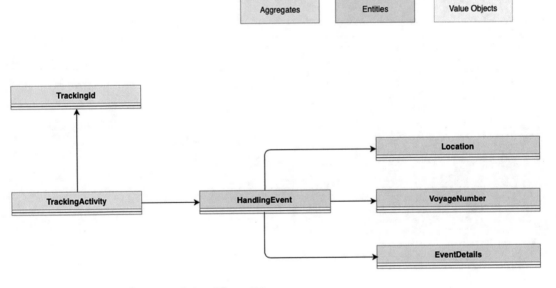

Figure 2-10. *Tracking Activity Class Diagram*

Note   *The source code for the book has the Core Domain Model demonstrated via package segregation. You can view the source code to get a clearer view of the types of objects within the domain model at* www.github.com/apress/ practical-ddd-in-enterprise-java.

Cargo Tracker: Domain Model Operations

We have outlined the Bounded Contexts of the Cargo Tracker and flushed out the Core Domain Model for each of them. The next step is to capture the Domain Model Operations that occur within a Bounded Context.

Operations within a Bounded Context might be

- **Commands** that request a change of state within the Bounded Context

- **Queries** that request the state of the Bounded Context

- **Events** that notify the state change of the Bounded Context

Figure 2-11 illustrates the systemic operations within the Bounded Context.

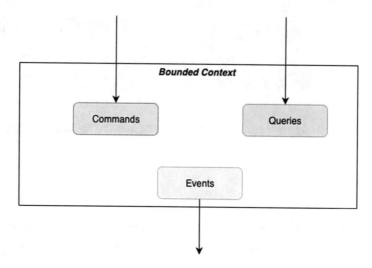

Figure 2-11. *Systemic Operations within a Bounded Context*

Figure 2-12 illustrates the Domain Model Operations for our Cargo Tracker's Bounded Contexts.

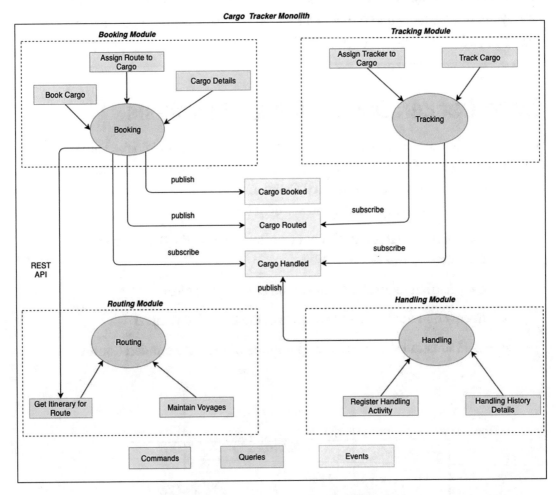

Figure 2-12. *Domain Model operations for our Cargo Tracker's Bounded Contexts*

Sagas

Sagas are used primarily when we adopt the microservices architectural style for developing our applications. The distributed nature of microservices application requires us to implement a mechanism to maintain data consistency for use cases that may span across multiple microservices. Sagas help us implement that. Sagas can be implemented in two ways either via ***Event Choreography*** or via ***Event Orchestration:***

- Implementation of choreography-based sagas is straightforward in the sense that **microservices** participating in a particular Saga will raise and subscribe to events directly.

- On the other hand, in orchestration-based Sagas, the lifecycle coordination happens through a central component. This central component is responsible for Saga creation, coordination of the flow across the various Bounded Contexts participating in the Saga, and finally the Saga Termination itself.

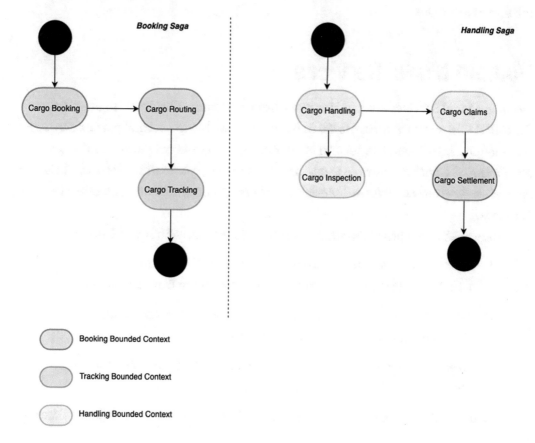

Figure 2-13. *Sagas within the Cargo Tracker Application*

Figure 2-13 illustrates a couple of Sagas within the Cargo Tracker application.

The Booking Saga involves the business operations within Cargo Booking, Cargo Routing, and Cargo Tracking. It starts with the cargo being booked to its subsequent routing and finally ends with the Tracking Identifier allocated to the booked cargo. This Tracking Identifier is used by the customers to track the progress of the cargo.

The Handling Saga involves the business operations within Cargo Handling, Inspection, Claims, and Final Settlement. It starts with the cargo being handled at the ports where it undergoes a voyage and claimed by the customer at the final destination and ends with the final settlement of the cargo (e.g., penalty for late delivery).

Both these Sagas span across multiple Bounded Contexts/Microservices, and the transactional consistency needs to be maintained across all these Bounded Contexts at the end of the Sagas.

Domain Model Services

Domain Model Services are used for two primary reasons. The first is to enable the **Bounded Context's Domain Model** to be made available to external parties **through** well-defined Interfaces. The second is interacting with external parties be it to **persist the Bounded Context's state to** Datastores (Databases), **publish the Bounded Context's state change events to external** Message Brokers, or communicate with other Bounded Contexts.

There are three types of Domain Model Services for any Bounded Context:

- **Inbound Services** where we implement well-defined interfaces which enable external parties to interact with the Domain Model

- **Outbound Services** where we implement all interactions with External Repositories/other Bounded Contexts

- **Application Services** which act as the façade layer between the Domain Model and both Inbound and Outbound services

Figure 2-14 illustrates the set of Domain Model Services within the Cargo Tracker Monolith.

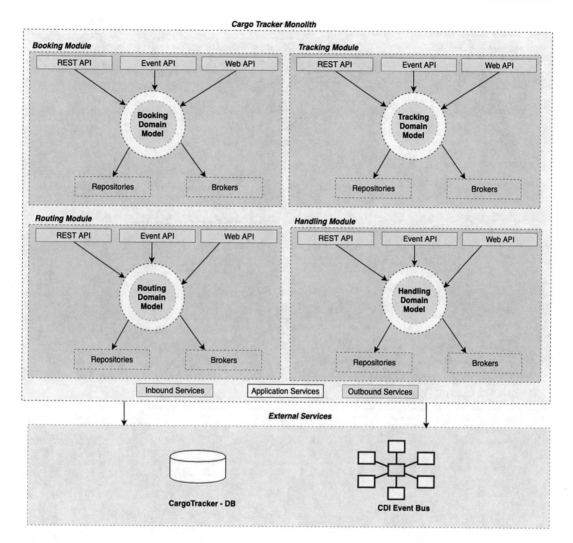

Figure 2-14. *Domain Model Services within the Cargo Tracker Monolith*

Figure 2-15 illustrates the set of Domain Model Services within the Cargo Tracker Microservices. Unlike the monolith, the microservices do not provide a native web interface.

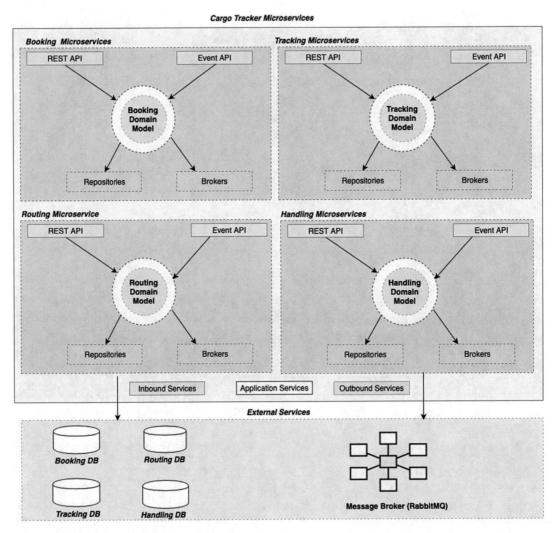

Figure 2-15. *Domain Model Services within the Cargo Tracker Microservices*

Domain Model Services Design

So how do we design these services? Which architectural pattern can we follow to implement these supporting services?

The hexagonal architectural pattern is a perfect fit to help us model/design and implement the Domain Model supporting services. Figure 2-16 illustrates the Hexagonal architectural pattern.

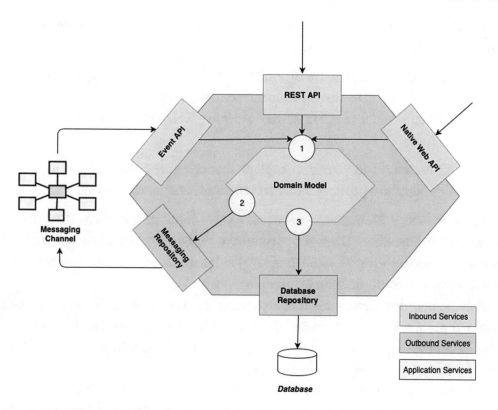

Figure 2-16. *Hexagonal Architectural Pattern*

The Hexagonal architecture uses the concept of ***ports and adaptors*** to implement the Domain Model Services. Let us expand on this concept a bit.

A port in the hexagonal architectural pattern could either be an inbound port or an outbound port:

- An inbound port provides an interface to the business operations of our domain model. This is typically implemented via the Application Services. Look at (1).

- An outbound port provides an interface to the technical operations required by our domain model. The Domain Model uses these interfaces to store or publish any kind of state from the sub-domain. Look at (2) and (3).

An adaptor in the hexagonal architectural pattern could either be an ***Inbound Adaptor or an Outbound Adaptor:***

- An inbound adaptor uses the inbound port to provide the capabilities for external clients to consume the domain model. These are implemented through REST API(s), Native Web API(s), or Event API(s).

- An outbound adaptor is an implementation of the outbound port for that specific repository. Look at Outbound Adaptors in the following.

To summarize, a "Domain Model" needs a set of supporting services also known as "Domain Model Services." These supporting services enable external clients to consume our domain model and at the same time also enable the domain model to store and publish states of the sub-domain in multiple repositories.

These supporting services are modeled using the Hexagonal Architectural Pattern wherein these services are mapped either as an "inbound/outbound port" or an "inbound/outbound adaptor." The hexagonal architectural pattern enables the "Domain Model" to be independent of these supporting services.

This rounds up our ***DDD-specific Design process***. We worked out the ***Sub-Domains/Bounded Contexts*** for our problem space, detailed out the ***Domain Model for each Bounded Context***, detailed out the ***Domain Model Operations*** that occur within the Bounded Context, and finally came up with the ***Domain Model Supporting Services*** required by the Domain Model.

This Design Process is followed irrespective of whether we are going to follow a Microservices- or a Monolithic-based architecture. We will expand on the design process and get into more detail as we start implementing the DDD artifacts identified earlier using the tools and techniques available within the Enterprise Java space.

Cargo Tracker: DDD Implementations

The subsequent chapters are going to detail the implementation of the Cargo Tracker application for the DDD artifacts we identified earlier.

As part of the implementations, we will be designing and developing the Cargo Tracker Application:

- As a DDD-based Monolith utilizing the Jakarta EE Platform

- As a DDD-based Microservices application utilizing the Eclipse MicroProfile Platform

- As a DDD-based microservices application utilizing the Spring Boot Platform

- As a DDD-based microservices application utilizing the Axon Framework

Let us proceed toward the first implementation of Cargo Tracker as a Monolith.

Summary

Summarizing our chapter

- We did an overview of our Cargo Tracker reference application and determined the Sub-Domains/Bounded Contexts for the application.

- We flushed out the Core Domain Model of the Cargo Tracker including identification of the Aggregates, Entities, and Value Objects. We also established the Domain Model operations and the Sagas associated with the Cargo Tracker application.

- We rounded off the chapter by determining the Domain Model Services required by the Cargo Tracker's Domain Model using the Hexagonal architectural pattern.

CHAPTER 3

Cargo Tracker: Jakarta EE

We now have a process in place for modeling the various DDD artifacts for any application and detailed out the same for the Cargo Tracker application.

To quickly recap

> *We identified Cargo Tracking as the main problem space/core domain and the Cargo Tracker application as the solution to address this problem space.*

> *We identified the various sub-domains/bounded contexts for the Cargo Tracker application.*

> *We detailed out the domain model for each of our bounded contexts including identification of aggregates, entities, value objects, and domain rules.*

> *We identified the supporting domain services required within the bounded contexts.*

> *We identified the various operations within our bounded contexts (Commands, Queries, Events, and Sagas).*

This rounds up the modeling phase for our DDD journey, and we have all the details in place to start our implementation phase.

Our book walks through four separate DDD implementations with Enterprise Java as the base for developing these implementations:

- A monolithic implementation using Java EE 8/Jakarta EE

- A microservices implementation based on Eclipse MicroProfile

- A microservices implementation based on Spring Boot

- A microservices implementation based on a pure play Command/ Query Responsibility Segregation (CQRS)/Event Sourcing (ES) design pattern using the Axon Framework

© Vijay Nair 2019

V. Nair, *Practical Domain-Driven Design in Enterprise Java*, https://doi.org/10.1007/978-1-4842-4543-9_3

39

The Enterprise Java landscape offers a vast ecosystem of tools, frameworks, and techniques that will help us in implementing the DDD concepts outlined in the previous chapters.

This chapter details the first DDD implementation of our Cargo Tracker application using the Java EE 8 platform as the foundation for the implementation. The Cargo Tracker application will be designed as a modular monolith, and we will map the DDD artifacts to the corresponding implementations available within the Java EE 8 platform.

First, here is an overview of the Java EE platform.

The Java EE Platform

The Java EE (Enterprise Edition) platform has been the standard for enterprise application development for close to 20 years. The platform proposes a set of specifications covering a range of technical capabilities required by enterprises for building applications in a scaleable, secure, robust, and standard way.

The goal of the platform is to simplify the developer experience by enabling them to build out the business functionalities while the platform does the heavy lifting of the system services via the implementation of the specifications using an Application Server.

Led by Oracle, the platform has wide acceptance and great community participation and has close to 15 vendor implementations of the various specifications. The current version of the platform is Java EE 8 with the Oracle GlassFish Application Server v. 5.0 providing the reference application.

Rebranding to Jakarta EE and the Way Forward

In 2017, Oracle along with the support of IBM and Red Hat decided to move the Java EE sources to the Eclipse Foundation under a new project **EE4J (Eclipse Enterprise for Java)**. The purpose of the movement was to create a nimbler governing process with a faster release cadence to keep up with the rapidly evolving technological landscape in the enterprise space.

EE4J is a top-level project within the Eclipse Foundation to which all the Java EE sources, Reference Implementations, and TCKs (Technology Compatibility Kits) are being transferred. The Jakarta EE platform is a project under EE4J and aims to be the future platform that will replace the current Java EE platform.

> *In short, all new specification releases or maintenance specification*
> *releases will now be made on Jakarta EE, and the Java EE 8 would*
> *be the last version of that platform.*

Jakarta EE has already seen tremendous momentum with multiple vendors signing up to the working committees and aims to modernize the stack to be relevant for traditional enterprise applications and at the same time align with new cloud-native/ microservices-based architectures.

The first version of the Jakarta EE platform aims to be an exact replica of the Java EE 8 platform with the focus primarily on the transfer process of the various specifications between Oracle and the Eclipse Foundation. The first reference implementation under the new Jakarta EE Platform brand has been released as Eclipse GlassFish 5.1 which is certified as Java EE 8 compatible.

This chapter would focus on the release of GlassFish which is Java EE 8 compatible and the first release on the Jakarta EE platform - Eclipse GlassFish 5.1. Our aim in this chapter is to implement the DDD concepts within the Cargo Tracker Reference Application based on a traditional monolithic architectural style.

Let us deep dive into the specifications.

Jakarta EE Platform Specifications

The Jakarta EE (based on Java EE 8) specifications are vast and aim to provide a standard set of capabilities that enterprises require to build applications. The specifications continuously evolve through multiple versions, and capabilities are added or modified either as new specifications or maintenance specifications.

The specifications are grouped into two profiles – Full Profile or Web Profile. The concept of profiles was introduced to categorize the capabilities required by applications. For pure web applications, the Web Profile specification provides the required set of capabilities (Java Persistence API [JPA], Contexts and Dependency Injection [CDI], Java API for RESTful Web Services [JAX-RS]), while for larger complex applications which might require, say, messaging capabilities or have legacy application integration requirements, the Full Profile provides the additional capabilities.

For our purposes, the Web Profile is more than adequate to help us implement Cargo Tracker in a monolithic architectural style, so we will expand only on that set of specifications.

The Web Profile set of specifications for Jakarta EE (based on Java EE 8) is illustrated in Figure 3-1 grouped by the area it covers. The official URL to access these specifications is www.oracle.com/technetwork/java/javaee/tech/index.html.

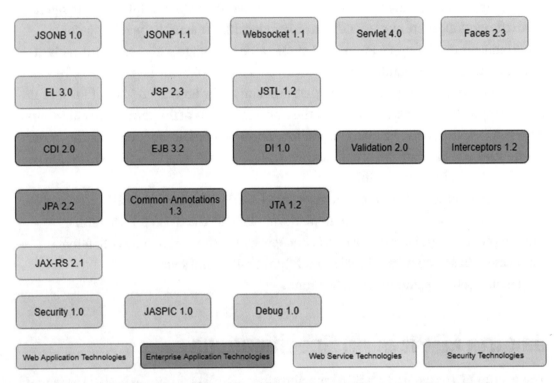

Figure 3-1. *Web Profile specifications for Jakarta EE (based on Java EE 8)*

Web Application Technologies

Web application technologies represent all those specifications within the Jakarta EE platform that cover

- HTTP protocol request/response processing capabilities

- HTML components to build browser-based thin client applications

- JSON data processing capabilities

Java Servlet

Servlets essentially receive HTTP(s) requests, process them, and send back responses to the client which is typically a web browser. The servlet specification is one of the most important specifications existing since Java EE 1.0 and serves as the fundamental technology for a web application.

A lot of web frameworks (e.g., JavaServer Faces [JSF], Spring Model View Controller [MVC]) use servlets as the foundational toolkit and abstract their usage, that is, directly utilizing servlets is pretty uncommon while utilizing a web framework.

In Java EE 8, the latest version of the specification is Servlet 4.0 which introduced a major feature to the Servlet API – support for HTTP/2. While traditional HTTP requests had a single request/response, with HTTP/2, you could have a single request but the server can choose to serve multiple responses at the same time resulting in resource optimization and an improved user experience.

JavaServer Faces

JavaServer Faces provides a component-based approach to build web applications. Based on a server-side rendering aspect, it implements the well-known MVC pattern with clean separations. Views are generally based on JSF's Facelets templating technology, Models are built using JSF Backing Beans, and the Controller is built on top of the Servlet API.

JSF has wide adoption and is consistently ranked among the top web frameworks adopted by enterprise customers for their web applications because of its solid design principles and the stability of the specification. Multiple implementations exist including Oracle's ADF Faces, PrimeFaces, and BootsFaces.

The latest version of the specification is JavaServer Faces 2.3.

JavaServer Pages

JavaServer Pages (JSP) was the first view technology proposed when the Java EE platform was created. JSPs are translated into servlets at runtime and help create dynamic web content within Java web applications. JSPs are no longer widely used due to the preference for JSF as the UI technology for Java web applications, and the specification has not been updated for a long time.

The latest version of the specification is JavaServer Pages 2.3.

Expression Language

The Expression Language (EL) specification helps in accessing and manipulating data. This is used by multiple specifications including JSP, JSF, and CDI. The EL is quite powerful and is adopted widely. Latest improvements include support for lambda expressions introduced in Java 8.

The latest version of the specification is EL 3.0.

JSP Standard Tag Library (JSTL)

JSTL offers a collection of utility tags that can be used in JSP pages. These utility tags cover tasks such as iterations/conditions/SQL access. The specification has not been updated for a while since the advent of JSF and is not widely used anymore.

The current version of the specification is at 1.2.

Java API for WebSocket

This specification is provided to enable integration of WebSockets within Java web applications. The specification details an API that covers both server-side and client-side implementations of WebSockets.

The specification underwent a maintenance released in Java EE 8, and the latest version is at 1.1.

Java API for JSON Binding

A new specification introduced in Java EE 8, it details an API that provides a binding layer to convert Java Objects to JSON messages and vice versa.

The first version of the specification is at version 1.0.

Java API for JSON Processing

This specification provides an API that can be used to access and manipulate JSON objects. The latest version of the specification in Java EE 8 was a major release with various enhancements such as JSON Pointer, JSON Patch, JSON Merge Patch, and JSON Collectors.

The current version of the specification is at version 1.1.

Enterprise Application Technologies

Enterprise application technologies represent all those specifications within the Jakarta EE platform that cover

- Building of enterprise business components
- Business Component Dependency Management/Injection capabilities
- Validation capabilities
- Transaction Management
- ORM (Object Relational Mapping) capabilities

Enterprise Java Beans (3.2)

Available since v. 1.0 of the Java EE platform, Enterprise Java Beans (EJBs) provide a standard way of implementing server-side business logic for enterprise applications. EJBs abstracted the developer from a bunch of infrastructural concerns (e.g., Transaction Processing, Lifecycle management) allowing them to focus only on the business logic. One of the most popular specifications, it does suffer a perception issue of being too complex and heavyweight to use. The specification has undergone major transformations to shed these tags. As of the latest version of the specification, it offers an extremely simple and streamlined programming model for building business objects.

The latest version of the specification is at version 3.2.

Contexts and Dependency Injection for Java (2.0)

CDIs were introduced in the Java EE specification to build a component and manage its dependencies via injection. The specification was introduced to restrict EJBs to peripheral infrastructural responsibilities while having core business logic written in CDI Beans. With recent releases of the platform, these infrastructural concerns can now be written within CDI Beans too. CDI has now become the foundational piece of technology for almost all other parts of the platform with EJBs slowly being pushed out of favor. The specification had a major release in Java EE 8 with support for asynchronous events, observer orderings, and alignments with Java 8 streams.

One of the most powerful aspects of CDI is the extension framework it provides to create capabilities which the standard set of specifications do not support currently.

These capabilities could include the following:

- Integration with new message brokers (e.g., Kafka)

- Integration with non-relational datastores (e.g., MongoDB, Cassandra)

- Integration with new age cloud infrastructure (e.g., AWS S3, Oracle Object Storage)

Some well-known CDI extensions include Apache DeltaSpike (`https://deltaspike.apache.org/`) and Arquillian (`http://arquillian.org/`).

The latest version of the specification is at version 2.0.

Bean Validation

This specification provides a Java API to implement validations within applications. This specification has a major release in Java EE 8 with support for new types of validations, integration of the new Java Time API, and so on.

The latest version of the specification is at version 2.0.

Java Persistence API (JPA)

This specification provides a Java API to implement ORM (Object Relational Mapping) facility between Java Objects and relational datastores. One of the more popular specifications, it has wide adoption and multiple implementations, the most famous of them being Hibernate.

The latest version of the specification is at version 2.2.

Java Transaction API (JTA)

This specification provides a Java API to implement programmatic transactional capability within your applications. The API supports distributed transactions across multiple repositories, one of the most important aspects for a monolith which has needs for high transactional consistencies.

The latest version of the specification is at version 1.2.

Common Annotations

This specification provides a set of annotations or rather markers which help the container in executing common tasks (e.g., Resource Injections, Lifecycle management).

The latest version of the specification is at version 1.3.

Interceptors

This specification helps developers to write interceptor methods on associated managed beans (EJBs, CDI). Common uses of interceptors are for centralized crosscutting concerns such as auditing and logging.

The latest version of the specification is at version 1.2.

Web Services in Jakarta EE

Web service technologies represent all those specifications within the Jakarta EE platform that cover building enterprise REST services. For now, there is one main API.

Java API for RESTful Web Services (JAX-RS)

This specification provides a standard Java API for developers to implement RESTful web services. Another popular specification, the latest version of the specification had a major release with support for Reactive Clients and Server-Side events.

The latest version of the specification is at version 2.1.

Security Technologies

Security technologies represent all those specifications within the Jakarta EE platform that cover securing enterprise business components.

Java EE Security API (1.0)

A new specification introduced in Java EE 8, this provides a standard Java API for security implementations centered around user management. New APIs were introduced for authentication management, identity store interactions, and security context implementations (retrieval of user information).

Jakarta EE Specification Summary

This completes our high-level overview of the Jakarta EE platform specifications based on Java EE 8. As can be seen, these specifications are comprehensive and provide almost every capability required to build out enterprise applications. The platform also provides for extension points in case it does not suffice any specific need of the enterprise.

The most important point is that these are standard specifications backed by multiple vendors to adhere to these standards. This gives enterprises extreme flexibility in choosing a deployment platform.

With the new governance structure in place under the Eclipse Foundation, the platform is gearing up itself for the next generation of enterprise applications being built.

Cargo Tracker as a Modular Monolith

The monolithic architectural style has been the foundation for enterprise projects for a very long time.

The main focus points for a monolithic architecture are the following:

- Strong transactional consistency

- Easier maintainability

- Centralized data management

- Shared responsibilities

With the recent advent of microservices, there is definitely a growing pressure on monolithic architectures. The microservices architectural style provides teams with a high degree of independence in terms of development, testing, and deployment of applications; but due care needs to be taken before you start dismantling a monolith and move it to a microservices-based architecture. Microservices are essentially distributed systems which in turn require a lot of investment in automation, monitoring, and compromises for consistency. Monoliths have considerable value for complex business applications.

However, architectural approaches toward monoliths have been changing by borrowing concepts from microservices especially in the area of structuring monolithic applications. This is where DDD plays a central role. Bounded Contexts as we have seen help us carve the business capabilities of a particular domain into independent *"solution areas."* Structuring these Bounded Contexts as separate modules within a monolith and using domain events to communicate between them help us achieve loose coupling enabling *"true modularity"* or termed *"modular monoliths."*

The advantage of going down the path of *"true modularity"* or *"modular monoliths"* using DDD is while it helps us reap the benefits of having a monolithic architecture, it helps maintain a level of independence which helps us transition to microservices down the line if required.

In the previous chapters, we have carved out our Business Capabilities/Sub-Domains for our Cargo Tracker application and solutioned them with Bounded Contexts. In this chapter, we will structure the Cargo Tracker application as a modular monolith with each Bounded Context modeled as a separate module.

Figure 3-2 shows the mapping of the Bounded Contexts to the corresponding modules within the Cargo Tracker monolith.

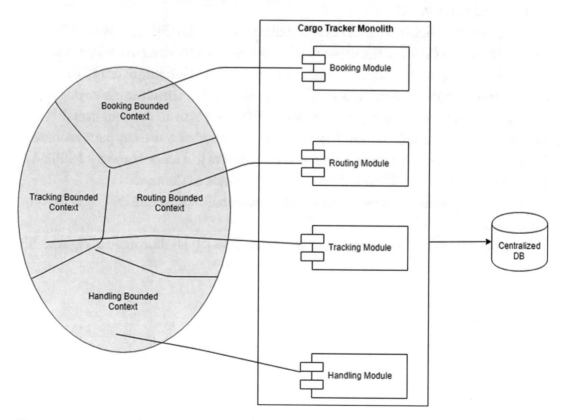

Figure 3-2. *Bounded Contexts as modules within the Cargo Tracker Monolith on a centralized DB*

With the set of specifications outlined and our intent clear for Cargo Tracker to be architected as a modular monolith based on DDD, let us proceed to implement it on the Java EE platform.

Bounded Context(s) with Jakarta EE

The Bounded Context is the starting point of our solution phase for our DDD implementation of the Cargo Tracker monolith. Each Bounded Context is going to be structured as a module within the monolith as its own independent deployable artifact.

The Cargo Tracker monolith's main deployment artifact will be a standard WAR (Web Archive) file which will be deployed onto an Application Server (Eclipse GlassFish). As stated previously, the application server provides an implementation for a specific version of the Jakarta EE specification (in this case, Java EE 8). Each Bounded Context's deployment artifact will be a standard JAR (Java Archive) file which will be bundled within the WAR file.

This WAR file would contain a set of JAR files with each JAR file representing the module/Bounded Context. The deployment architecture is illustrated in Figure 3-3.

Implementing the Bounded Contexts involves a logical grouping of our DDD artifacts into a single deployable artifact. The logical grouping involves identifying a package structure where we place the various DDD artifacts to achieve our overall solution for the Bounded Context. That is, we do not specifically use any particular Java EE specification(s) to implement a Bounded Context. We just identify a well-identified package structure for our DDD artifacts within the Bounded Context.

The package structure needs to mirror the hexagonal architecture that we laid out in Chapter 2 (Figure 2-16).

The package structure for any of our Bounded Context(s) is illustrated in Figure 3-3.

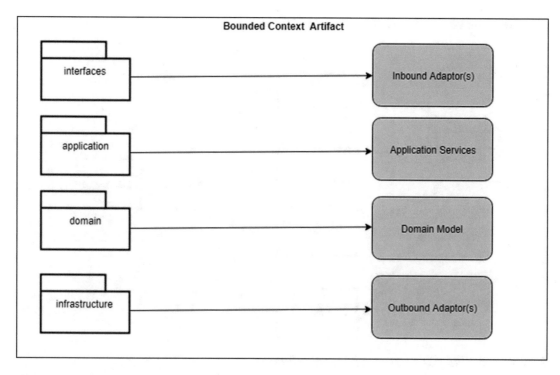

Figure 3-3. Package structure for the Bounded Contexts

Let us expand on the package structure.

interfaces

This package contains all the possible inbound services a Bounded Context provides classified by protocol.

They serve two main purposes:

- Protocol negotiation on behalf of the domain model (e.g., REST API(s), Web API(s), WebSocket(s), FTP(s))

- View adapters for data (e.g., Browser View(s), Mobile View(s))

As an example, the Booking Bounded Context provides multiple types of services. One example is a Web API for the native UI within the Cargo Tracker application to book a cargo/modify a cargo as well as listing of cargos for a customer. Similarly, the Handling Bounded Context provides a RESTful API for any kind of handling operations which are consumed by the Handling Mobile Application. All of these services would be a part of the "interfaces" package.

The package structure is illustrated in Figure 3-4.

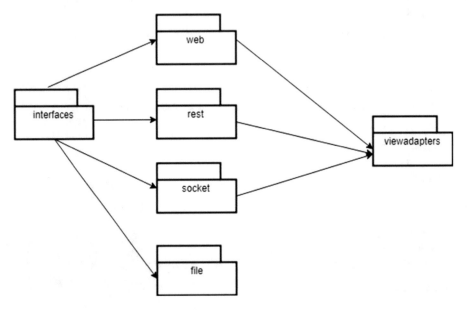

Figure 3-4. *Package structure for interfaces*

application

This package contains the Application services a Bounded Context's domain model would require.

Application services classes serve multiple purposes:

- Act as ports for input interfaces and output repositories

- Commands, Queries, Events, and Saga participants

- Transaction initiation, control, and termination

- Centralized concerns (e.g., Logging, Security, Metrics) for the underlying domain model

- Data transfer object transformation

- Callouts to other Bounded Contexts

The package structure is illustrated in Figure 3-5.

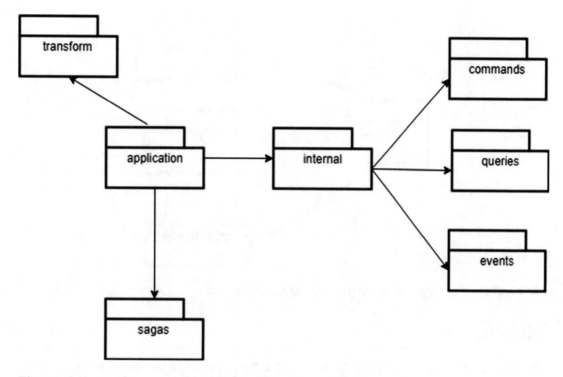

Figure 3-5. *Package structure for Application services*

domain

This package contains the Bounded Context's domain model.

The following are the core classes of our Bounded Contexts:

- Aggregates

- Entities

- Value Objects

- Domain Rules

The package structure is illustrated in Figure 3-6.

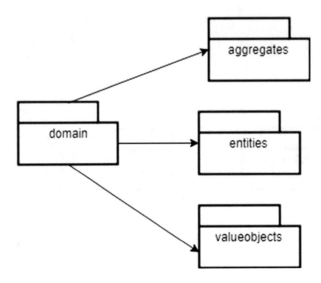

Figure 3-6. *Package structure for our domain model*

infrastructure

This package contains the infrastructural components required by the Bounded Context's domain model to communicate to any external repositories (e.g., Relational Database(s), NoSQL Databases, Message Queues, Event Infrastructure).

The package structure is illustrated in Figure 3-7.

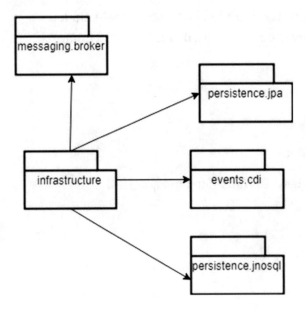

Figure 3-7. *Package structure for the infrastructure components*

Shared Kernels

Sometimes the domain model may need to be shared across multiple Bounded Contexts. Shared kernels within DDD offer us a robust mechanism to share domain models reducing the amount of duplicated code. Shared kernels are easier to implement within a monolith rather than a microservices-based application which advocates a much higher level of independency.

It does come up with a fair degree of challenges though as multiple teams need to agree on what aspect of the domain model would need to be shared across Bounded Contexts.

In our case within the Cargo Tracker monolith, we will keep all the events (package – events.cdi) that are raised by the various Bounded Contexts within a shared kernel.

This is illustrated in Figure 3-8.

Figure 3-8. *Shared infrastructure containing all the CDI events*

We now have our Bounded Contexts neatly grouped by modules in a package structure with clearly separated concerns.

Implementing the Domain Model with Jakarta EE

Our core domain model is the central feature of our Bounded Context and as stated earlier has a set of artifacts associated with it. Implementation of these artifacts is done with the help of the tools that Java EE provides.

To quickly summarize, the domain model artifacts that we need to implement are the following:

- Aggregates

- Entities

- Value Objects

Let's walk through each of these artifacts and see what corresponding tool(s) Java EE provides for us to implement these.

Aggregates

Aggregates are at the center of our domain model. To quickly recap, we have four aggregates within each of our Bounded Contexts as shown in Figure 3-9.

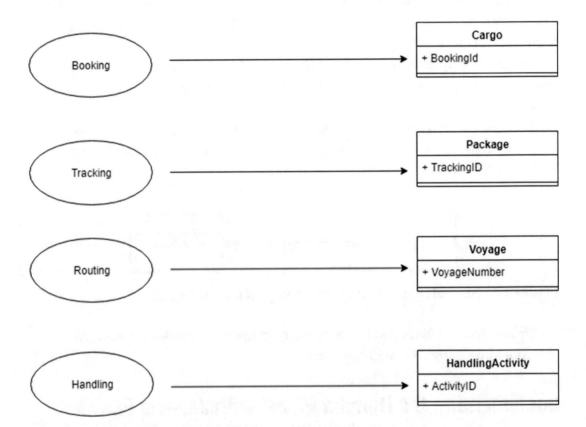

Figure 3-9. *Aggregates within our Bounded Context*

Implementation of an Aggregate covers the following aspects:

- Aggregate Class Implementation

- Domain Richness (Business Attributes, Business Methods)

- State Construction

- State Persistence

- Inter-Aggregate References

- Events

Aggregate Class Implementation

To implement our root aggregate, we will use JPA (Java Persistence API) from the Java EE framework as the main tool. Each of our root aggregate classes is implemented as a JPA entity. There are no specific annotations that JPA provides to annotate a specific class as a root aggregate, so we use the JPA-provided standard annotation "@Entity".

Listing 3-1 of the Cargo Root aggregate is shown in the following:

Listing 3-1. Cargo Root Aggregate

```
package com.practicalddd.cargotracker.booking.domain.model.aggregate;

import javax.persistence.Entity;
@Entity // JPA provided annotation
public class Cargo implements Serializable{
@Id
@GeneratedValue
private Long id; // Surrogate Key
@Embedded //To retain domain richness use an Embedded class instead of the
          direct Java implementation
private BookingId bookingId // Globally unique identifier of the Cargo Root
                            Aggregate (Booking Id)
}
```

Listing 3-2 shows the BookingID aggregate identifier:

Listing 3-2. Booking ID Aggregate Identifier

```
@Embeddable
public class BookingId implements Serializable{
@Column(name="booking_id", unique=true,updateable=false)
private String id;
public BookingId(){
}
public BookingId(String id){
     this.id = id;
}
}
```

```
public String getBookingId(){
return id;
}
```

For our aggregate identifier implementation, we choose to have a technical/surrogate key (Primary Key) and a corresponding business key (Unique Key). The business key conveys the business intent of the aggregate identifier clear, that is, Booking Identifier of a newly booked cargo and is the key that is exposed to consumers of the domain model. The technical key on the other hand is a pure internal representation of the aggregate identifier and is useful for use cases such as inter-aggregate references.

JPA provides us the @Id annotation to denote the primary key of our root aggregate.

Domain-Rich Aggregate vs. Anemic Aggregates

The basic premise of DDD is to have the domain richness expressed and centralized within the domain model, and our aggregate forms the centerpiece of our domain model.

The aggregate should be domain rich and convey the intent of the Bounded Context using clear business concepts.

An aggregate could also end up being anemic, that is, one with only getters and setters. This is considered to be anti-pattern in the DDD world.

To summarize

- Anemic aggregates give no purpose or intent of the domain.

- The pattern is intended only to capture the attributes and is most useful in representing data transfer objects rather than core business objects.

- Anemic aggregates result in domain logic leaking into the surrounding services which results in polluting the intent of the surrounding services.

- Anemic aggregates result in unmaintainable code over a period of time.

We should avoid anemic aggregates as far as possible and restrict them to their intended usage, that is, pure data objects.

Domain-rich aggregates on the other hand as the name suggests are **rich**. They express clearly the intent of the sub-domain they represent in terms of business attributes and business methods. Let us explain this in a bit more detail in the sections that follow.

Business Attribute Coverage

The root aggregate should cover all the business attributes required by the Bounded Context to function. These attributes should be modeled in business terms rather than technical terms.

Let us walk through the example of our Cargo root aggregate.

A cargo will have

- An Origin Location

- A Booking Amount

- A Route Specification (Origin Location/Destination Location/ Destination Arrival Deadline)

- An Itinerary

- Delivery Progress

The Cargo root aggregate class captures these as separate classes within the main aggregate class.

Listing 3-3 of the Cargo Root aggregate demonstrates these annotations:

Listing 3-3. Cargo root aggregate - Business attribute coverage

```
@ManyToOne // JPA Provided annotation
private Location origin;
@Embedded // JPA Provided annotation
private CargoBookingAmount bookingAmount;
@Embedded // JPA Provided annotation
private RouteSpecification routeSpecification;
@Embedded // JPA Provided annotation
private Itinerary itinerary;
@Embedded // JPA Provided annotation
private Delivery delivery;
```

Notice how we use business terms to express these dependent classes which clearly express the intent of the Cargo root aggregate.

The Java Persistence API (JPA) provides us a set of structural (e.g., Embedded/Embeddable) and relational (e.g., ManyToOne) annotations which help in defining the root aggregate class in pure business concepts.

Associated classes are modeled either as Entity Objects or Value Objects. We shall detail these concepts later; but to quickly summarize, Entity Objects within a Bounded Context have an identity of their own but always exist within a root aggregate, that is, they cannot exist independently and they never change during the complete lifecycle of the aggregate. Value Objects on the other hand have no identity of their own and are easily replaceable in any instance of an aggregate.

Business Method Coverage

Another important aspect of aggregates is the expression of domain logic via business methods. This adds to the domain richness aspect that is most important in the DDD world.

Aggregates need to capture the domain logic that is required for the particular sub-domain to function. For example, when we request for a cargo aggregate to be loaded, the cargo aggregate should have its delivery progress derived and presented to the consumer. This should be via domain methods within the aggregate rather than implement it within the supporting layers.

Business methods are implemented as simple methods within the aggregate and work with the current state of the aggregate. Listing 3-4 illustrates this concept for a couple of business methods. Notice how the aggregate handles this domain logic rather than the supporting layers:

Listing 3-4. Cargo root aggregate - Business methods

```
public class Cargo{
    public void deriveDeliveryProgress() {
        //Implementation goes here
    }
    public void assignToRoute(Itinerary itinerary){
      //implementation goes here
    }
}
```

Please refer to the chapter's source code for a complete implementation.

Aggregate State Construction

Aggregate state construction could be either for a new aggregate or when we have to load an existing aggregate.

Creating a new aggregate is as simple as using constructors on the JPA Entity class. Listing 3-5 shows the constructor for creating a new instance of our cargo root aggregate class:

Listing 3-5. Cargo root aggregate construction

```
public Cargo(BookingId bookingId, RouteSpecification routeSpecification) {
      this.bookingId = bookingId;
      this.origin = routeSpecification.getOrigin();
      this.routeSpecification = routeSpecification;
   }
```

Another mechanism of creating a new aggregate is using the Factory Design Pattern, that is, utilizing static factories which return us a new aggregate.

In our Handling Bounded Context, we construct the Handling Activity root aggregate depending upon the type of activity being performed. Certain handling activity types do not require a voyage. When a customer claims a cargo, the corresponding handling activity does not require a voyage. However, when a cargo is being unloaded at a port, the associated handling activity mandates a voyage. Hence, a factory to create various types of Handling Activity aggregates is the recommended approach here.

Listing 3-6 shows a factory that creates instances of the Handling Activity aggregates. The factory class is implemented using a CDI Bean, while the aggregate instance is created using a regular constructor:

Listing 3-6. Handling Activity root aggregate

```
package com.practicalddd.cargotracker.handling.domain.model.aggregate;

@ApplicationScoped // CDI scope of the factory (Application scope indicates
                a single instance at the application level)
public class HandlingActivityFactory implements Serializable{
      public HandlingActivity createHandlingActivity(Date registrationTime,
          Date completionTime, BookingId bookingId,
          VoyageNumber voyageNumber, UnLocode unlocode,
```

```
                HandlingActivity.Type type){
                if (voyage == null) {
                    return new HandlingActivity(cargo, completionTime,
                            registrationTime, type, location);
                    } else {
                    return new HandlingActivity(cargo, completionTime,
                            registrationTime, type, location, voyage);
                }
            }
        }
    }
```

Loading an existing aggregate, that is, sourcing an aggregate's state, can be done in two ways:

- Domain Sourced in which we construct the aggregate state by loading the current state of the aggregate directly from the datastore

- Event Sourced in which we construct the aggregate state by loading an empty aggregate and replaying all the events that occurred on that particular aggregate

For our monolithic implementation, we will use a state-sourced aggregate.

A state-sourced aggregate is loaded using an infrastructural data repository class that takes in the primary identifier of the aggregate and loads the entire object hierarchy of the aggregate including its related entities and value objects from the datastore (e.g., a relational database or NoSQL database).

Loading of state-sourced aggregates is generally done in the Application services (see section on Application services in the following).

Loading a state-sourced cargo aggregate is shown in Listing 3-7. This is typically placed in an Application services:

Listing 3-7. Cargo root aggregate - loading state via repositories

```
Cargo cargo = cargoRepository.find(bookingId);
```

This code piece uses the CargoRepository infrastructure class which takes in a Cargo Booking ID and loads the object hierarchy of the cargo which includes the cargo's Booking Amount, the cargo's Route Specification, the cargo's Itinerary, and the cargo's Delivery progress. As part of this implementation, we will use a JPA-specific implementation (JPACargoRepository class) which loads the cargo aggregate from a relational database.

To quickly summarize

- New Aggregates can be constructed using regular constructors or using static factories.

- Existing Aggregates are constructed using Domain Sourcing, that is, loading of the aggregate and its object hierarchy state directly from the Database using repository classes.

Aggregate State Persistence

The persistence operation of an aggregate should affect the state of that aggregate only. Generally, the aggregate does not persist itself but relies on repositories to perform these operations, in this case our JPA repositories. In case multiple aggregates need to be persisted, this would need to be in one of the Application services classes.

Inter-Aggregate References

Inter-aggregate references are relations that exist between aggregates across bounded contexts. In a monolithic implementation, these are implemented as associations using the annotations that JPA provides.

As an example in our Handling Bounded Context's root aggregate HandlingActivity, we have a many-to-one association with the cargo via the cargo's booking id as a join column.

Listing 3-8 shows the association:

Listing 3-8. Root Aggregate associations

```
public class HandlingActivity implements Serializable {
        @ManyToOne
        @JoinColumn(name = "cargo_ id")
        @NotNull
        private Cargo cargo; // Aggregate reference linked via
                                association
}
```

So whenever we load a `HandlingActivity` aggregate from the datastore, its corresponding cargo association is loaded via the association defined earlier.

There are possibly other ways to design aggregate references, for example, you could just use the primary key identifier for the cargo aggregate, that is, the booking id, and retrieve the details of the cargo through a service call. Alternatively, you could store a subset of the cargo details required within the handling bounded context and get notified of changes in the cargo aggregate through events fired by the Booking Bounded context which owns the Cargo aggregate.

The choice of aggregate associations always raises a point of debate. In terms of a purist DDD approach, this is strictly avoidable since this indicates a leakage and the boundary of the Bounded Context needs to be relooked at. Sometimes, however, it is necessary to adopt a pragmatic approach considering the application needs (e.g., transactional consistencies) and the capabilities of the underlying platform (e.g., Event Infrastructure).

Our microservices implementations adopt the purist approach, while for the Cargo Tracker monolith, we implement aggregate references via JPA associations.

Aggregate Events

As per true DDD, domain events always need to be published by aggregates. If an event is published by any other part of the application (e.g., Application services class), it is deemed a technical event rather than a business domain event. While this definition is up for debate, the definition of a domain event is one that originates from an aggregate as only it is aware of the state change happening.

Java EE does not offer us any direct capability to publish a domain event from our aggregate layer built on top of JPA, so we move this part of the implementation to the Application services layer. In the subsequent chapters, we will see capabilities provided by the underlying toolkit which does support publishing of domain events from our aggregate layer (e.g., as part of the Spring Framework, the Spring Data Commons project provides us the annotation `@DomainEvents` which we can add to a JPA aggregate). While theoretically you can use `EntityListener` classes to listen to lifecycle events of the underlying aggregate, it represents a change in the Entity data rather than a business event itself.

A summary of our aggregate implementation using Java EE is shown in Figure 3-10.

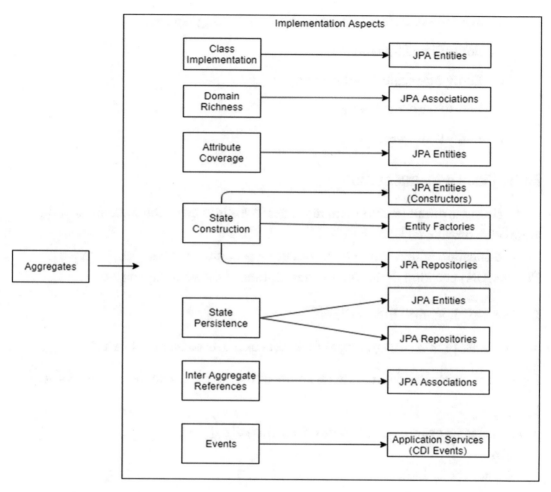

Figure 3-10. Aggregate implementation summary

Entities

Entities within a Bounded Context have an identity of their own but always exist within a root aggregate, that is, they cannot exist independently. An Entity object never changes during the complete lifecycle of the aggregate.

As an example seen in Chapter 2, within our Booking Bounded Context, we have one Entity Object – the Origin Location of the cargo. The origin location of the cargo never changes during the entire lifecycle of the cargo and hence is a suitable candidate to be modeled as an Entity object.

Implementation of Entity objects covers the following aspects:

- Entity Class Implementation

- Entity-Aggregate Relationships

- Entity State Construction

- Entity State Persistence

Entity Class Implementation

Entity classes are implemented separately as JPA Entities using the standard @Entity annotation provided by JPA.

The Location Entity class, which contains a generated primary key, a United Nations (UN) Location Code, and the description, is shown in Listing 3-9:

Listing 3-9. Location Entity Class

```
package com.practicalddd.cargotracker.booking.domain.model.entities;

import com.practicalddd.cargotracker.booking.domain.model.entities.UnLocode;

@Entity
public class Location implements Serializable {
    @Id
    @GeneratedValue
    private Long id;
    @Embedded
    private UnLocode unLocode;
    @NotNull
    private String name;
}
```

Entity identifiers utilize the same concept as Aggregate identifiers – a technical/surrogate key and a business key.

Entity-Aggregate Relationships

Entity classes have a strong association with their root aggregates, that is, they cannot exist without a root aggregate. Modeling the association with the root aggregate is done using standard JPA association annotations.

Within the Cargo root aggregate, the Location entity class is utilized to denote the Origin Location of the cargo. The Origin Location within the Booking Bounded Context cannot exist without a cargo being present.

Listing 3-10 shows the association between the Location Entity class and the Cargo root aggregate:

Listing 3-10. Cargo root aggregate associations

```
public class Cargo implements Serializable {
     @ManyToOne
     @JoinColumn(name = "origin_id", updatable = false)
     //Not the responsibility of Location to update the root aggregate
     i.e. Cargo
     private Location origin;
}
```

Entity State Construction/Persistence

Entities are always constructed/persisted ONLY along with the underlying root aggregate when these operations are performed on the root aggregate.

The Cargo origin location is always constructed when the Cargo aggregate is constructed. The same for persistence, when we persist a new cargo booking, we persist the Origin location along with it.

A summary of our entity implementation using Java EE is shown in Figure 3-11.

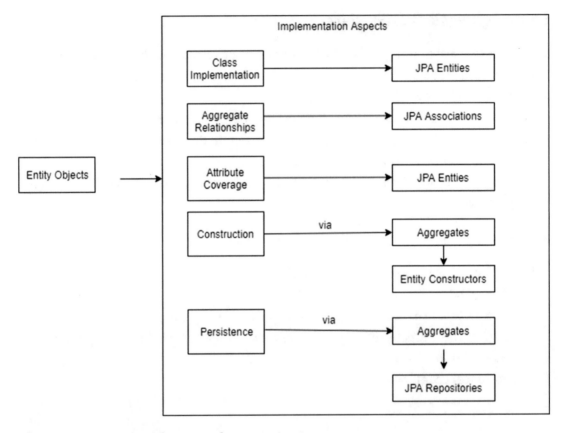

Figure 3-11. *Entity Object implementation summary*

Value Objects

Value Objects exist within the scope of a Bounded Context's aggregate. They have no identity of their own and are replaceable in any instance of an aggregate.

Repeating our examples seen in Chapter 2, within our Booking Bounded Context, we have multiple Value Objects that are part of the Cargo root aggregate:

- – The Route Specification of the cargo

- – The Itinerary of the cargo

- – The Delivery Progress of the cargo

Each of these is easily replaceable in our Cargo root aggregate. Let us walk through the scenarios and the rationale why we have these as value objects and not as entities because it is an important domain modeling decision:

- When a new cargo is booked, we will have a new route specification, an empty itinerary, and no delivery progress.

- As the cargo is assigned an itinerary, the empty itinerary value object is replaced by an allocated itinerary object.

- As the cargo progresses through multiple ports as part of its itinerary, the delivery value object is updated and replaced within the root aggregate.

- Finally, if the customer chooses to change the delivery location of the cargo or the deadline for delivery, the route specification changes, a new itinerary is allocated, and the delivery progress is updated.

In each of these scenarios, it becomes quite obvious that these objects need to be replaced within the root aggregate, and hence they are modeled as Value Objects.

Implementation of Value Objects covers the following aspects:

- Value Object Class Implementation

- Value Object-Aggregate Relationship

- Value Object Construction

- Value Object Persistence

Value Object Class Implementation

Value Objects are implemented as JPA Embeddable objects using the @Embeddable annotation provided by JPA.

Since Value Objects do not have an identity of their own, they do not have any primary identifier.

Listing 3-11 shows our Value Objects – RouteSpecification, Itinerary, and Delivery – implemented as JPA Embeddable objects:

Listing 3-11. Delivery Value Objects

```
@Embeddable
public class RouteSpecification implements Serializable{

    @ManyToOne
    @JoinColumn(name = "spec_origin_id", updatable = false)
    private Location origin;
    @ManyToOne
    @JoinColumn(name = "spec_destination_id")
    private Location destination;

   @Temporal(TemporalType.DATE)
   @Column(name = "spec_arrival_deadline")
   @NotNull
   private LocalDate arrivalDeadline;
}

@Embeddable
public class Delivery implements Serializable{
    public static final LocalDate ETA_UNKOWN = null;
    public static final HandlingActivity NO_ACTIVITY = new
    HandlingActivity();
    @Enumerated(EnumType.STRING)
    @Column(name = "transport_status")
    @NotNull
    private TransportStatus transportStatus;
    @ManyToOne
    @JoinColumn(name = "last_known_location_id")
    private Location lastKnownLocation;
    @ManyToOne
    @JoinColumn(name = "current_voyage_id")
    private Voyage currentVoyage;
    @NotNull
    private boolean misdirected;
```

```
    private LocalDate eta;
    @Embedded
    private HandlingActivity nextExpectedActivity;
    @Column(name = "unloaded_at_dest")
    @NotNull
    private boolean isUnloadedAtDestination;
    @Enumerated(EnumType.STRING)
    @Column(name = "routing_status")
    @NotNull
    private RoutingStatus routingStatus;
    @Column(name = "calculated_at")
    @NotNull
    private LocalDateTime calculatedAt;
    @ManyToOne
    @JoinColumn(name = "last_event_id")
    private HandlingEvent lastEvent;
}

@Embeddable
public class Itinerary implements Serializable{
    public static final Itinerary EMPTY_ITINERARY = new Itinerary();
    @OneToMany(cascade = CascadeType.ALL, orphanRemoval = true)
    @JoinColumn(name = "booking_id")
    @OrderBy("loadTime")
    @Size(min = 1)
    private List<Leg> legs = Collections.emptyList();
}
```

Value Object-Aggregate Relationship

Value Objects cannot exist without the root aggregate, but since they have no identifier, they are easily replaceable within an aggregate instance.

Associations between Value Objects and Aggregates are implemented using the @Embedded annotation provided by JPA.

Listing 3-12 shows our Value Objects – `RouteSpecification`, `Itinerary`, and `Delivery` – associated with our Cargo root aggregate as embedded objects:

Listing 3-12. Cargo root aggregate's Value Objects

```
@Embedded
private RouteSpecification routeSpecification;
@Embedded
private Itinerary itinerary;
@Embedded
private Delivery delivery;
```

Value Object Construction/Persistence

Value Objects are always constructed/persisted ONLY along with the underlying root aggregate when these operations are performed on the root aggregate.

When we book a new cargo, at that point of time, the aggregate does not have an itinerary assigned; and if we attempt to derive the delivery progress, it will come up as empty since it has not been routed yet. Notice how we map these business concepts within our root aggregate in Listing 3-13. We assign an empty itinerary and a delivery snapshot based on an empty handling history to our cargo aggregate.

Listing 3-13 shows how value objects Itinerary and Delivery are created when a cargo root aggregate is constructed:

Listing 3-13. Value Objects state construction

```
public Cargo(BookingId bookingId, RouteSpecification routeSpecification) {
        this.bookingId = bookingId;
        this.origin = routeSpecification.getOrigin();
        this.routeSpecification = routeSpecification;
        this.itinerary = Itinerary.EMPTY_ITINERARY; // Empty Itinerary since
                                        the cargo is not routed yet
                        this.delivery = new Delivery(this.
                        routeSpecification, this.itinerary,
                        HandlingHistory.EMPTY); // Delivery
                        snapshot derived based on an empty handling
                        history since this is a new cargo booking
}
```

A summary of our Value Object implementation using Jakarta EE is shown in Figure 3-12.

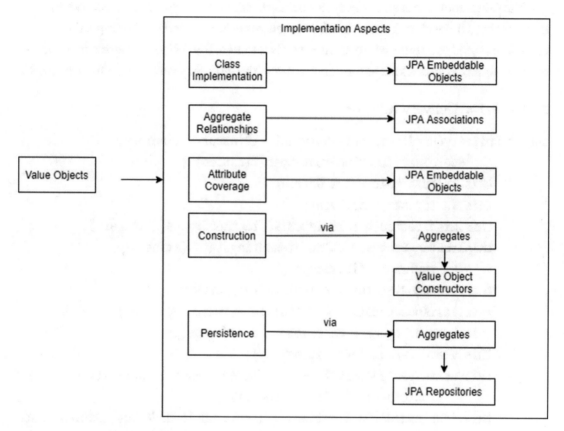

Figure 3-12. *Value Object implementation summary*

Domain Rules

Domain rules assist the aggregate in any kind of business logic execution within the scope of a bounded context. While these rules typically enrich the state of the aggregate, they do not themselves persist the changes in the state. They present the new state changes to the Application services which examine the state changes to take corresponding actions. As seen in the previous chapter, these rules could exist within the domain model or outside the domain model (within the services layer).

A business rule (within the domain model) generally finds its place within a Value Object as a private routine. Let's explain this through an example.

The Cargo root aggregate is always associated with a `Delivery` value object. When either of these three changes, that is, when a new route is specified for the cargo, the cargo is assigned to a route; or when the cargo is handled, the delivery progress must be recalculated. Let's take a look at the constructor of the `Delivery` value object in Listing 3-14:

Listing 3-14. Delivery value object

```
public Delivery(HandlingEvent lastEvent, Itinerary itinerary,
          RouteSpecification routeSpecification) {
      this.calculatedAt = new Date();
      this.lastEvent = lastEvent;
      this.misdirected = calculateMisdirectionStatus(itinerary);
      this.routingStatus = calculateRoutingStatus(itinerary,
              routeSpecification);
      this.transportStatus = calculateTransportStatus();
      this.lastKnownLocation = calculateLastKnownLocation();
      this.currentVoyage = calculateCurrentVoyage();
      this.eta = calculateEta(itinerary);
      this.nextExpectedActivity = calculateNextExpectedActivity(
              routeSpecification, itinerary);
      this.isUnloadedAtDestination = calculateUnloadedAtDestination(route
      Specification);
    }
```

These calculations are domain rules which examine the current state of the aggregate to determine the next state of the aggregate.

Again, as we have seen before, a domain rule within the domain model relies only on existing aggregate state for its execution. In case this rule requires data other than aggregate state, the domain rule should be pushed to the services layer.

A summary of our implementation is shown in Figure 3-13.

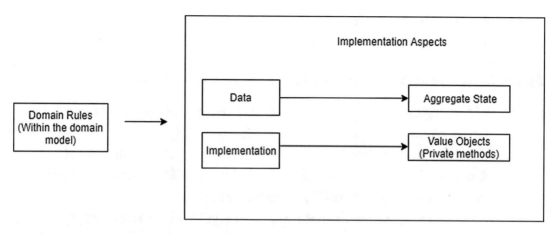

Figure 3-13. *Domain Rule implementation summary*

Commands

A Command within a Bounded Context is any operation that changes the aggregate state. Java EE does not offer us anything specific for denoting a command operation, so in our implementation, this is spread across Application services and the domain model. The domain model part changes the aggregate state, while the Application services persist the changes.

For the command Change destination, this involves associating the cargo root aggregate with a new route specification and new delivery status.

Listing 3-15 shows the implementation part within the cargo root aggregate:

Listing 3-15. Command example within the Cargo root aggregate

```
public void specifyNewRoute(RouteSpecification routeSpecification) {
    Validate.notNull(routeSpecification, "Route specification is
    required");
    this.routeSpecification = routeSpecification;
    this.delivery = delivery.updateOnRouting(this.routeSpecification,
        this.itinerary);
}
```

Listing 3-16 shows the implementation part within the booking bounded context's Application services:

Listing 3-16. Command example within the Cargo root aggregate

```
public void changeDestination(BookingId bookingId, UnLocode unLocode) {
        Cargo cargo = cargoRepository.find(bookingId);
        Location newDestination = locationRepository.find(unLocode);
        RouteSpecification routeSpecification = new RouteSpecification(
                cargo.getOrigin(), newDestination,
                cargo.getRouteSpecification().getArrivalDeadline());
        cargo.specifyNewRoute(routeSpecification); //Call to domain model
        cargoRepository.store(cargo); //Store the State
}
```

A summary of our implementation is shown in Figure 3-14.

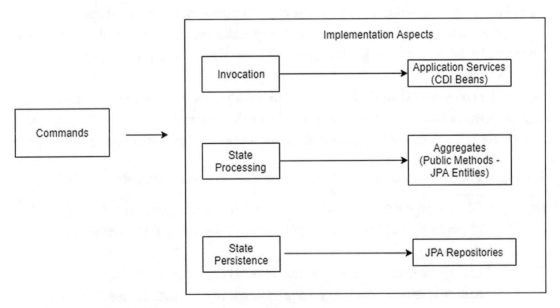

Figure 3-14. *Command implementation summary*

Queries

A Query within a Bounded Context is any operation that retrieves the state of the aggregate. JPA provides us Named Queries which we can mark on the aggregate JPA entity to query the state of the aggregate. JPA repositories can use the Named Queries to retrieve the state of the aggregate.

Listing 3-17 shows the usage of named queries within the Cargo root aggregate. We got named queries for finding all cargos, finding a cargo by a specific booking id, and finally getting all booking ids:

Listing 3-17. Named queries within the Cargo root aggregate

```
@Entity
@NamedQueries({
    @NamedQuery(name = "Cargo.findAll",
            query = "Select c from Cargo c"),
    @NamedQuery(name = "Cargo.findByBookingId",
            query = "Select c from Cargo c where c.bookingId = :bookingId"),
    @NamedQuery(name = "Cargo.getAllBookingIds",
            query = "Select c.bookingId from Cargo c") })
public class Cargo implements Serializable {}
```

Listing 3-18 shows the usage of the named query findByBookingId within the Cargo JPA repository:

Listing 3-18. Named queries within the Cargo root aggregate

```
@Override
public Cargo find(BookingId bookingId) {
        Cargo cargo;
try {
        cargo = entityManager.createNamedQuery("Cargo.findByBookingId",
                Cargo.class)
            .setParameter("bookingId", bookingId)
            .getSingleResult();
    } catch (NoResultException e) {
```

```
        logger.log(Level.FINE, "Find called on non-existant Booking
        ID.", e);
        cargo = null;
    }
  return cargo;
}
```

A summary of our implementation is shown in Figure 3-15.

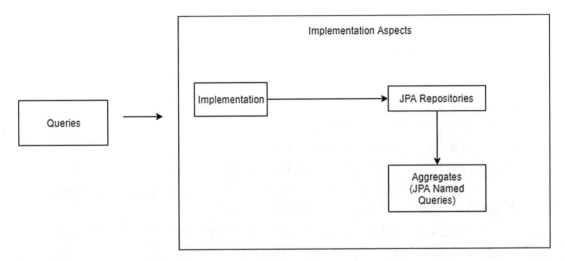

Figure 3-15.   *Query implementation summary*

Implementing Domain Model Services with Jakarta EE

As stated before, we have three types of supporting services that the core domain model requires.

Inbound Services

Inbound services (or Inbound Adaptors as denoted in the Hexagonal Architectural Pattern) act as the outermost gateway for our core domain model.

Within the Cargo Tracker, we have implemented two types of inbound services based on the type of consumers of the domain model:

- HTTP API(s) implemented using RESTful web services

- Native Web API(s) implemented using JSF (JavaServer Faces) Managed Beans

We could have additional inbound services/adaptors classified by the protocol that needs to be supported, for example, we could have a WebSocket-based inbound service for real-time updates or a file-based inbound service for batch uploads. All of these protocols should be modeled as part of inbound services.

Let us take examples of each type of the inbound services within our Cargo Tracker application and see how they are implemented using Jakarta EE.

RESTful API(s)

Jakarta EE provides the capabilities to implement RESTful API(s) using the JAX-RS specification. This specification is one of the most widely used within the platform.

An example of a RESTful API within the Cargo Tracker Application using JAX-RS is shown in Listing 3-19:

Listing 3-19. REST API example

```
package com.practicalddd.cargotracker.handling.interfaces.rest;
@Path("/handling")
public class HandlingService{
    @POST
    @Path("/reports")
    @Consumes("application/json")
    public void submitReport(@NotNull @Valid HandlingReport handlingReport){
    }
}
```

This RESTful API is exposed as part of the Handling Bounded Context and processes the handling of the cargo at the port of transit. The path of the API is at /handling/reports; it consumes a JSON structure and is a POST request, typical RESTful constructs which JAX-RS supports.

Native Web API(s)

The second type of inbound service implemented is via Native Web API(s). The Cargo Admin Web Interface is a thin browser-based interface implemented using JavaServer Faces (JSF), the standard for building HTML applications within the Jakarta EE platform.

JSF is based on the popular MVC (Model View Controller) with the model implemented using JSF Managed Beans based on CDI (Component Dependency Injection). The model acts as the inbound service layer for the web interfaces.

An example of a Native Web API within the Cargo Tracker Application using JSF/CDI is shown in Listing 3-20:

Listing 3-20. Web API example

```
package com.practicalddd.cargotracker.booking.interfaces.web;

@Named //Name of the bean
@RequestScoped //Scope of the bean
public class CargoAdmin {
        public String bookCargo() {
                //Invoke the domain model to book a new cargo
        }
}
```

The Cargo Admin class is implemented as a Web API using JSF and CDI Beans. It exposes a set of operations (e.g., bookCargo) to the Cargo Admin Web Interface which is used by a clerk to perform various operations (e.g., booking of a cargo). The Cargo Admin Web Interface can invoke the operations on these CDI Beans.

A summary of the implementation is illustrated in Figure 3-16.

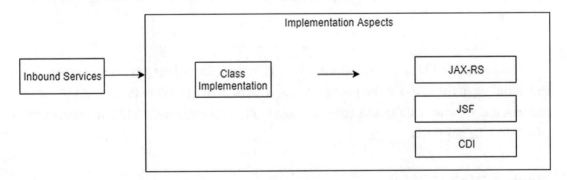

Figure 3-16. *Inbound Services implementation summary*

Application Services

Application services are built using CDI (Component Dependency Injection) components available within the Jakarta EE platform. While we have touched upon the topic of CDI earlier, we did not get into a lot of details around it. Let us cover that aspect now.

Introduced first in Java EE 6.0, CDI has effectively replaced EJBs as the de facto tool within the Jakarta EE platform to build business components. CDI manages the lifecycle and interactions of components with support for type safe dependency injection. In addition, CDI provides a comprehensive SPI (Service Provider Framework) allowing portable extensions to be built and integrated within the Jakarta EE platform.

Building an Application services using CDI involves the following steps. We will take the Cargo Booking Application services as an example:

- Create a regular Java interface with the operations that the Application services provides. Listing 3-21 demonstrates this:

Listing 3-21. Booking Application services interface

```
package com.practicalddd.cargotracker.booking.application;

public interface BookingService {
 BookingId bookNewCargo(UnLocode origin, UnLocode destination, LocalDate
arrivalDeadline);
List<Itinerary> requestPossibleRoutesForCargo(BookindId bookingId);
 void assignCargoToRoute(Itinerary itinerary, BookingId bookingId);
 void changeDestination(BookingId bookingId, UnLocode unLocode);

}
```

- Provide an implementation of the interface marked with CDI-specific annotations. CDI annotations are typically used for giving a scope to the component along with a name (in case there are multiple implementations of a specific interface).

    We provide an implementation of the Booking Service interface and give it an Application Scope, that is, a single instance for the entire application.

Listing 3-22 demonstrates this:

Listing 3-22. Booking Application services implementation

```
package com.practicalddd.cargotracker.booking.application.internal;

@ApplicationScoped //CDI Annotation to determine scope
public class  DefaultBookingService implements BookingService {
    BookingId bookNewCargo(UnLocode origin, UnLocode destination,
    LocalDate arrivalDeadline){
        //Implementation provided here
    }
  List<Itinerary> requestPossibleRoutesForCargo(BookindId bookingId){
        //Implementation provided here
    }
  void assignCargoToRoute(Itinerary itinerary, BookingId bookingId){
        //Implementation provided here
    }
  void changeDestination(BookingId bookingId, UnLocode unLocode){
        //Implementation provided here
    }
}
```

- An Application services will have a set of dependencies, for example, it would need to access the repository infrastructure classes to retrieve the aggregate details as part of a particular operation. Listing 3-6 did briefly touch upon this wherein within the Application services, we used a Cargo Repository class to load the Cargo aggregate. The Application services class is provided the dependency of the Cargo Repository class via the CDI "Inject" annotation

Listing 3-23 demonstrates this:

Listing 3-23. Booking Application services dependencies

```
package com.practicalddd.cargotracker.booking.application.internal;

@Inject //Inject the dependency of the Cargo Repository infrastructure
private CargoRepository cargoRepository;

@ApplicationScoped //CDI Annotation to determine scope
public class DefaultBookingService implements BookingService {
 @Override
 public List<Itinerary> requestPossibleRoutesForCargo(BookingId bookingId) {
 Cargo cargo = cargoRepository.find(bookingId); //Use the Cargo Repository
        //Subsequent implemtnation here.
 }
}
```

A summary of the implementation is illustrated in Figure 3-17.

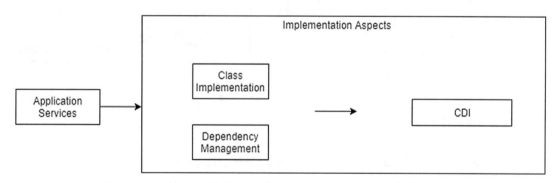

Figure 3-17. *Application Services implementation summary*

Application Services: Events

As we have stated earlier, domain events within DDD in the true sense have to be generated by the aggregate. Since Jakarta EE does not provide us a mechanism to generate domain events by the aggregate, we need to push this capability to the Application services.

The Event Infrastructure is based on CDI Events. Introduced in CDI 2.0, it offers a very clean implementation of an event notification/observer model. This results in loose coupling between the various Bounded Contexts which in turn helps us achieve our desired design of true modular monoliths.

The CDI eventing model is displayed in Figure 3-18.

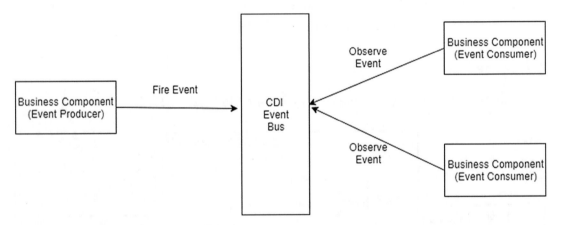

Figure 3-18. *CDI Eventing model*

The CDI Event bus is not a specialized event bus; it is an internal implementation of the Observer Pattern implemented within the container with enhanced support including Transactional Observers, Conditional Observers, Ordering, and both synchronous and asynchronous events.

Let us walk through an implementation within the Cargo Tracker application. The Handling Bounded context fires a "Cargo Inspected" event every time a cargo is inspected as part of the handling activity. The Tracking Bounded Context observes this event and updates the tracking progress of the cargo accordingly.

The flow is summarized in Figure 3-19.

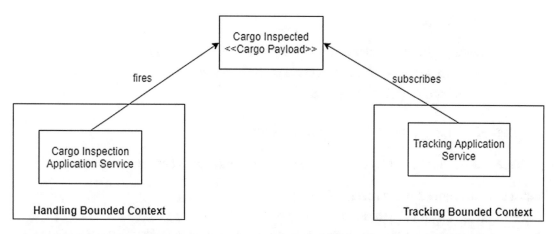

Figure 3-19. *Event flows between the Handling Bounded Context and the Tracking Bounded Context*

In terms of actual implementation, the following steps are followed:

– *Create an Event Class (via Stereotypes).*

Listing 3-24 demonstrates this. We create a "Cargo Inspected" event class:

Listing 3-24. Cargo Inspected event class stereotype

```
package com.practicalddd.cargotracker.handling.infrastructure.events.cdi;

import static java.lang.annotation.ElementType.FIELD;
import static java.lang.annotation.ElementType.PARAMETER;
import static java.lang.annotation.RetentionPolicy.RUNTIME;
import java.lang.annotation.Retention;
import java.lang.annotation.Target;
import javax.inject.Qualifier;

@Qualifier // Stereotype annotations
@Retention(RUNTIME) //Stereotype annotations
@Target({FIELD, PARAMETER}) //Stereotype annotations
public @interface CargoInspected { //Event
}
```

   −   *Fire the event.*

Listing 3-25 demonstrates the firing of the "Cargo Inspected" event from the Application services, in this case the Cargo Inspected Application services:

Listing 3-25. Firing the cargo inspected event

```
package com.practicalddd.cargotracker.handling.application.internal;

import javax.enterprise.event.Event;
import javax.inject.Inject;
import com.practicalddd.cargotracker.infrastructure.events.cdi.
CargoInspected; //Import the stereotype event class

public class DefaultCargoInspectionService implements
CargoInspectionService{

@Inject
@CargoInspected
private Event<Cargo> cargoInspected; //The event that will get fired.
                                     The payload is the Cargo aggregate

    /**
     * Method which will process the inspection of the cargo and fire a
       subsequent event
     */
    public void inspectCargo(BookingId bookingId) {
            //Load the Cargo
            Cargo cargo = cargoRepository.find(bookingId);

            //Process the inspection

            // Fire the event post inspection
            cargoInspected.fire(cargo);
    }
}
```

— *Observe the event.*

The Cargo Tracking service within the Tracking Bounded Context observes the event and accordingly updates the tracking progress of the cargo.

Listing 3-26 demonstrates this:

Listing 3-26. Observing the Cargo Inspected event

```
package com.practicalddd.cargotracker.tracking.application.internal;

import javax.enterprise.event.Event;
import javax.inject.Inject;
import com.practicalddd.cargotracker.infrastructure.events.cdi.
CargoInspected;

public class DefaultTrackingService implements TrackingService{

@Inject
@CargoInspected
private Event<Cargo> cargoInspected; //Subscription to the event

    /**
     * Method which observes the CDI event and processes the payload
     */
    public void onCargoInspected(@Observes @CargoInspected Cargo cargo) {
        //Process the event
    }
}
```

A summary of the implementation is illustrated in Figure 3-20.

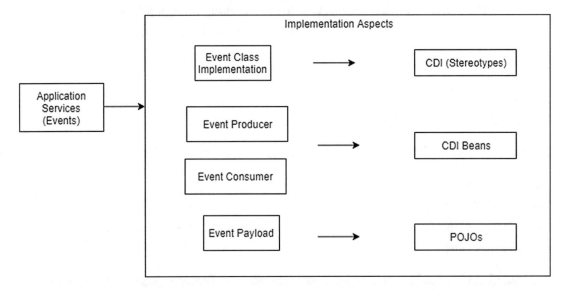

Figure 3-20. *Application Services Event implementation summary*

Outbound Services

Within the Cargo Tracker monolith, we use outbound services primarily to communicate with the underlying database repository. The outbound services are implemented as "Repository" classes and are part of the infrastructure layer.

Repository classes are built using JPA and use CDI for their lifecycle management. JPA provides a managed resource named "EntityManager" which abstracts the database configuration details (e.g., Datasource).

A repository class generally revolves around a specific aggregate and deals with all database operations for that aggregate including the following:

- Persistence of a new aggregate and its associations

- Update of an aggregate and its associations

- Querying the aggregate and its associations

Listing 3-27 demonstrates an example of a repository class JPACargoRepository:

Listing 3-27. Cargo Repository class implementation

```java
package com.practicalddd.cargotracker.booking.infrastructure.persistence.jpa;

//JPA Annotations
import javax.enterprise.context.ApplicationScoped;
import javax.persistence.EntityManager;
import javax.persistence.NoResultException;
import javax.persistence.PersistenceContext;

@ApplicationScoped
public class  JpaCargoRepository implements CargoRepository, Serializable {

@PersistenceContext
    private EntityManager entityManager; //Managed resource used by the
Repository class to interact with the database

// Store a cargo
@Override
    public void store(Cargo cargo) {
        entityManager.persist(cargo);
    }

//Find all cargos. Uses a Named Query defined on the Cargo root aggregate.
See also Queries
@Override
    public List<Cargo> findAll() {
        return entityManager.createNamedQuery("Cargo.findAll", Cargo.class)
                .getResultList();
    }

//Find a specific cargo. Uses a Named Query defined on the Cargo root
aggregate
@Override
    public Cargo find(BookingId bookingId) {
        Cargo cargo;
```

```
try {
    cargo = entityManager.createNamedQuery("Cargo.findByBookingId",
        Cargo.class)
        .setParameter("bookingId", bookingId)
        .getSingleResult();
} catch (NoResultException e) {
    logger.log(Level.FINE, "Find called on non-existant Booking
    ID.", e);
    cargo = null;
}
    return cargo;
}

}
```

The implementation summary is illustrated in Figure 3-21.

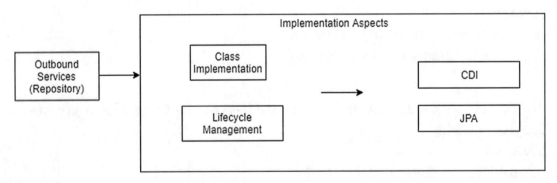

Figure 3-21. *Outbound Services implementation summary*

This rounds off our implementation of the Cargo Tracker as a modular monolith using Jakarta EE 8.

Implementation Summary

We now have a complete DDD implementation of the monolithic Cargo Tracker application with the various DDD artifacts implemented using the corresponding specifications available within Java EE.

The implementation summary is denoted in Figure 3-22.

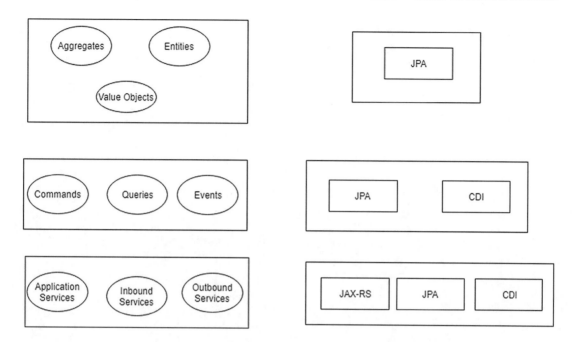

Figure 3-22. *DDD artifact implementation summary using Java EE*

Summary

Summarizing our chapter

- We started by establishing the details about the Jakarta EE platform and the various capabilities it provides.

- We then rationalized the decision behind the implementation of Cargo Tracker as a modular monolith using Domain Driven Design.

- We rounded off by deep diving into the development of the various DDD artifacts – first the domain model and then the domain model supporting services using the technologies available on the Jakarta EE platform.

CHAPTER 4

Cargo Tracker: Eclipse MicroProfile

To quickly recap

We identified Cargo Tracking as the main problem space/core domain and the Cargo Tracker application as the solution to address this problem space.

We identified the various sub-domains/bounded contexts for the Cargo Tracker application.

We detailed out the domain model for each of our bounded contexts including identification of aggregates, entities, value objects, and domain rules.

We identified the supporting domain services required within the bounded contexts.

We identified the various operations within our bounded contexts (Commands, Queries, Events, and Sagas).

We implemented a monolithic version of Cargo Tracker using Jakarta EE.

This chapter details the second DDD implementation of our Cargo Tracker application using the new Eclipse MicroProfile platform. The Cargo Tracker application will be designed using a microservices-based architecture. As before, we will map the DDD artifacts to the corresponding implementations available within the Eclipse MicroProfile platform.

First, here is an overview of the Eclipse MicroProfile platform.

© Vijay Nair 2019
V. Nair, *Practical Domain-Driven Design in Enterprise Java*, https://doi.org/10.1007/978-1-4842-4543-9_4

Eclipse MicroProfile

As the Microservices architectural style started gaining rapid traction among enterprises, there was an urgent need for the Java EE platform to evolve to cater to these requirements. Handicapped by the release process coupled with the fact that the Java EE platform was more focused on traditional monolithic applications, a group of existing Java EE vendors decided to form a more optimized platform suited for Microservices architecture with an accelerated release cycle.

This new platform, christened as MicroProfile, was first released in 2016 and joined the Eclipse Foundation, thus getting the name "Eclipse MicroProfile." The aim of the MicroProfile platform was to utilize the strong foundational specifications from the Java EE platform and enhance them with a set of cloud-native/microservices-specific specifications, thus aiming to be a complete microservices platform powered by Jakarta EE.

The platform in a short span of time has gained wide acceptance and great community participation and has close to nine vendor implementations of the various specifications. The specifications have been extremely well-thought-of, considering both present and future challenges presented in the microservices landscape.

The Microservices Architectural Style

The microservices architectural style has quickly become the foundation for building next-generation enterprise applications. The Microservices architectural style promotes independence along the complete software development and delivery lifecycle significantly accelerating the delivery velocity for enterprise applications. A quick summary of the advantages of microservices is illustrated in Figure 4-1.

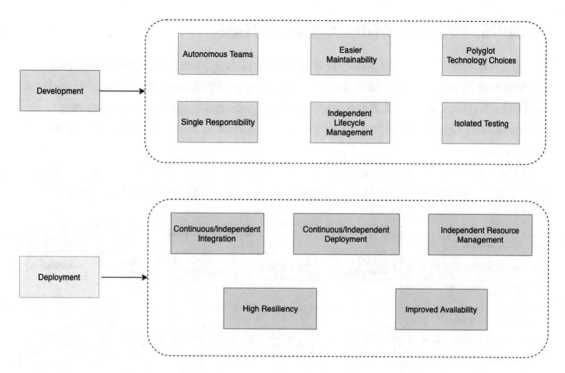

Figure 4-1. *Advantages of a Microservices-based Architecture*

The microservices architecture does come with its own set of complexities. The inherent distributed nature of Microservices architecture results in ***implementation complexities*** in the areas of

- Transaction Management

- Data Management

- Application Patterns (e.g., reporting, auditing)

- Deployment Architecture

- Distributed Testing

As this architectural style becomes more popular, these areas are being addressed in various ways using open source frameworks as well as proprietary vendor software.

Eclipse MicroProfile: Capabilities

The Eclipse MicroProfile platform provides a very strong foundational platform for applications planning to move to the microservices architectural style. Coupled with DDD which offers us well-defined processes and patterns to design and develop microservices, the combination offers a strong platform to build microservices-based applications.

Before we deep dive into the technical components of the MicroProfile platform, let us articulate the requirements of a microservices platform as illustrated in Figure 4-2.

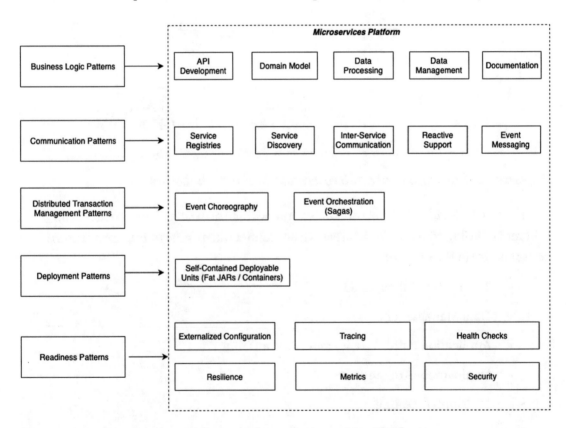

Figure 4-2. *Requirements of a complete microservices platform*

The requirements are split across various areas which cater to the unique requirements of a microservices platform.

The set of specifications that the Eclipse MicroProfile platform provides is illustrated in Figure 4-3. The specifications are grouped into two categories:

- *A Core Set* which helps in catering to specific requirements of Cloud-Native/Microservices architectural styles. These specifications provide solutions in the areas of Configuration, Health Checks, Communication Patterns, Monitoring, Security, and Resiliency.

- *A Supporting Set* which helps in catering to traditional requirements of applications, be it Microservices or Monoliths. This includes capability to build Business Logic, API Design, Data Management, and Data Processing.

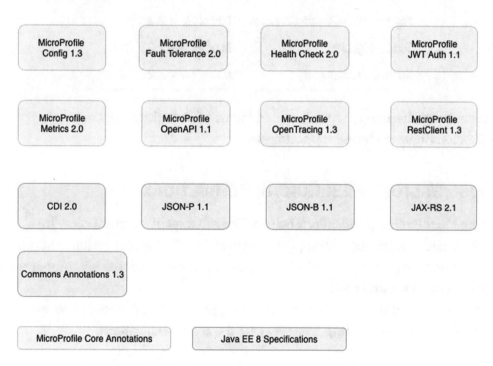

Figure 4-3. *Eclipse MicroProfile specifications*

Unlike the main Java EE/Jakarta EE platform, there are no profiles within the MicroProfile project. There are just a single set of specifications which any vendor needs to implement to be MicroProfile compliant.

Here are the current set of vendors who implement MicroProfile specifications.

Implementation Name	Implementation Version
Helidon (Oracle)	MicroProfile 2.2
SmallRye (Community)	MicroProfile 2.2
Thorntail (Red Hat)	MicroProfile 3.0
Open Liberty (IBM)	MicroProfile 3.0
WebSphere Liberty (IBM)	MicroProfile 3.0
Payara Server (Payara Services)	MicroProfile 2.2
Payara Micro (Payara Services)	MicroProfile 2.2
TomEE (Apache)	MicroProfile 2.0
KumuluzEE (Kumuluz)	MicroProfile 2.2

Let us deep dive into the specifications. We will first walk through the core specifications followed by the supporting set.

Eclipse MicroProfile: Core Specifications

The core MicroProfile specifications help implement a set of technical concerns that cloud-native/Microservices applications mandate. The set of specifications are designed and thought out to enable developers wanting to adopt the Microservices style implement these features easily.

From a microservices requirements mapping perspective, the shaded boxes as illustrated in Figure 4-4 are implemented with the core specifications.

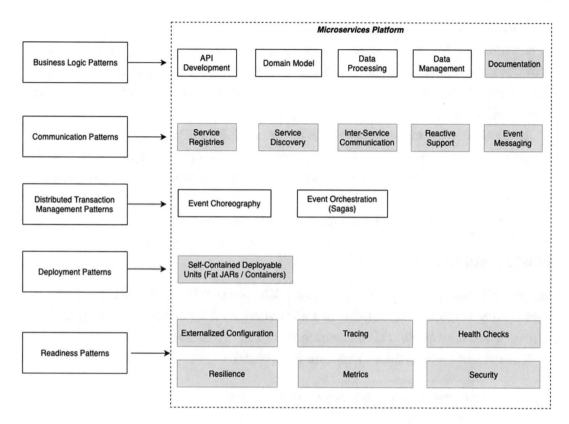

Figure 4-4. *Eclipse MicroProfile core specifications mapped to the microservices requirements*

Let us walk through the core specification set of MicroProfile.

Eclipse MicroProfile Config

The configuration specification defines an easy-to-use mechanism for implementing application configuration required by microservices. Every microservices would require some kind of configuration (e.g., Resource Locations such as other service URLs or Database Connectivity, Business Configurations, Feature Flags). The configuration information can also be different depending upon which environment the microservices is being deployed to (e.g., development, testing, production). The microservices artifact should not be changed to accommodate the different patterns of configuration.

MicroProfile config defines a standard way of aggregating and injecting configuration information required by a microservices without the need for repackaging the artifact. It provides a mechanism for injecting default configuration with mechanisms to override the defaults via external means (Environment Variables, Java Command Line Variables, Container Variables).

In addition to injecting configuration information, MicroProfile Config also defines a standard way of implementing Configuration Sources, that is, the repository where the configuration information is stored. Configuration Sources could be GIT repositories or Databases.

The current version of the specification is at v. 1.3.

Eclipse MicroProfile Health Check

The MicroProfile Health Check specification defines a standard runtime mechanism of determining the status and visibility of a microservices. It is intended to be used within a containerized environment via a machine-to-machine mechanism.

The current version of the specification is at v. 2.0.

Eclipse MicroProfile JWT Authentication

The MicroProfile JSON Web Token (JWT) Authentication specification defines a standard security mechanism for implementing authentication and authorization (RBAC [Role-Based Access Control]) for microservices endpoints using JSON Web Token (JWT).

The current version of the specification is at v. 1.1.

Eclipse MicroProfile Metrics

The MicroProfile Metrics specification defines a standard mechanism for microservices to emit metrics that are recognizable by monitoring tools.

The current version of the specification is at v. 2.0.

Eclipse MicroProfile OpenAPI

The MicroProfile OpenAPI specification defines a standard mechanism for generating OpenAPI-compliant contracts/documents for microservices.

The current version of the specification is at v. 1.1.

Eclipse MicroProfile OpenTracing

The MicroProfile OpenTracing specification defines a standard mechanism for implementing distributed tracing within microservices applications.

The current version of the specification is at v. 1.3.

Eclipse MicroProfile Type Safe Rest Client

The MicroProfile Rest Client specification defines a standard mechanism for implementing RESTful invocations between microservices.

The current version of the specification is at v. 1.3.

This rounds off the core set of specifications provided by Eclipse MicroProfile. As can be seen, the specifications are extremely well-thought-out and offer a comprehensive and complete set of features to help build standards-based Microservices applications.

Eclipse MicroProfile: Supporting Specifications

While the core set of specifications help us implement the crosscutting microservices concerns, the supporting specifications help us build the Business Logic aspects of microservices. This includes the Domain Model, API(s), Data Processing, and Data Management.

From a microservices requirements mapping perspective, the boxes in orange as illustrated in Figure 4-5 are implemented with the supporting specifications.

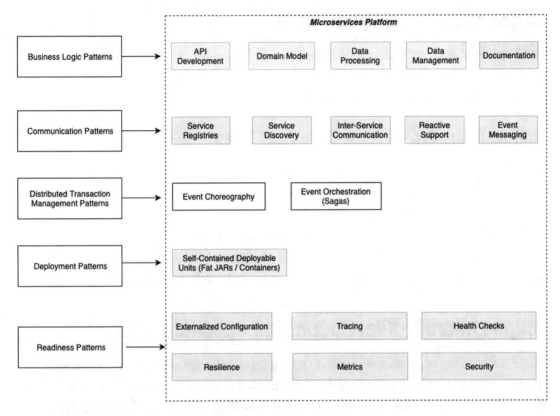

Figure 4-5. *Eclipse MicroProfile supporting specifications*

Next, we'll see a quick overview of the supporting specifications.

Contexts and Dependency Injection for Java (2.0)

As stated in the previous chapter, CDI was introduced in the Java EE specification to build a component and manage its dependencies via injection. CDI has now become the foundational piece of technology for almost all other parts of the platform with EJBs slowly being pushed out of favor.

The latest version of the specification is at version 2.0.

Common Annotations

This specification provides a set of annotations or rather markers which help the runtime container in executing common tasks (e.g., Resource Injections, Lifecycle management).

The latest version of the specification is at version 1.3.

Java API for RESTful Web Services (JAX-RS)

This specification provides a standard Java API for developers to implement RESTful web services. Another popular specification, the latest version of the specification had a major release with support for Reactive Clients and Server-Side events.

The latest version of the specification is at version 2.1.

Java API for JSON Binding

A new specification introduced in Java EE 8, it details an API that provides a binding layer to convert Java Objects to JSON messages and vice versa.

The first version of the specification is at version 1.0.

Java API for JSON Processing

This specification provides an API that can be used to access and manipulate JSON objects. The latest version of the specification in Java EE 8 was a major release with various enhancements such as JSON Pointer, JSON Patch, JSON Merge Patch, and JSON Collectors.

The current version of the specification is at version 1.1.

As can been seen, the platform does not provide out-of-the-box support for distributed transaction management using Orchestration-based Sagas. We would need to implement Distributed Transactions using *Event Choreography*. The MicroProfile platform in a future release is planning an implementation of the saga orchestration patterns as part of the MicroProfile LRA (Long Running Action) specification.

Eclipse MicroProfile Specification Summary

This completes our high-level overview of the Eclipse MicroProfile platform specifications. These specifications are comprehensive and provide almost every capability required to build out enterprise applications that want to adopt a microservices architectural style. The platform also provides for extension points in case it does not suffice any specific need of the enterprise.

Just like the Jakarta EE platform, the most important point is that these are standard specifications backed by multiple vendors. This gives enterprises flexibility in choosing a microservices platform.

Cargo Tracker Implementation: Eclipse MicroProfile

To restate, the goal of the chapter is ***implementation of Cargo Tracker as a Microservices application utilizing Domain Driven Design and the Eclipse MicroProfile platform.***

As part of the implementation, we are going to be using ***DDD as the foundation*** to help us ***design and develop*** our microservices. As we navigate through the implementation, we will map and implement the DDD artifacts with the corresponding tools available within the Eclipse MicroProfile platform.

The two foundational pieces of any DDD-based architecture are the Domain Model and the Domain Model services. Figure 4-6 illustrates this. The previous chapter demonstrated the usage of DDD to help us implement Cargo Tracker as a monolith. This chapter will demonstrate the usage of DDD to help us achieve our stated goal of implementing Cargo Tracker as a microservices application.

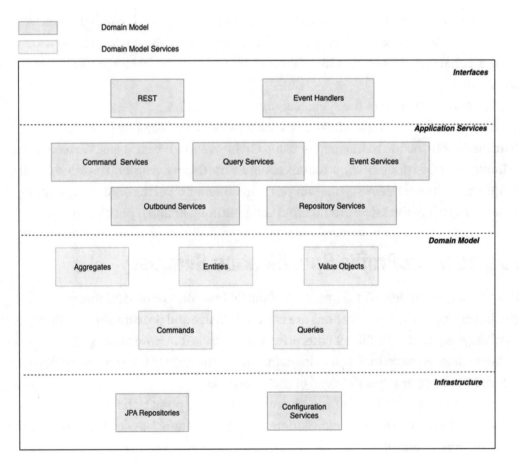

Figure 4-6. *DDD artifact implementation summary*

There might be some repetitions from the previous chapter due to the commonality of implementations of some of the DDD artifacts. It is suggested that you read this chapter as you would be implementing a microservices project from scratch using Eclipse MicroProfile.

Implementation Choice: Helidon MP

The first step is to choose the MicroProfile implementation that we will use to implement the DDD artifacts. We do have a wide choice of implementations available as laid out before. For our implementation, we choose to use the Helidon MP project (`https://helidon.io`) from Oracle.

The Helidon MP project supports the Eclipse MicroProfile specifications; it is designed to be simple to use and runs on a fast reactive web server with very little overhead. In addition to the support for the Core/Supporting set of specifications, it also provides a set of extensions which include support for gRPC, Jedis (Redis library), HikariCP (Connection Pool library), and JTA/JPA.

An overview of the capabilities provided by the Helidon MP project is illustrated in Figure 4-7.

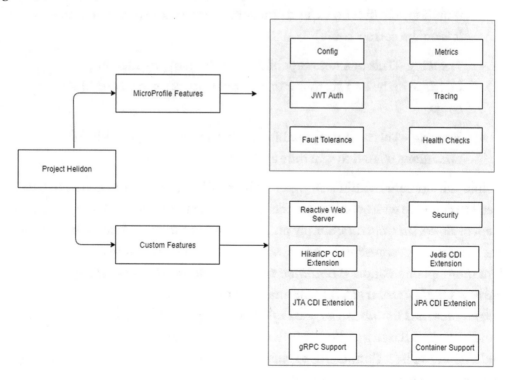

Figure 4-7. *Helidon MP support for the MicroProfile specifications and additional extensions*

The current version of Helidon MP is 1.2 which supports Eclipse MicroProfile 2.2.

Cargo Tracker Implementation: Bounded Context(s)

Our implementation begins first with splitting the Cargo Tracker monolith into a set of microservices. For this purpose, we carve the Cargo Tracker Domain into a set of ***Business Capabilities/Sub-Domains***. Figure 4-8 illustrates the business capabilities of the Cargo Tracker Domain.

- ***Booking*** – This business capability/sub-domain is responsible for all the operations related to the booking of a new cargo, assigning a route to the cargo, and any updates to the cargo (e.g., change of destination/cancellation).

- ***Handling*** – This business capability/sub-domain is responsible for all operations related to the handling of cargo at the various ports that are part of the cargo's voyage. This includes registering of handling activities on a cargo or inspecting the cargo (e.g., to check if it is on the correct route).

- ***Tracking*** – This business capability/sub-domain provides an interface to the end customer to accurately track the progress of a cargo.

- ***Routing*** – This business capability/sub-domain is responsible for all operations related to schedule and route maintenance.

While sub-domains within DDD operate in what is known as the "***problem space,***" we need to come up with solutions for them too. We achieve this in DDD by using the concept of ***Bounded Contexts***. Simply put, Bounded Contexts operate in the "***solution space,***" that is, they represent the actual solution artifact for our problem space.

For our implementation, ***a Bounded Context is modeled as containing a single or a set of Microservice(s)***. This makes sense for obvious reasons since the ***independence that Bounded Contexts offer*** satisfies the fundamental aspect required of a microservices-based architecture. All the operations that manage the state of the Bounded Context, be it Commands to change state, Queries to retrieve state, or Events to publish state, are part of the Microservices.

From a deployment perspective as illustrated in Figure 4-8, each Bounded Context is a separate self-contained deployable unit. The deployable unit could be packaged in the form of a *fat JAR file or a Docker Container image*. Since Helidon MP provides first-class support for Docker, we will utilize that as our packaging choice.

Microservices will need a *DataStore* to store their state. We choose to adopt the *Database per service pattern*, that is, each of our microservices will have its own separate DataStore. Just like we have a polyglot choice of technology for our application tier, we have a polyglot choice for the DataStore too. We could choose to have a plain Relational Database (e.g., Oracle, MySQL, PostgreSQL), a NoSQL Database (e.g., MongoDB, Cassandra), or even an in-memory datastore (e.g., Redis). The choice depends primarily on the scalability requirements and the type of use case the microservices intends to cater to. For our implementation, we decide to go with MySQL as the choice of DataStore.

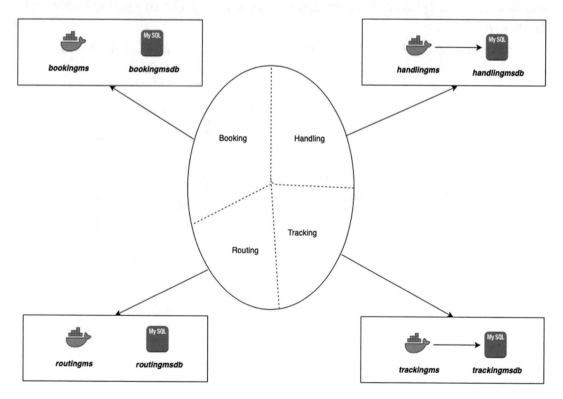

Figure 4-8. *Bounded Context artifacts*

Before we proceed further on the implementation, here is a short note on the language that we will use going further. The Bounded Context terminology is a DDD-specific terminology, and since this is a book around DDD, it makes sense to use DDD terminologies primarily. This chapter is also about a microservices implementation. As we have stated, this implementation *models a Bounded Context as a Microservices*. So going forward, our usage of the term Bounded Context essentially denotes the same as a Microservices.

Bounded Contexts: Packaging

Packaging the Bounded Contexts involves a logical grouping of our DDD artifacts into a single deployable self-sufficient artifact. Each of our Bounded Context is going to be built as an *Eclipse MicroProfile application*. Eclipse MicroProfile applications are self-sufficient in the sense that they contain all the *dependencies, configuration, and runtime,* that is, they do not have any external dependency (like an Application Server) for them to run.

The anatomy of an Eclipse MicroProfile application is illustrated in Figure 4-9.

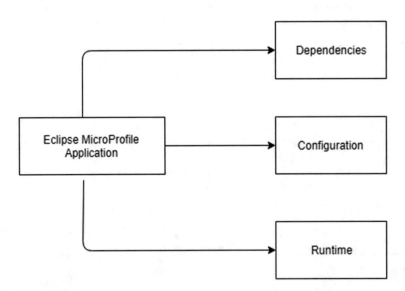

Figure 4-9. *Anatomy of an Eclipse MicroProfile application*

Helidon MP offers a Maven archetype (helidon-quickstart-mp) to help us scaffold an Eclipse MicroProfile application. Listing 4-1 shows the Helidon MP Maven command that we would use to generate the MicroProfile application for the *Booking Bounded Context*:

Listing 4-1. Helidon MP quickstart archetype

```
mvn archetype:generate -DinteractiveMode=false -DarchetypeGroupId=io.
helidon.archetypes -DarchetypeArtifactId=helidon-quickstart-
mp -DarchetypeVersion=1.2 -DgroupId=com.practicalddd.cargotracker
-DartifactId=bookingms -Dpackage=com.practicalddd.cargotracker.bookingms
```

The source code generated by the archetype contains a **"Main"** class. The Main class contains a main method which brings up the Helidon MP web server when we run the application. Figure 4-10 illustrates the code generated by the quickstart archetype.

In addition to the main class, it also generates a **sample REST resource file (Greeter)** to help test the application, **a microprofile configuration file (microprofile-config. properties)** which can be used to set up configuration information for the application, and a **beans.xml file for CDI integration**.

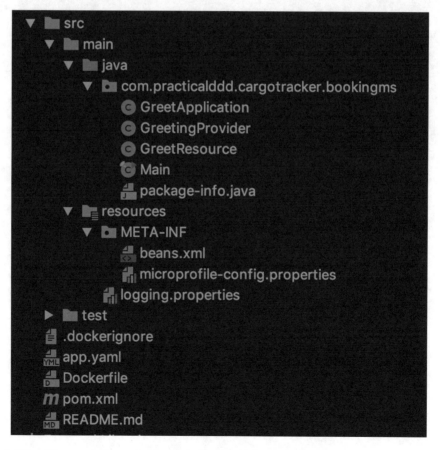

Figure 4-10. Generated project using the Helidon archetype

We can run the application in two ways:

- As a JAR file

  Building the project will result in a JAR file (**bookingms.jar**). Running it as a simple JAR file using the command "**java -jar bookingms.jar**" will bring up Helidon MP's web server on the configured port (8080) and make the Greeter REST resource available at **http://<<Machine-Name>>:8080/greet**.

  We can use the curl utility to test the Greeter REST resource using the command

  curl -X GET http://<<Machine-Name>>:8080/greet.

  This will display the message "Hello World". This indicates that the Booking Microservices Helidon MP application instance is up and running correctly as a JAR file.

- As a Docker image

  An alternative that Helidon MP provides is the capability to build and run the MicroProfile application as a Docker image. This is keeping in line with the principle of the MicroProfile application providing capabilities to build cloud-native applications.

  Building the Docker image is done using the command

  docker build -t bookingms.

  Running the Docker image is done using the command

  docker run --rm -p 8080:8080 bookingms:latest.

  We can use the curl utility again to test the Greeter REST resource using the command

  curl -X GET http://<<Machine-Name>>:8080/greet.

  This will display the message "Hello World". This indicates that the Booking Microservices Helidon MP application instance is up and running correctly as a Docker image.

Since our preferred approach is to use containers, we will build and run all the microservices within the Cargo Tracker application as Docker images.

Bounded Contexts: Package Structure

With the packaging aspect decided, the next step is to decide the package structure of each of our Bounded Context, that is, to arrive at a logical grouping of the various DDD MicroProfile artifacts into a single deployable artifact. The logical grouping involves identifying a package structure where we place the various DD MicroProfile artifacts to achieve our overall solution for the Bounded Context.

The high-level package structure for any of our Bounded Context is illustrated in Figure 4-11.

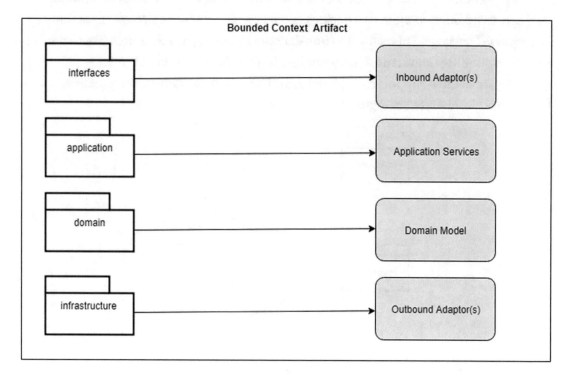

Figure 4-11. *Package structure for the Bounded Contexts*

Let us expand on the package structure a bit.

interfaces

This package encloses all the inbound interfaces to our Bounded Context classified by the communication protocol. The main purpose of ***interfaces*** is to negotiate the protocol on behalf of the Domain Model (e.g., REST API(s), WebSocket(s), FTP(s), Custom Protocol).

As an example, the Booking Bounded Context provides REST APIs for sending ***State Change Requests,* that is, *Commands,*** to it (e.g., Book Cargo Command, Assign Route to Cargo Command). Similarly, the Booking Bounded Context provides REST APIs for sending ***State Retrieval Requests,* that is, *Queries,*** to it (e.g., Retrieve Cargo Booking Details, List all Cargos). This is grouped into the "***rest***" package.

It also has Event Handlers which subscribe to the various Events that are generated by other Bounded Contexts. All Event Handlers are grouped into the "***eventhandlers***" package. In addition to these two packages, the interface package also contains the "***transform***" package. This is used to translate the incoming API Resource/Event data to the corresponding Command/Query model required by the Domain Model.

Since we need to support REST, Events, and data transformation, the package structure is as illustrated in Figure 4-12.

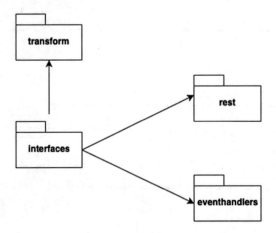

Figure 4-12. *Package structure for interfaces*

application

Application services act as the façade for the Bounded Context's Domain Model. They provide façade services to dispatch Commands/Queries to the underlying Domain Model. They are also the place where we place outbound calls to other Bounded Contexts as part of the processing of a Command/Query.

To summarize, Application Services

- Participate in Command and Query Dispatching.

- Invoke infrastructural components where necessary as part of the Command/Query processing.

- Provide Centralized concerns (e.g., Logging, Security, Metrics) for the underlying Domain Model.

- Make callouts to other Bounded Contexts.

The package structure is illustrated in Figure 4-13.

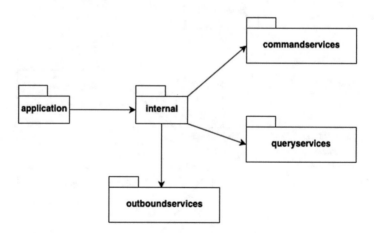

Figure 4-13. *Package structure for Application services*

domain

This package contains the Bounded Context's Domain Model. This is the heart of the Bounded Context's Domain Model which contains the implementation of the core Business Logic.

The core classes of our Bounded Contexts are as follows:

- Aggregates

- Entities

- Value Objects

- Commands

- Events

The package structure is illustrated in Figure 4-14.

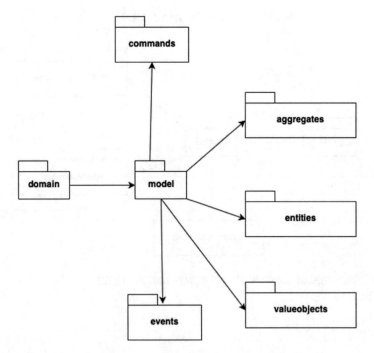

Figure 4-14. *Package structure for our domain model*

infrastructure

The infrastructure package serves four main purposes:

- When a Bounded Context receives an operation related to its state (Change of State, Retrieval of State), it **needs an underlying repository to process the operation**; in our case, this repository is our MySQL Database instance(s). The infrastructure package contains all the necessary components required by the Bounded Context to communicate to the underlying repository. As part of our implementation, we intend to use either JPA or JDBC to implement these components.

- When a Bounded Context needs to communicate a state change event, it needs an underlying Event Infrastructure to publish the state change event. In our implementation, we intend to use a **message broker as the underlying Event Infrastructure** (RabbitMQ). The infrastructure package contains all the necessary components required by the Bounded Context to communicate to the underlying message broker.

- When a Bounded Context needs to communicate with another Bounded Context synchronously, it needs an underlying infrastructure to support a service-to-service communication via REST. The infrastructure package contains all the necessary components required by the Bounded Context to communicate to other Bounded Contexts.

- The final aspect that we include in the infrastructural layer is any kind of MicroProfile-specific configuration.

The package structure is illustrated in Figure 4-15.

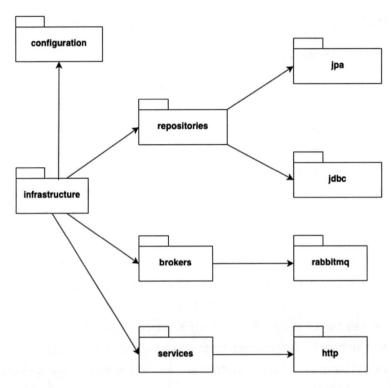

Figure 4-15. *Package structure for the infrastructure components*

A complete summary of the entire package structure for any of our Bounded Context is illustrated in Figure 4-16.

Figure 4-16. *Package structure for any of our Bounded Context*

This completes the implementation of the Bounded Contexts of our Cargo Tracker microservices application. Each of our Bounded Contexts is implemented as a MicroProfile application using the Helidon MP project with a Docker image as an artifact. The Bounded Contexts are neatly grouped by modules in a package structure with clearly separated concerns.

Let us step into the implementation of the Cargo Tracker Application.

Cargo Tracker Implementation

The next section of this chapter is going to detail the implementation of the Cargo Tracker application as a microservices application utilizing DDD and Eclipse MicroProfile (Helidon MP).

A high-level overview of the logical grouping of our various DDD artifacts is illustrated in Figure 4-17. As seen, we need to implement two groups of artifacts:

- The ***Domain Model*** which will contain our ***Core Domain/Business Logic***

- The ***Domain Model Services*** which contain ***supporting services for our Core Domain Model***

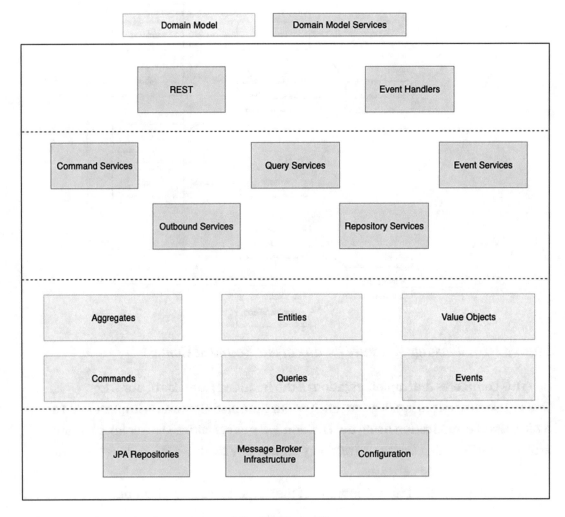

Figure 4-17. *Logical grouping of the DDD artifacts*

In terms of actual implementation of the Domain Model, this translates to the various *Value Objects, Commands, and Queries* of a specific Bounded Context/ Microservices.

In terms of actual implementation of the Domain Model Services, this translates to *the Interfaces, Application Services, and Infrastructure* that the Domain Model of the Bounded Context/Microservices requires.

Going back to our Cargo Tracker application, Figure 4-18 illustrates our microservices solution in terms of the various Bounded Contexts and the operations it supports. As seen, this contains the various *Commands that each Bounded Context will process*, the *Queries that each Bounded Context will serve,* and the *Events that each Bounded Context will subscribe/publish*. Each of the microservices is a separate deployable artifact with its own storage.

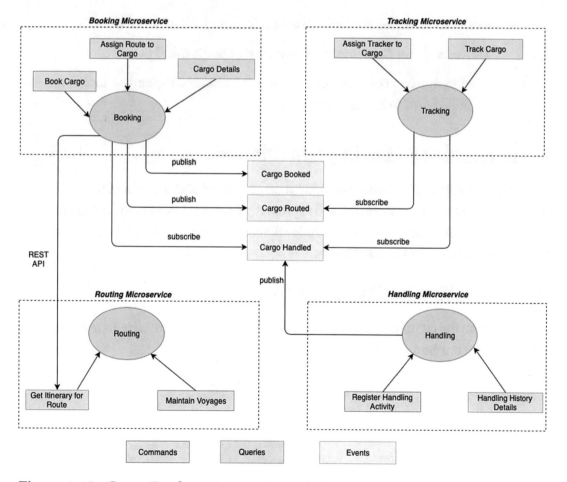

Figure 4-18. *Cargo Tracker Microservices solution*

Note   Certain code implementations will contain only summaries/snippets to help understand the implementation concepts. The source code for the chapter contains the full implementation of the concepts.

Domain Model: Implementation

Our Domain Model is the central feature of our Bounded Context and as stated earlier has a set of artifacts associated with it. Implementation of these artifacts is done with the help of the tools that Eclipse MicroProfile provides.

To quickly summarize, the Domain Model artifacts that we need to implement are as follows:

- ***Core Domain Model*** – Aggregates, Entities, and Value Objects

- ***Domain Model Operations*** – Commands, Queries, and Events

Let's walk through each of these artifacts and see what corresponding tool(s) Eclipse Microprofile provides us to implement these.

Core Domain Model: Implementation

The implementation of the Core Domain for any Bounded Context covers the identification of those artifacts that will express the business intent of the Bounded Context clearly. At a high level, this includes the identification and implementation of Aggregates, Entities, and Value Objects.

Aggregates/Entities/Value Objects

Aggregates are the centerpiece of our Domain Model. To recap, we have four aggregates within each of our Bounded Contexts as illustrated in Figure 4-19.

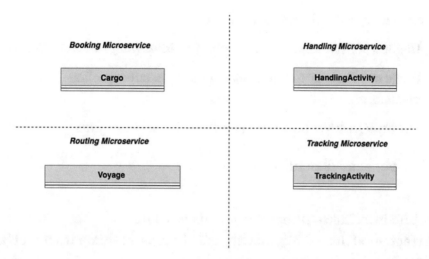

Figure 4-19. *Aggregates within our Bounded Context(s)/Microservices*

Implementation of an Aggregate covers the following aspects:

- Aggregate Class Implementation

- Domain Richness via Business Attributes

- Implementing Entities/Value Objects

Aggregate Class Implementation

Since we intend to use MySQL as our Datastore for each of our Bounded Contexts, we intend to use JPA (Java Persistence API) from the Java EE specification. JPA provides a standard way of defining and implementing Entities/Services which interact with underlying SQL Datastores.

JPA Integration: Helidon MP

Helidon MP provides us support to utilize JPA through an external integration mechanism. To include this support, we need to add some additional configuration/dependencies:

pom.xml

Listing 4-2 shows the changes that need to be done in the ***pom.xml dependencies file*** that Helidon MP generates.

The dependency list includes the following:

- Helidon MP JPA Integration Support (***helidon-integrations-cdi-jpa***)

- Usage of ***HikariCP*** for our Datasource connection pooling mechanism

- The MySQL driver library for Java (***mysql-connector-java***)

Listing 4-2. pom.xml dependencies

```
<dependency>
    <groupId>io.helidon.integrations.cdi</groupId>
    <artifactId>helidon-integrations-cdi-datasource-hikaricp</artifactId>
</dependency>
<dependency>
    <groupId>mysql</groupId>
    <artifactId>mysql-connector-java</artifactId>
</dependency>
<dependency>
    <groupId>io.helidon.integrations.cdi</groupId>
    <artifactId>helidon-integrations-cdi-jpa</artifactId>
</dependency>
<dependency>
    <groupId>io.helidon.integrations.cdi</groupId>
    <artifactId>helidon-integrations-cdi-jpa-weld</artifactId>
</dependency>
<dependency>
    <groupId>io.helidon.integrations.cdi</groupId>
    <artifactId>helidon-integrations-cdi-eclipselink</artifactId>
</dependency>
<dependency>
    <groupId>jakarta.persistence</groupId>
    <artifactId>jakarta.persistence-api</artifactId>
</dependency>
<dependency>
    <groupId>io.helidon.integrations.cdi</groupId>
    <artifactId>helidon-integrations-cdi-jta</artifactId>
```

```
</dependency>
<dependency>
    <groupId>io.helidon.integrations.cdi</groupId>
    <artifactId>helidon-integrations-cdi-jta-weld</artifactId>
</dependency>
<dependency>
    <groupId>javax.transaction</groupId>
    <artifactId>javax.transaction-api</artifactId>
</dependency>
microprofile-config
```

We need to configure the Connection properties for each of our MySQL Database instances. Listing 4-3 shows the configuration properties that need to be added. You would need to replace the values with your MySQL Instance(s) Details as necessary:

Listing 4-3. Configuration information for the datasource connectivity

```
javax.sql.DataSource.<<BoundedContext-Name>>.dataSourceClassName=com.mysql.
cj.jdbc.MysqlDataSource
javax.sql.DataSource.<<BoundedContext-Name>>.dataSource.
url=jdbc:mysql://<<Machine-Name>>:<<Machine-Port>>/<<MySQL-Database-
Instance-Name>>
javax.sql.DataSource.<<BoundedContext-Name>>.dataSource.user=
<<MySQL-Database-Instance-UserID>>
javax.sql.DataSource.<<BoundedContext-Name>>.dataSource.password=
<<MySQL-Database-Instance-Password>>
persistence.xml
```

The final step is to configure a JPA "***persistence-unit***" mapped to the Datasource configured in the ***microprofile-config*** file as seen in Listing 4-4:

Listing 4-4. Configuration information for the persistence unit

```
<persistence version="2.2"  xmlns="http://xmlns.jcp.org/xml/ns/
persistence  xmlns:xsi="http://www.w3.org/2001/XMLSchema-instance"
xsi:schemaLocation="http://xmlns.jcp.org/xml/ns/persistence  http://xmlns.
jcp.org/xml/ns/persistence/persistence_2_2.xsd">
```

```
<persistence-unit name="<<BoundedContext-Name>>" transaction-type="JTA">
    <jta-data-source><<BoundedContext-Datasource>></jta-data-source>
</persistence-unit>
</persistence>
```

We are now ready to implement JPA within our MicroProfile applications. Unless stated otherwise, all our Aggregates within all our Bounded Contexts implement the same mechanism.

Each of our root aggregate classes is implemented as a JPA entity. There are no specific annotations that JPA provides to annotate a specific class as a root aggregate, so we take a regular POJO and use the JPA-provided standard annotation @Entity. Taking the Booking Bounded Context as an example which has Cargo as the root Aggregate, Listing 4-5 shows the minimalistic code required for a JPA Entity:

Listing 4-5. Cargo root aggregate implemented as a JPA Entity

```
package com.practicalddd.cargotracker.bookingms.domain.model.aggregates;
import javax.persistence.*;
@Entity //JPA Entity Marker
public class Cargo {
}
```

Every JPA Entity requires an identifier. For our Aggregate Identifier implementation, we choose to have a ***technical/surrogate identifier (Primary Key)*** for our Cargo Aggregate derived from a MySQL sequence. In addition to the technical identifier, we also choose to have a ***Business Key***.

The Business key conveys the business intent of the aggregate identifier clear, that is, Booking Identifier of a newly booked cargo, and is the key that is exposed to external consumers of the Domain Model (more on this later). The technical key on the other hand is a pure internal representation of the aggregate identifier and is useful to maintain relationships ***within a Bounded Context*** between the Aggregates and its Dependent Objects (see Value Objects/Entities in the following).

Continuing with our example of the Cargo Aggregate within the Booking Bounded Context, we add the Technical and Business Keys to the Class implementation until now.

Listing 4-6 demonstrates this. The *"@Id"* annotation identifies the primary key on our Cargo Aggregate. There is no specific annotation to identify the Business Key, so we just implement it as a regular POJO (***BookingId***) and ***embed*** it within our Aggregate using the "*@**Embedded**"* annotation provided by JPA:

Listing 4-6. Cargo root aggregate identifier implementation

```
package com.practicalddd.cargotracker.bookingms.domain.model.aggregates;
import javax.persistence.*;
@Entity
public class Cargo {
    @Id //Identifier Annotation provided by JPA
    @GeneratedValue(strategy = GenerationType.AUTO) // Rely on a MySQL
    generated sequence
    private Long id;
    @Embedded //Annotation which enables usage of Business Objects instead
    of primitive types
    private BookingId bookingId; // Business Identifier
}
```

Listing 4-7 shows the implementation of the BookingId Business Key Class:

Listing 4-7. BookingId business key class implementation

```
package com.practicalddd.cargotracker.bookingms.domain.model.aggregates;
import javax.persistence.*;
import java.io.Serializable;
/**
 * Business Key Identifier for the Cargo Aggregate
 */
@Embeddable
public class BookingId implements Serializable {
    @Column(name="booking_id")
    private String bookingId;
    public BookingId(){}
    public BookingId(String bookingId){this.bookingId = bookingId;}
    public String getBookingId(){return this.bookingId;}
}
```

We now have a bare-bones implementation of an Aggregate (Cargo) using JPA. The other aggregates have the same mechanism of implementation barring the Handling Activity Bounded Context. Since it is an event log, we decide to implement only one key for the Aggregate, that is, the Activity Id.

Figure 4-20 summarizes our bare-bones implementation of all our Aggregates.

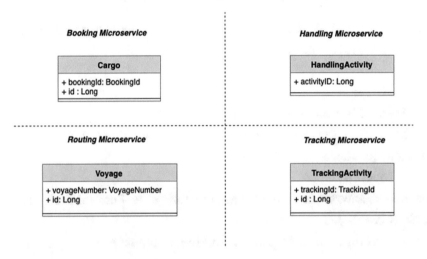

Figure 4-20. Bare-Bones implementation of our Aggregates

Domain Richness: Business Attributes

With the bare-bones implementation ready, let us move onto the meat of the Aggregate – Domain richness. ***The Aggregate of any Bounded Context should be able to express the Business Language of the Bounded Context clearly***. Essentially, what it means in pure technical terms is that our Aggregate should not be anemic, that is, only containing getter/setter methods.

An ***anemic aggregate*** goes against the fundamental principle of DDD since it essentially would mean ***the Business Language being expressed in multiple layers of an application*** which in turn leads to an unmaintainable piece of software in the long run.

So how do we implement a Domain-Rich Aggregate? The short answer is ***Business Attributes and Business Methods***. Our focus in this section is going to be on the Business Attributes aspect while we will cover the Business Methods part as part of the Domain Model Operations implementation.

Business Attributes of an Aggregate capture the state of an Aggregate as attributes depicted using Business Terms rather than Technical Terms.

Let us walk through the example of our Cargo aggregate.

Translating state to business concepts, the Cargo Aggregate has the following attributes:

- *Origin Location* of the cargo.

- *Booking Amount* of the cargo.

- *Route specification* (Origin Location, Destination Location, Destination Arrival Deadline).

- *Itinerary* that the cargo is assigned to based on the Route Specification. The Itinerary consists of multiple *Legs* that the cargo might be routed through to get to the destination.

- *Delivery Progress* of the cargo against its Route Specification and Itinerary assigned to it. The Delivery Progress provides details on the *Routing Status, Transport Status, Current Voyage of the cargo, Last Known Location of the cargo, Next Expected Activity, and the Last Activity that occurred on the cargo*.

Figure 4-21 illustrates the Cargo Aggregate and its relationships with its dependent objects. Notice how we are able to clearly represent the Cargo Aggregate in *pure Business Terms*.

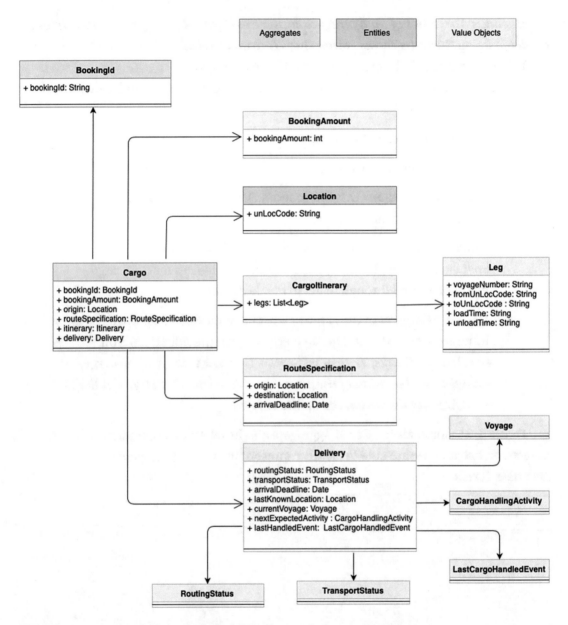

Figure 4-21. *Cargo Aggregate and its dependent associations*

JPA provides us a set of annotations *(@Embedded, @Embeddable)* to help implement our Aggregate class using Business Objects.

Listing 4-8 shows the example of our Cargo Aggregate with all the ***Dependencies modeled as Business Objects:***

Listing 4-8. Business object dependencies for the Cargo root aggregate

```
package com.practicalddd.cargotracker.bookingms.domain.model.aggregates;
import javax.persistence.*;

import com.practicalddd.cargotracker.bookingms.domain.model.entities.*;
import com.practicalddd.cargotracker.bookingms.domain.model.valueobjects.*;
@Entity
public class Cargo {
    @Id
    @GeneratedValue(strategy = GenerationType.AUTO)
    private Long id;
    @Embedded
    private BookingId bookingId; // Aggregate Identifier
    @Embedded
    private BookingAmount bookingAmount; //Booking Amount
    @Embedded
    private Location origin; //Origin Location of the Cargo
    @Embedded
    private RouteSpecification routeSpecification; //Route Specification of
    the Cargo
    @Embedded
    private CargoItinerary itinerary; //Itinerary Assigned to the Cargo
    @Embedded
    private Delivery delivery; // Checks the delivery progress of the cargo
    against the actual Route Specification and Itinerary
}
```

Dependent classes for an Aggregate are ***modeled either as Entity Objects or Value Objects***. To recap, Entity Objects within a Bounded Context have an identity of their own but always exist within a root aggregate, that is, they cannot exist independently, and they never change during the complete lifecycle of the aggregate. Value Objects on the other hand have no identity of their own and are easily replaceable in any instance of an aggregate.

Continuing with our example, within the Cargo Aggregate, we have the following:

- *"Origin"* of the cargo as an ***Entity Object*** (Location). This cannot change within a Cargo Aggregate Instance and hence is modeled as an Entity Object.

- ***Booking Amount*** of the cargo, ***Route Specification*** of the cargo, ***Cargo Itinerary*** assigned to the cargo, and the ***Delivery of the cargo*** as Value Objects. These objects are replaceable in any Cargo Aggregate Instance and hence are modeled as Value Objects.

Let us walk through the scenarios and the rationale why we have these as value objects and not as entities because it is an ***important domain modeling decision***:

- When a new cargo is booked, we will have ***a new Route Specification***, ***an empty Cargo Itinerary***, and ***no delivery progress***.

- As the cargo is assigned an itinerary, the ***empty Cargo Itinerary*** is replaced by an ***allocated Cargo Itinerary***.

- As the cargo progresses through multiple ports as part of its itinerary, the ***Delivery*** progress is updated and replaced within the root aggregate.

- Finally, if the customer chooses to change the delivery location of the cargo or the deadline for delivery, the ***Route Specification changes***, a ***new Cargo Itinerary*** will be assigned, the ***Delivery is recalculated***, and the ***Booking Amount changes***.

They are ***all replaceable and hence modeled as Value Objects***. That is the ***thumb rule for modeling Entities and Value Objects within an Aggregate***.

Implementing Entity Objects/Value Objects

Entity Objects/Value Objects are implemented as JPA Embeddable objects using the *"@Embeddable"* annotation provided by JPA. They are then embedded into the Aggregate using the "*@Embedded*" annotation.

Listing 4-9 shows the mechanism of embedding into the Aggregate class.

Let us look at the implementation of the Cargo Aggregate's Entity Objects/Value Objects.

Listing 4-9 demonstrates the ***Location Entity Object***. Notice the package name (***grouped under model.entities***):

Listing 4-9. Location entity class implementation

```
package com.practicalddd.cargotracker.bookingms.domain.model.entities;
import javax.persistence.Column;
import javax.persistence.Embeddable;
/**
 * Location Entity class represented by a unique 5-digit UN Location code.
 */
@Embeddable
public class Location {
    @Column(name = "origin_id")
    private String unLocCode;
    public Location(){}
    public Location(String unLocCode){this.unLocCode = unLocCode;}
    public void setUnLocCode(String unLocCode){this.unLocCode = unLocCode;}
    public String getUnLocCode(){return this.unLocCode;}
}
```

Listing 4-10 demonstrates examples of the ***Booking Amount/Route Specification Value Object(s)***. Notice the package name (***grouped under model.valueobjects***):

Listing 4-10. Booking Amount Value object implementation

```
package com.practicalddd.cargotracker.bookingms.domain.model.valueobjects;
import javax.persistence.Column;
import javax.persistence.Embeddable;
/**
 * Domain model representation of the Booking Amount for a new Cargo.
 * Contains the Booking Amount of the Cargo
 */
@Embeddable
public class BookingAmount {
    @Column(name = "booking_amount", unique = true, updatable= false)
    private Integer bookingAmount;
```

```
    public BookingAmount(){}
    public BookingAmount(Integer bookingAmount){this.bookingAmount =
    bookingAmount;}
    public void setBookingAmount(Integer bookingAmount){this.bookingAmount =
    bookingAmount;}
    public Integer getBookingAmount(){return this.bookingAmount;}
}
```

Listing 4-11 demonstrates the *Route Specification Value Object*:

Listing 4-11. Route Specification Value object implementation

```
package com.practicalddd.cargotracker.bookingms.domain.model.valueobjects;
import com.practicalddd.cargotracker.bookingms.domain.model.entities.
Location;
import javax.persistence.*;
import javax.validation.constraints.NotNull;
import java.util.Date;
/**
 * Route Specification of the Booked Cargo
 */
@Embeddable
public class RouteSpecification {
    private static final long serialVersionUID = 1L;
    @Embedded
    @AttributeOverride(name = "unLocCode", column = @Column(name =
    "spec_origin_id"))
    private Location origin;
    @Embedded
    @AttributeOverride(name = "unLocCode", column = @Column(name =
    "spec_destination_id"))
    private Location destination;
    @Temporal(TemporalType.DATE)
    @Column(name = "spec_arrival_deadline")
    @NotNull
    private Date arrivalDeadline;
    public RouteSpecification() { }
```

```
/**
 * @param origin origin location
 * @param destination destination location
 * @param arrivalDeadline arrival deadline
 */
public RouteSpecification (Location origin, Location destination,
                           Date arrivalDeadline) {
    this.origin = origin;
    this.destination = destination;
    this.arrivalDeadline = (Date) arrivalDeadline.clone();
}
public Location getOrigin() {
    return origin;
}
public Location getDestination() {
    return destination;
}

public Date getArrivalDeadline() {
    return new Date(arrivalDeadline.getTime());
}
}
```

The remaining Value Objects (***RouteSpecification, CargoItinerary, and Delivery***) are implemented in the same way using the "***@Embeddable***" annotation and embedded into the Cargo Aggregate using the "***@Embedded***" annotation.

Note   Please refer to the chapter's source code for the complete implementation.

Let us look at abbreviated class diagrams for the other Aggregates (HandlingActivity, Voyage, and Tracking). Figures 4-22, 4-23, and 4-24 illustrate this.

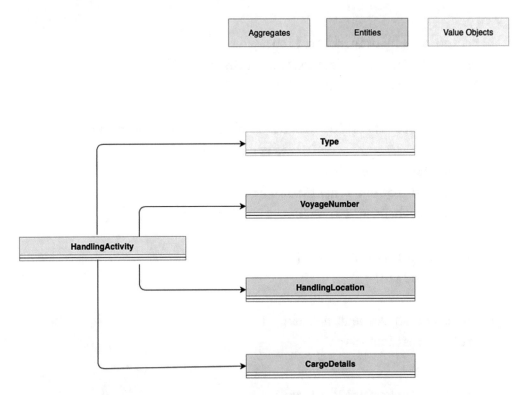

Figure 4-22. *Handling Activity and its dependent associations*

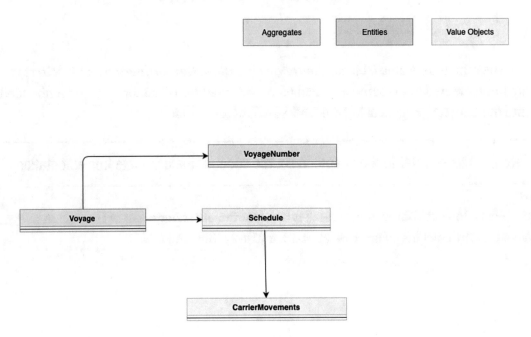

Figure 4-23. *Voyage and its dependent associations*

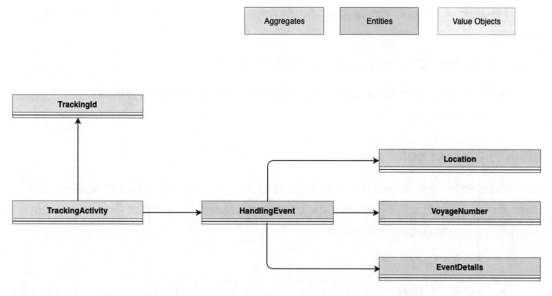

Figure 4-24. *Tracking Activity and its dependent associations*

This completes the implementation of the Core Domain Model. Let us look at the implementation of the Domain model operations next.

Note   The source code for the book has the Core Domain Model demonstrated via package segregation. You can view the source code to get a clearer view of the types of objects within the domain model at github.com/practicalddd.

Domain Model Operations

Domain Model operations within a Bounded Context deal with any kind of operations associated with the state of the Aggregate of the Bounded Context. This includes operations that change the status of an Aggregate (***Commands***), retrieve the current state of the Aggregate (***Queries***), or notify the Aggregate state change(***Events***).

Commands

Commands are responsible for changing the state of the Aggregate within a Bounded Context.

Implementation of Commands within a Bounded Context involves the following steps:

- Identification/implementation of Commands

- Identification/implementation of Command Handlers to process Commands

Identification of Commands

Identification of Commands revolves around identifying any operation that affects the state of the Aggregate. For example, the Booking Command Bounded Context has the following operations or commands:

- Book a Cargo

- Route a Cargo

Both these operations result in a change of state of the Cargo Aggregate within the Bounded Context and are hence identified as Commands.

Implementation of Commands

Once identified, implementing the identified Commands within the MicroProfile implementation is done using regular POJOs. Listing 4-12 demonstrates the implementation of the BookCargoCommand class for the Book Cargo Command:

Listing 4-12. BookCargoCommand class implementation

```
package com.practicalddd.cargotracker.bookingms.domain.model.commands;
import java.util.Date;
/**
 * Book Cargo Command class
 */
public class BookCargoCommand {

    private String bookingId;
    private int bookingAmount;
    private String originLocation;
    private String destLocation;
    private Date destArrivalDeadline;
```

```java
    public BookCargoCommand(){}

    public BookCargoCommand(int bookingAmount,
                          String originLocation, String destLocation,
                          Date destArrivalDeadline){

        this.bookingAmount = bookingAmount;
        this.originLocation = originLocation;
        this.destLocation = destLocation;
        this.destArrivalDeadline = destArrivalDeadline;
    }

    public void setBookingId(String bookingId){this.bookingId = bookingId;}

    public String getBookingId(){return this.bookingId;}

    public void setBookingAmount(int bookingAmount){
        this.bookingAmount = bookingAmount;
    }

    public int getBookingAmount(){
        return this.bookingAmount;
    }

    public String getOriginLocation() {return originLocation; }

    public void setOriginLocation(String originLocation)
    {this.originLocation = originLocation; }

    public String getDestLocation() { return destLocation; }

    public void setDestLocation(String destLocation) { this.destLocation =
    destLocation; }

    public Date getDestArrivalDeadline() { return destArrivalDeadline; }

    public void setDestArrivalDeadline(Date destArrivalDeadline)
    { this.destArrivalDeadline = destArrivalDeadline; }
}
```

Identification of Command Handlers

Every Command will have a corresponding Command Handler. The purpose of the Command Handler is ***to process the input command and set the state of the Aggregate***. Command Handlers are ***the only place within the Domain Model where Aggregate state is set***. This is a strict rule that needs to be followed to help implement a rich Domain Model.

Implementation of Command Handlers

Since the Eclipse MicroProfile platform does not provide any out-of-the-box capabilities to implement Command Handlers, our methodology of implementation will be to ***just identify the routines on the Aggregates which can be denoted as Command Handlers***. For our first command ***Book Cargo,*** we identify the ***constructor of the Aggregate as our Command Handler;*** and for our second command ***Route Cargo,*** we create a new routine "***assignToRoute()***" as our Command Handler.

Listing 4-13 shows the snippet of code of the constructor of the Cargo Aggregate. The constructor accepts the ***BookCargoCommand*** as an input parameter and sets the corresponding state of the Aggregate:

Listing 4-13. BookCargoCommand command handler

```
/**
 * Constructor Command Handler for a new Cargo booking
 */
public Cargo(BookCargoCommand bookCargoCommand){
    this.bookingId = new BookingId(bookCargoCommand.getBookingId());
    this.routeSpecification = new RouteSpecification(
                new Location(bookCargoCommand.getOriginLocation()),
                new Location(bookCargoCommand.getDestLocation()),
                bookCargoCommand.getDestArrivalDeadline()
        );
    this.origin = routeSpecification.getOrigin();
    this.itinerary = CargoItinerary.EMPTY_ITINERARY; //Empty Itinerary
    since the Cargo has not been routed yet
    this.bookingAmount = bookingAmount;
    this.delivery = Delivery.derivedFrom(this.routeSpecification,
            this.itinerary, LastCargoHandledEvent.EMPTY);
}
```

Listing 4-14 shows the snippet of code for the **assignToRoute()** Command Handler. It accepts the **RouteCargoCommand** class as input and sets the state of the Aggregate:

Listing 4-14. RouteCargoCommand command handler

```
/**
 * Command Handler for the Route Cargo Command. Sets the state of the
   Aggregate and registers the
 * Cargo routed event
 * @param routeCargoCommand
 */
public void assignToRoute(RouteCargoCommand routeCargoCommand) {
    this.itinerary = routeCargoCommand.getCargoItinerary();
    // Handling consistency within the Cargo aggregate synchronously
    this.delivery = delivery.updateOnRouting(this.routeSpecification,
            this.itinerary);

}
```

Figure 4-25 illustrates the class diagram for our Command Handler implementation.

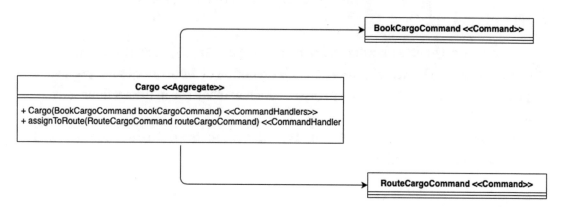

Figure 4-25. *Class diagram for the Command Handler implementation*

In summary, Command Handlers play a very important role of managing the Aggregate state within a Bounded Context. The actual invocation of Command Handlers happens via Application Services which we shall see in the sections that follow.

Queries

Queries within the Bounded Context are responsible for ***providing the state of the Bounded Context's Aggregate*** to external consumers.

To implement Queries, we utilize ***JPA Named Queries,*** that is, queries that can be defined on an Aggregate to retrieve state in various forms. Listing 4-15 demonstrates the snippet of code from the Cargo Aggregate that defines the queries that need to be made available. In this case, we have three queries – ***Find All Cargos, Find a Cargo by its Booking Identifier, and Final Booking Identifiers for all Cargos:***

Listing 4-15. Named Queries within the Cargo root aggregate

```
@NamedQueries({
        @NamedQuery(name = "Cargo.findAll",
                query = "Select c from Cargo c"),
        @NamedQuery(name = "Cargo.findByBookingId",
                query = "Select c from Cargo c where c.bookingId =
                :bookingId"),
        @NamedQuery(name = "Cargo.findAllBookingIds",
                query = "Select c.bookingId from Cargo c") })
public class Cargo{}
```

In summary, Queries play the role of presenting the Aggregate state within a Bounded Context. The actual invocation and execution of these queries happens via Application Services and Repository classes which we shall see in the sections that follow.

This completes the implementation of Queries within the Domain Model. We shall now see how to implement Events.

Events

An event within a Bounded Context is any operation that publishes the ***Bounded Context's Aggregate State Changes as Events***. Since Commands change the state of an Aggregate, it is safe to assume that any Command operation within a Bounded Context will result in a corresponding Event. The subscribers of these events could be either other Bounded Contexts within the same domain or Bounded Contexts belonging to any other external domains.

Domain Events play a central role within a microservices architecture, and it is important to implement them in a robust manner. The distributed nature of a microservices architecture mandates the usage of Events via a ***choreography mechanism*** to ***maintain state and transactional consistency*** between the various Bounded Contexts of a microservices-based application.

Figure 4-26 illustrates examples of the events that flow between the various Bounded Contexts of the Cargo Tracker Application.

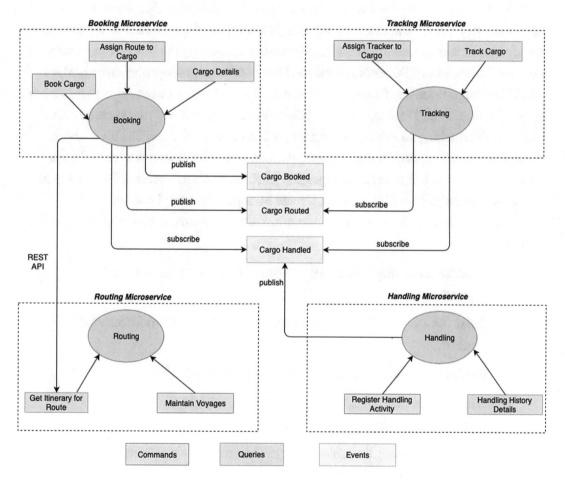

Figure 4-26. *Flow of Events in a Microservices architecture*

Let us explain this a bit more using an example Business case.

When a cargo is assigned a route, this means that the cargo can now be tracked which requires a Tracking Identifier to be issued to the cargo. The assigning of route to the cargo is handled within the Booking Bounded Context, while issuing the tracking identifier is handled within the Tracking Bounded Context. In the monolithic way of doing things, the process of assigning a route to the cargo and issuing the tracking identifier happens together since *we can maintain the same transactional context across multiple Bounded Contexts due to the shared model for processes, runtimes, and Datastores*.

However, in a microservices architecture, it is not possible to achieve the same since it is a *shared nothing architecture*. When a cargo is assigned a route, the Booking Bounded Context is only responsible for ensuring that the Cargo Aggregate's state reflects the new route. The Tracking Bounded Context needs to know about this change of state so that it can issue the Tracking Identifier accordingly to *complete the business use case*. This is where *Domain Events and Event Choreography* play an important role. If the Cargo Bounded Context can raise the event that the Cargo Aggregate has been assigned a Route, the Tracking Bounded Context can subscribe to that specific event and issue the tracking identifier to complete this business use case. The mechanism of *raising events* and *delivering events* to various Bounded Contexts to complete a business use case is the *event choreography pattern*. In short, Domain Events/Event Choreography helps in building Event-Driven Microservices applications.

There are four stages to the implementation of a robust event-driven choreography architecture:

- *Register* the Domain Events that need to be raised from a Bounded Context.

- *Raise* the Domain Events that need to be published from a Bounded Context.

- *Publish* the Events that are raised from a Bounded Context.

- *Subscribe* to the Events that have been published from other Bounded Contexts.

Considering the capabilities provided by the MicroProfile platform, the implementation is split across multiple areas:

- Raising of Events is implemented by the *Application Services.*

- Publishing of Events is implemented *by the Outbound Services.*

- Subscribing to Events is handled *by the Interface/Inbound services.*

As part of our implementation for Domain Events, we will use **CDI Events as the logical infrastructure** for Event publishing/subscribing, while we will use **RabbitMQ to provide us the physical infrastructure** to achieve Event choreography.

The only area that we will cover in this section, since we are in the phase of implementing the Domain Model, is the creation of the Event Classes that participate in the choreography across multiple Bounded Contexts. The subsequent sections of the chapter will deal with each of the other aspects *(Application Services will cover the implementation of raising of these Events, Outbound services will cover the implementation of the publishing of Events, and Inbound Services will cover the implementation of subscribing to the Events)*.

Event classes within the Domain Model are created as custom annotations using the "*@interface*" annotation. We will see the usages of these Events in the sections that follow when we implement the other areas of the event choreography architecture.

Listing 4-16 demonstrates the CargoBookedEvent implemented as a custom annotation:

Listing 4-16. CargoBookedEvent stereotype annotation

```
import javax.inject.Qualifier;
import java.lang.annotation.Retention;
import java.lang.annotation.Target;
import static java.lang.annotation.ElementType.FIELD;
import static java.lang.annotation.ElementType.PARAMETER;
import static java.lang.annotation.RetentionPolicy.RUNTIME;
/**
 * Event Class for the Cargo Booked Event. Implemented as a custom
   annotation
 */
@Qualifier
@Retention(RUNTIME)
@Target({FIELD, PARAMETER})
public @interface CargoBookedEvent {
}
```

Similarly, Listing 4-17 demonstrates the implementation of the CargoRoutedEvent event class:

Listing 4-17. CargoRoutedEvent stereotype annotation

```
import javax.inject.Qualifier;
import java.lang.annotation.Retention;
import java.lang.annotation.Target;

import static java.lang.annotation.ElementType.FIELD;
import static java.lang.annotation.ElementType.PARAMETER;
import static java.lang.annotation.RetentionPolicy.RUNTIME;

/**
 * Event Class for the Cargo Routed Event. Wraps up the Cargo
 */

@Qualifier
@Retention(RUNTIME)
@Target({FIELD, PARAMETER})
public @interface CargoRoutedEvent {
}
```

This completes the ***demonstration of concepts to implement the Core Domain Model***. Let us now move onto ***implementing the Domain Model Services***.

Domain Model Services

Domain Model Services are used for two primary reasons. The first is to enable the Bounded Context's state to be ***made available to external parties*** through ***well-defined Interfaces***. The second is ***interacting with external parties*** be it to persist the Bounded Context's state to ***Datastores*** (Databases), publish the Bounded Context's state change events to external ***Message Brokers,*** or to ***communicate with other Bounded Contexts***.

There are three types of Domain Model Services for any Bounded Context:

- ***Inbound Services*** where we implement well-defined interfaces which enable external parties to interact with the Domain Model

- ***Outbound Services*** where we implement all interactions with External Repositories/other Bounded Contexts

– ***Application Services*** which act as the façade layer between the
Domain Model and both Inbound and Outbound services

Figure 4-27 illustrates the Domain Model Services implementation.

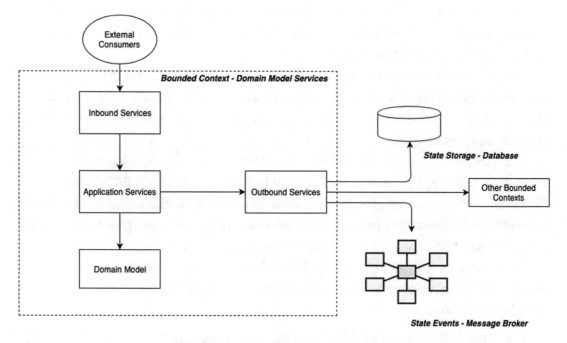

Figure 4-27. *Domain Model Services implementation summary*

Inbound Services

Inbound services (or Inbound Adaptors as denoted in the Hexagonal Architectural
Pattern) act as the outermost gateway for our Core Domain Model. As stated, it involves
the implementation of well-defined interfaces which enable external consumers to
interact with the core domain model.

The type of inbound services ***depends upon the types of operations*** we need to
expose to ***enable the external consumers of the Domain Model***.

Considering that we are implementing the microservices architectural pattern for
our Cargo Tracker application, we provide two types of Inbound Services:

– ***An API Layer based on REST*** which is used by external consumers to
invoke operations on the Bounded Context (***Commands/Queries***)

– ***An Event Handling Layer based on CDI Events*** which consumes
Events from the Message Broker and processes them

REST API

The responsibility of the REST API is to receive HTTP requests on behalf of the Bounded Context from external consumers. This request could be for Commands or Queries. The responsibility of the REST API layer is to translate it into the Command/Query Model recognized by the Bounded Context's Domain Model and delegate it to the Application Services Layer to further process it.

Looking back at Figure 4-5 which detailed out all the operations for the various Bounded Contexts *(e.g., Book Cargo, Assign Route to Cargo, Handle Cargo, Track Cargo)*, all these operations will have corresponding REST APIs which will accept these requests and process them.

Implementation of the REST API in Eclipse MicroProfile is by utilizing the REST capabilities provided by Helidon MP based on *JAX-RS* (Java API for RESTful Web Services). As the name suggests, this specification provides capabilities to build RESTful web services. *Helidon MP provides an implementation for this specification*, and this capability automatically gets added when we create the scaffold project.

Let us walk through an example of a REST API built using JAX-RS. Listing 4-18 depicts the *CargoBookingController class* which provides a REST API for our *Cargo Booking Command*.

- The REST API is available at the URL "*/cargobooking*".

- It has a single POST method that accepts a BookCargoResource which is the input payload to the API.

- It has a dependency on the CargoBookingCommandService which is an Application services which acts as a façade (see implementation in the following). This dependency is injected into the API class utilizing the "*@Inject*" annotation. This annotation is available as part of CDI.

- It transforms the Resource Data (*BookCargoResource*) to the Command Model (*BookCargoCommand*) using an Assembler utility class (*BookCargoCommandDTOAssembler*).

- After transforming, it delegates the process to the CargoBookingCommandService for further processing.

- It returns back a Response to the external consumer with the Booking Identifier of the newly booked cargo with a *Response Status of "200 OK"*.

Listing 4-18. CargoBooking controller class implementation

```
package com.practicalddd.cargotracker.bookingms.interfaces.rest;
import com.practicalddd.cargotracker.bookingms.application.internal.
commandservices.CargoBookingCommandService;
import com.practicalddd.cargotracker.bookingms.domain.model.aggregates.
BookingId;
import com.practicalddd.cargotracker.bookingms.interfaces.rest.dto.
BookCargoResource;
import com.practicalddd.cargotracker.bookingms.interfaces.rest.transform.
BookCargoCommandDTOAssembler;

import javax.enterprise.context.ApplicationScoped;
import javax.inject.Inject;
import javax.ws.rs.POST;
import javax.ws.rs.Path;
import javax.ws.rs.Produces;
import javax.ws.rs.core.MediaType;
import javax.ws.rs.core.Response;

@Path("/cargobooking")
@ApplicationScoped
public class CargoBookingController {
    private CargoBookingCommandService cargoBookingCommandService;
    // Application Service Dependency

    /**
     * Inject the dependencies (CDI)
     * @param cargoBookingCommandService
     */
    @Inject
    public CargoBookingController(CargoBookingCommandService
    cargoBookingCommandService){
        this.cargoBookingCommandService = cargoBookingCommandService;
    }
```

```
/**
 * POST method to book a cargo
 * @param bookCargoResource
 */

@POST
@Produces(MediaType.APPLICATION_JSON)
public Response bookCargo(BookCargoResource bookCargoResource){
    BookingId bookingId  = cargoBookingCommandService.bookCargo(
            BookCargoCommandDTOAssembler.toCommandFromDTO(book
            CargoResource));

    final Response returnValue = Response.ok()
            .entity(bookingId)
            .build();
    return returnValue;
    }
}
```

Listing 4-19 shows the implementation for the **BookCargoResource** class:

Listing 4-19. BookCargo resource class for the controller

```
package com.practicalddd.cargotracker.bookingms.interfaces.rest.dto;

import java.time.LocalDate;

/**
 * Resource class for the Book Cargo Command API
 */
public class BookCargoResource {

    private int bookingAmount;
    private String originLocation;
    private String destLocation;
    private LocalDate destArrivalDeadline;

    public BookCargoResource(){}
```

```java
public BookCargoResource(int bookingAmount,
                    String originLocation, String destLocation,
                    LocalDate destArrivalDeadline){

    this.bookingAmount = bookingAmount;
    this.originLocation = originLocation;
    this.destLocation = destLocation;
    this.destArrivalDeadline = destArrivalDeadline;
}

public void setBookingAmount(int bookingAmount){
    this.bookingAmount = bookingAmount;
}

public int getBookingAmount(){
    return this.bookingAmount;
}

public String getOriginLocation() {return originLocation; }

public void setOriginLocation(String originLocation) {this.
originLocation = originLocation; }

public String getDestLocation() { return destLocation; }

public void setDestLocation(String destLocation) { this.destLocation =
destLocation; }

public LocalDate getDestArrivalDeadline() { return destArrivalDeadline; }

public void setDestArrivalDeadline(LocalDate destArrivalDeadline) {
this.destArrivalDeadline = destArrivalDeadline; }

}
```

Listing 4-20 shows the implementation for the ***BookCargoCommandDTOAssembler***
class:

Listing 4-20. DTO Assembler class implementation

```
package com.practicalddd.cargotracker.bookingms.interfaces.rest.transform;

import com.practicalddd.cargotracker.bookingms.domain.model.commands.
BookCargoCommand;
import com.practicalddd.cargotracker.bookingms.interfaces.rest.dto.
BookCargoResource;

/**
 * Assembler class to convert the Book Cargo Resource Data to the Book
   Cargo Model
 */
public class BookCargoCommandDTOAssembler {

    /**
     * Static method within the Assembler class
     * @param bookCargoResource
     * @return BookCargoCommand Model
     */
    public static BookCargoCommand toCommandFromDTO(BookCargoResource
    bookCargoResource){

        return new BookCargoCommand(
                    bookCargoResource.getBookingAmount(),
                    bookCargoResource.getOriginLocation(),
                    bookCargoResource.getDestLocation(),
                    java.sql.Date.valueOf(bookCargoResource.
                    getDestArrivalDeadline()));
    }
}
```

Listing 4-21 shows the implementation for the ***BookCargoCommand*** class:

Listing 4-21. BookCargoCommand class implementation

```
package com.practicalddd.cargotracker.bookingms.domain.model.commands;

import java.util.Date;

/**
 * Book Cargo Command class
 */
public class BookCargoCommand {

    private int bookingAmount;
    private String originLocation;
    private String destLocation;
    private Date destArrivalDeadline;

    public BookCargoCommand(){}

    public BookCargoCommand(int bookingAmount,
                          String originLocation, String destLocation,
                          Date destArrivalDeadline){

        this.bookingAmount = bookingAmount;
        this.originLocation = originLocation;
        this.destLocation = destLocation;
        this.destArrivalDeadline = destArrivalDeadline;
    }

    public void setBookingAmount(int bookingAmount){
        this.bookingAmount = bookingAmount;
    }

    public int getBookingAmount(){
        return this.bookingAmount;
    }
```

```
public String getOriginLocation() {return originLocation; }

public void setOriginLocation(String originLocation)
{this.originLocation = originLocation; }

public String getDestLocation() { return destLocation; }

public void setDestLocation(String destLocation) { this.destLocation =
destLocation; }

public Date getDestArrivalDeadline() { return destArrivalDeadline; }

public void setDestArrivalDeadline(Date destArrivalDeadline)
{ this.destArrivalDeadline = destArrivalDeadline; }
}
```

Figure 4-28 demonstrates the class diagram for our implementation.

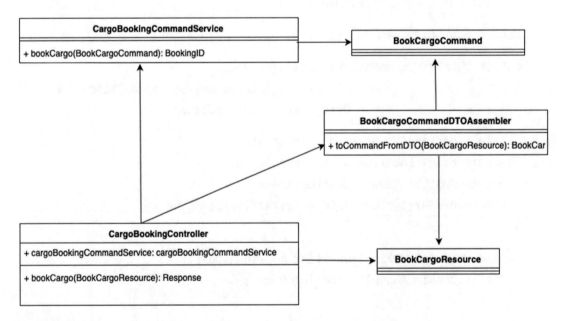

Figure 4-28. *Class diagram for the REST API implementation*

All our inbound REST API implementations follow the same approach which is illustrated in Figure 4-29.

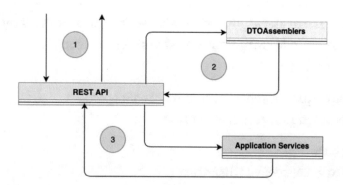

Figure 4-29. *Inbound Services implementation process summary*

1. The inbound request for a Command/Query comes to the REST API. API classes are implemented using JAX-RS capabilities provided by Helidon MP.

2. The REST API class uses a utility Assembler component to convert the Resource Data format to the Command/Query Data format required by the Domain Model.

3. The Command/Query Data is sent to the Application Services for further processing.

Event Handlers

The other type of interfaces that exist within our Bounded Contexts are the Event Handlers. Within a Bounded Context, Event Handlers are responsible for processing Events that the Bounded Context is interested in. These Events are raised by other Bounded Contexts within the applicationThese. "***EventHandlers***" are created within the subscribing Bounded Context which resides within the ***inbound/interface*** layer. The Event Handlers receive the Event along with the Event payload data and process them as a regular operation.

Listing 4-22 demonstrates the "***CargoRoutedEventHandler***" which resides within the Tracking Bounded Context. It ***observes*** the "***CargoRoutedEvent***" and receives the "***CargoRoutedEventData***" as the payload:

Listing 4-22. CargoRouted event handler implementation

```
package com.practicalddd.cargotracker.trackingms.interfaces.events;

import com.practicalddd.cargotracker.shareddomain.events.CargoRoutedEvent;
import com.practicalddd.cargotracker.shareddomain.events.
CargoRoutedEventData;

import javax.enterprise.context.ApplicationScoped;
import javax.enterprise.event.Observes;

@ApplicationScoped
public class CargoRoutedEventHandler {

    public void receiveEvent(@Observes @CargoRoutedEvent
    CargoRoutedEventData eventData) {
        //Process the Event
    }
}
```

All our Event Handler implementations follow the same approach as illustrated in Figure 4-30.

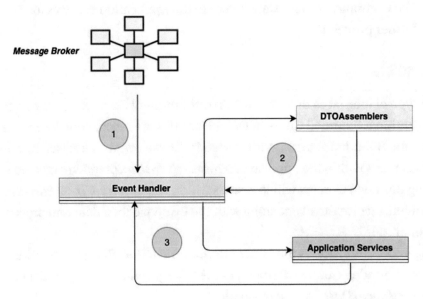

Figure 4-30. *Implementation process summary for Event Handler implementations*

1. Event Handlers receive inbound events from a Message Broker.

2. Event Handlers use a utility Assembler component to convert the Resource Data format to the Command Data format required by the Domain Model.

3. The Command Data is sent to the Application Services for further processing.

The implementation for mapping the Inbound Events to the corresponding physical queues of our Message Broker (RabbitMQ) is covered as part of the **Outbound Services – Message Broker** implementation.

Application Services

Application Services act as a façade or a port between the Inbound/Outbound Services and the Core Domain Model within a Bounded Context.

Within a Bounded Context, Application services are responsible for ***receiving requests from the Inbound Services*** and delegating them to the corresponding services, that is, Commands are delegated to **Command Services**, Queries are delegated to **Query Services**, and requests to communicate with other Bounded Contexts are delegated to **Outbound Services**. As part of the processing of a Command/Query/External Bounded Context Communication, Application services might be required to communicate with **Repositories, Message Brokers, or other Bounded Contexts. Outbound Services** are used to help in this communication.

Finally, since the MicroProfile specification does not provide the capability to raise Domain Events directly from the Domain Model, we rely on **Application Services to raise Domain Events.** The Domain Events are published onto the message brokers using Outbound Services.

Application Services classes are implemented **using CDI Managed Beans. Helidon MP provides an implementation for CDI,** and this capability automatically gets added when we create the scaffold project.

Figure 4-31 depicts the responsibilities of the Application Services.

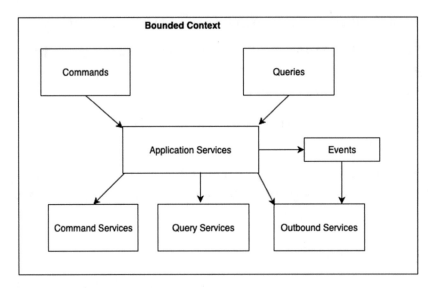

Figure 4-31. *Responsibilities of the Application Services*

Application Services: Command/Query Delegation

As part of this responsibility, Application services within a Bounded Context receive requests for processing Commands/Queries. These requests come in typically from the Inbound Services (API Layer). As part of the processing, Application services first utilize the ***CommandHandlers/QueryHandlers*** (see section on the Domain Model) of the Domain model to set state or query state. They then utilize the Outbound Services to persist state or execute queries on the state of the Aggregate.

Let us walk through an example of a Command Delegator Application Services Class, the ***Cargo Booking Command Application Services Class,*** which handles all Commands related to the Booking Bounded Context. We will also look at one of the Commands in more detail, ***the Book Cargo Command,*** which is an instruction to book a new cargo:

- The Application services class is implemented as a CDI Bean with a scope attached to it (in this case ***@Application***).

- The Application services class is provided with the necessary dependencies via the @Inject annotation. In this case, the CargoBookingCommandApplicationService class has dependencies on an ***outbound service repository class*** (***CargoRepository***) which it uses to persist the newly created cargo. It also has a dependency on the "***CargoBookedEvent***" which needs to be raised once the cargo is persisted. The CargoBookedEvent is a stereotype class and has the cargo as its payload event. We will look at Domain events in more detail in the sections that follow, so for now let us proceed.

- The Application Services delegates the processing to the *"bookCargo"* method. Before the processing of the method, the Application services ensures that a new Transaction is opened via the *"@Transactional"* annotation.

- The Application services class stores the newly booked cargo in the Booking MySQL Database table (CARGO) and fires the *Cargo Booked Event*.

- It returns back a response to the inbound interface with the Booking Identifier of the newly booked cargo.

Listing 4-23 demonstrates the *Cargo Booking Command Application Services Class* implementation:

Listing 4-23. Cargo Booking Command Application services implementation class

```
package com.practicalddd.cargotracker.bookingms.application.internal.
commandservices;

import com.practicalddd.cargotracker.bookingms.domain.model.aggregates.
BookingId;
import com.practicalddd.cargotracker.bookingms.domain.model.aggregates.
Cargo;
import com.practicalddd.cargotracker.bookingms.domain.model.commands.
BookCargoCommand;
import com.practicalddd.cargotracker.bookingms.domain.model.entities.
Location;
import com.practicalddd.cargotracker.bookingms.domain.model.events.
CargoBookedEvent;
import com.practicalddd.cargotracker.bookingms.domain.model.valueobjects.
BookingAmount;
import com.practicalddd.cargotracker.bookingms.domain.model.valueobjects.
RouteSpecification;
```

```java
import com.practicalddd.cargotracker.bookingms.infrastructure.repositories.
jpa.CargoRepository;

import javax.enterprise.context.ApplicationScoped;
import javax.enterprise.event.Event;
import javax.inject.Inject;
import javax.transaction.Transactional;

/**
 * Application Service class for the Cargo Booking Command
 */
@ApplicationScoped // Scope of the CDI Managed Bean. Application Scope
indicates a single instance for the service class.
public class CargoBookingCommandService   // CDI Managed Bean
{

    @Inject
    private CargoRepository cargoRepository; // Outbound Service to connect
    to the Booking Bounded Context MySQL Database Instance

    @Inject
    @CargoBookedEvent
    private Event<Cargo> cargoBooked; // Event that needs to be raised when
    the Cargo is Booked

    /**
     * Service Command method to book a new Cargo
     * @return BookingId of the Cargo
     */
    @Transactional // Inititate the Transaction
    public BookingId bookCargo(BookCargoCommand bookCargoCommand){

        BookingId bookingId = cargoRepository.nextBookingId();

        RouteSpecification routeSpecification = new RouteSpecification(
                new Location(bookCargoCommand.getOriginLocation()),
                new Location(bookCargoCommand.getDestLocation()),
                bookCargoCommand.getDestArrivalDeadline()
        );
```

```
        BookingAmount bookingAmount = new BookingAmount(bookCargoCommand.
        getBookingAmount());
        Cargo cargo = new Cargo(
                bookingId,
                bookingAmount,
                routeSpecification);
        cargoRepository.store(cargo); //Store the Cargo

        cargoBooked.fire(cargo); // Fire the Cargo Booked Event

        return bookingId;
    }

    // All other implementations of Commands for the Booking Bounded
    Context

}
```

Listing 4-24 demonstrates the ***Cargo Booking Query Application Services Class*** implementation which serves all queries related to the Booking Bounded Context. The implementation is the same as the Cargo Booking Command Application Services Class except for the ***fact that it does not raise any Domain Event*** since it just queries the state of a Bounded Context and does not change its state:

Listing 4-24. Cargo Booking Query Application services implementation

```
package com.practicalddd.cargotracker.bookingms.application.internal.
queryservices;

import com.practicalddd.cargotracker.bookingms.domain.model.aggregates.
BookingId;
import com.practicalddd.cargotracker.bookingms.domain.model.aggregates.
Cargo;
import com.practicalddd.cargotracker.bookingms.infrastructure.repositories.
jpa.CargoRepository;

import javax.enterprise.context.ApplicationScoped;
import javax.inject.Inject;
import javax.transaction.Transactional;
import java.util.List;
```

```java
/**
 * Application Service which caters to all queries related to the Booking
   Bounded Context
 */
@ApplicationScoped
public class CargoBookingQueryService {

    @Inject
    private CargoRepository cargoRepository; // Inject Dependencies

    /**
     * Find all Cargos
     * @return List<Cargo>
     */
    @Transactional
    public List<Cargo> findAll(){
        return cargoRepository.findAll();
    }

    /**
     * List All Booking Identifiers
     * @return List<BookingId>
     */
    public List<BookingId> getAllBookingIds(){
        return cargoRepository.getAllBookingIds();
    }

    /**
     * Find a specific Cargo based on its Booking Id
     * @param bookingId
     * @return Cargo
     */
    public Cargo find(String bookingId){
        return cargoRepository.find(new BookingId(bookingId));
    }
}
```

Figure 4-32 illustrates the class diagram for the implementation.

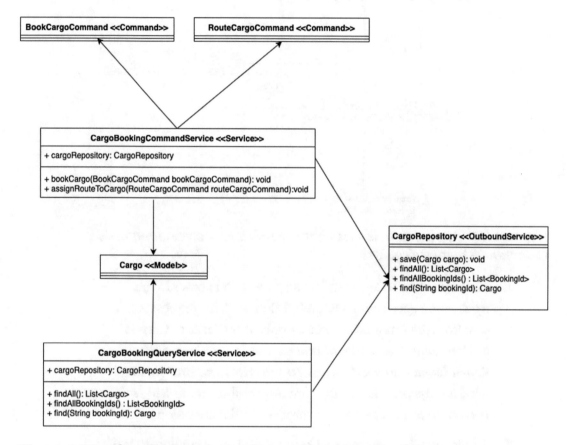

Figure 4-32. *Class diagram for implementation of Application Services as Command/Query Delegators*

All our Application Services implementations (Commands/Queries) follow the same approach which is illustrated in Figure 4-33.

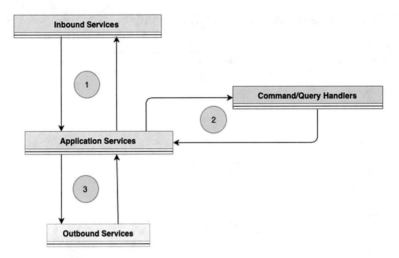

Figure 4-33. *Application Services implementation process summary as Command/Query Delegators*

1. The request for a Command/Query operation comes to the Application Services of a Bounded Context. This request is sent from the Inbound Services. Application Services Classes are ***implemented as CDI Managed Beans***, they have all their ***dependencies injected using CDI Injection Annotation***, they ***have a scope***, and finally they are responsible for ***creating a transactional context*** to start processing the operation.

2. Application Services rely on Command/Query Handlers to set/query Aggregate state.

3. As part of the processing of an operation, Application Services would need to interact with External Repositories. They rely on Outbound Services to perform these interactions.

Application Services: Raising Domain Events

The other role that Application Services play is to raise the Domain Events generated whenever the Bounded Context processes a Command.

In the previous chapter, we implemented Domain Events using the CDI 2.0 Eventing model. Based on an event notification/observer model, the event bus acts as the coordinator for the Event Producers and Consumers. In the monolithic implementation, we used a pure internal implementation of the Event Bus, and Events were being produced and consumed within the same thread of execution.

In the microservices world, this is something that will not work. Since each microservices is deployed separately, there needs to be a ***centralized message broker*** which coordinates the events across Event Producers and Consumers across multiple Bounded Contexts/microservices as illustrated in Figure 4-34. Our implementation will use RabbitMQ as the centralized message broker.

In the case of Eclipse MicroProfile since we use CDI Events, this basically translates to

- Firing of CDI Events and publishing them as messages to RabbitMQ or

- Observing CDI Events and consuming them as messages from RabbitMQ

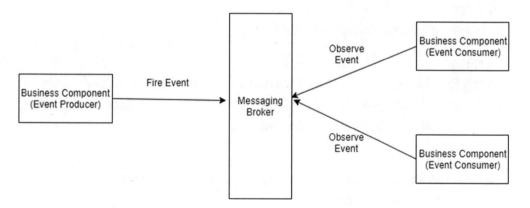

Figure 4-34. *Domain Events summary*

We have spoken about the business use case of the Tracking Bounded Context requiring to subscribe to the Cargo Routed event from the Booking Bounded Context to assign a Tracking Identifier to the booked cargo. Let us walk through the implementation of this business use case to demonstrate the publishing of Events by Application Services.

Listing 4-25 demonstrates the code section from the ***CargoBookingCommandService*** class that processes the command to assign a route to the cargo and then fires the "***CargoRouted***" event:

Listing 4-25. Firing the CargoRouted event from the Application services class

```
package com.practicalddd.cargotracker.bookingms.application.internal.
commandservices;

import javax.enterprise.event.Event; // CDI Eventing

/**
 * Application Service class for the Cargo Booking Command
 */
@ApplicationScoped
public class CargoBookingCommandService {

    @Inject
    private CargoRepository cargoRepository;

    @Inject
    @CargoRoutedEvent // Custom annotation for the Cargo Routed Event
    private Event<CargoRoutedEventData> cargoRouted; // Event that needs to
    be raised when the Cargo is Routed

     /**
     * Service Command method to assign a route to a Cargo
     * @param routeCargoCommand
     */
    @Transactional
    public void assignRouteToCargo(RouteCargoCommand routeCargoCommand){

        Cargo cargo = cargoRepository.find(new BookingId(routeCargoCommand.
        getCargoBookingId()));
        CargoItinerary cargoItinerary = externalCargoRoutingService.
        fetchRouteForSpecification(new RouteSpecification(
                new Location(routeCargoCommand.getOriginLocation()),
                new Location(routeCargoCommand.getDestinationLocation()),
                routeCargoCommand.getArrivalDeadline()
        ));
```

```
    routeCargoCommand.setCargoItinerary(cargoItinerary);
    cargo.assignToRoute(routeCargoCommand);
    cargoRepository.store(cargo);

    cargoRouted.fire(new CargoRoutedEventData(routeCargoCommand.
    getCargoBookingId()));
  }
}
```

There are three steps that we need to implement to fire CDI events and their payloads:

- Inject the Application Services with the Event that needs to be fired. This is done by using the custom annotation for the Event implemented as part of the Domain Model operations (***Events***). In this case, we inject the ***CargoRoutedEvent*** custom annotation to the ***CargoBookingCommandService***.

- We create an Event Payload Data object which will be the payload for the Event that is published. In this case, it is the ***CargoRoutedEventData*** object.

- We use the "***fire()***" ***method provided by CDI to raise the event*** and wrap the payload to be sent along with the event.

Figure 4-35 illustrates the class diagram for the Application Services implementation raising a Domain Event.

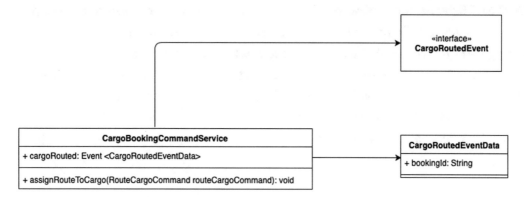

Figure 4-35. *Class diagram for Application Services implementation for raising Domain Events*

All our implementations for Application services responsible for raising domain Events follow the same approach. This is illustrated in Figure 4-36.

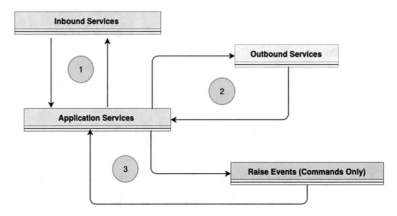

Figure 4-36. *Process summary for Application Services responsible for raising Domain Events*

This completes the demonstration of implementation of Raising of Domain Events. The implementation of raising of Domain Events is still at a logical level. We still need to publish these events to a physical Message Broker (RabbitMQ in our case) to complete our eventing architecture. We use ***Binder Classes*** to achieve this, and it is covered as part of our ***Outbound Services - Broker implementation***.

Outbound Services

Outbound Services provide capabilities to interact with ***services external to a Bounded Context***. The ***external service could be the Datastore*** where we store the Bounded Context's Aggregate State, it could be the ***message broker where we publish the Aggregate state***, or it could be an ***interaction with another Bounded Context***.

Figure 4-37 illustrates the responsibilities of the Outbound Services. They receive requests to communicate with the external services as part of an operation (Commands, Queries, Events). They use APIs (Persistence APIs, REST APIs, Broker APIs) based on the external service type to interact with them.

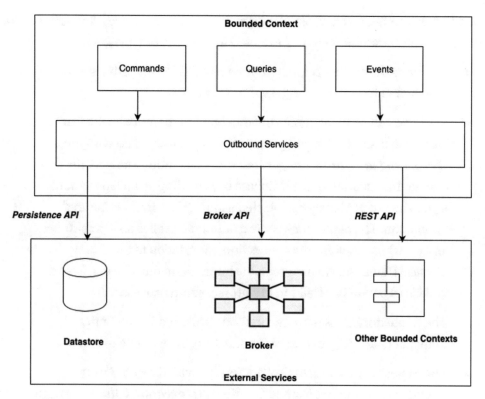

Figure 4-37. *Outbound Services*

Let us look at implementing these Outbound Service types.

Outbound Services: Repositories

The outbound services for Database access are implemented as *"Repository" classes*. A repository class is built around a specific aggregate and deals with all database operations for that aggregate including the following:

- Persistence of a new aggregate and its associations

- Update of an aggregate and its associations

- Querying the aggregate and its associations

Let us walk through an example of a Repository class, the ***Cargo Repository Class,*** which handles all Database operations related to the ***Cargo Aggregate***:

- The Repository class is implemented as a CDI Bean with a scope attached to it (in this case ***@Application***).

- Since we will be using JPA as the mechanism to interact with our Database Instance, we will provide the Repository class with the ***JPA-managed Entity Manager Resource***. The Entity Manager Resource enables interactions with a Database by providing an encapsulation layer. The Entity Manager is injected using "***@PersistenceContext***" annotation. The persistence context annotation relies on a persistence. xml file which contains the connection information to the actual physical Database. We have seen the implementation of a persistence. xml file as part of our Helidon MP project setup process.

- The Repository class uses the methods provided by the Entity Manager (***persist()***) to persist/update Cargo Aggregate instances.

- The Repository class uses the methods provided by the Entity Manager to create JPA Named Queries (***createNamedQueries()***) and run them to return results.

Listing 4-26 shows the implementation of the Cargo Repository class:

Listing 4-26. Cargo repository class implementation

```
package com.practicalddd.cargotracker.bookingms.infrastructure.
repositories.jpa;

import com.practicalddd.cargotracker.bookingms.domain.model.aggregates.
BookingId;
import com.practicalddd.cargotracker.bookingms.domain.model.aggregates.Cargo;

import javax.enterprise.context.ApplicationScoped;
import javax.persistence.EntityManager;
import javax.persistence.NoResultException;
import javax.persistence.PersistenceContext;

import java.util.ArrayList;
import java.util.List;
```

```java
import java.util.UUID;
import java.util.logging.Level;
import java.util.logging.Logger;

/**
 * Repository class for the Cargo Aggregate. Deals with all repository
   operations
 * related to the state of the Cargo
 */
@ApplicationScoped
public class CargoRepository {

    private static final long serialVersionUID = 1L;

    private static final Logger logger = Logger.getLogger(
            CargoRepository.class.getName());

    @PersistenceContext(unitName = "bookingms")
    private EntityManager entityManager;

    /**
     * Returns the Cargo Aggregate based on the Booking Identifier of a Cargo
     * @param bookingId
     * @return
     */
    public Cargo find(BookingId bookingId) {
        Cargo cargo;
        try {
            cargo = entityManager.createNamedQuery("Cargo.findByBookingId",
                    Cargo.class)
                    .setParameter("bookingId", bookingId)
                    .getSingleResult();
        } catch (NoResultException e) {
            logger.log(Level.FINE, "Find called on non-existant Booking
            ID.", e);
            cargo = null;
        }
```

```java
        return cargo;
    }

    /**
     * Stores the Cargo Aggregate
     * @param cargo
     */
    public void store(Cargo cargo) {
        entityManager.persist(cargo);
    }

    /**
     * Gets next Booking Identifier
     * @return
     */

    public BookingId nextBookingId() {
        String random = UUID.randomUUID().toString().toUpperCase();

        return new BookingId(random.substring(0, random.indexOf("-")));
    }

    /**
     * Find all Cargo Aggregates
     * @return
     */
    public List<Cargo> findAll() {
        return entityManager.createNamedQuery("Cargo.findAll", Cargo.class)
                .getResultList();
    }

    /**
     * Get all Booking Identifiers
     * @return
     */
```

```
public List<BookingId> getAllBookingIds() {
    List<BookingId> bookingIds = new ArrayList<BookingId>();

    try {
        bookingIds = entityManager.createNamedQuery(
                "Cargo.getAllTrackingIds", BookingId.class).
                getResultList();
    } catch (NoResultException e) {
        logger.log(Level.FINE, "Unable to get all tracking IDs", e);
    }

    return bookingIds;
    }
}
```

All our Repository implementations follow the same approach which is illustrated in Figure 4-38.

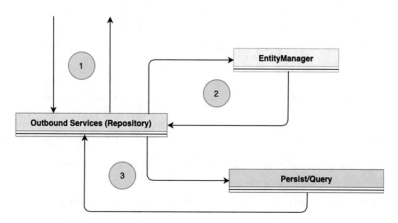

Figure 4-38. *Repository implementation process summary*

1. Repositories receive requests to change/query Aggregate state.

2. Repositories use the Entity Manager to perform database operations on the Aggregate (storing, querying).

3. The Entity Manager performs the operation and returns the results back to the Repository class.

Outbound Services: REST API(s)

Usage of REST API(s) as a mode of communication between microservices is quite a common requirement. While we have seen event choreography as one mechanism to do it, sometimes a synchronous call between Bounded Contexts is all what is required.

Let us explain this through an example. As part of the Cargo Booking process, we need to allocate the cargo an itinerary depending upon the route specification. The data required to generate an optimal itinerary is maintained as part of the Routing Bounded Context which maintains vessel movements, itineraries, and schedules. This requires the Booking Bounded Context's Booking Service to make an outbound call to the Routing Bounded Context's Routing Service which provides a REST API to retrieve all possible itineraries depending upon the cargo's Route Specification.

This is illustrated in Figure 4-39.

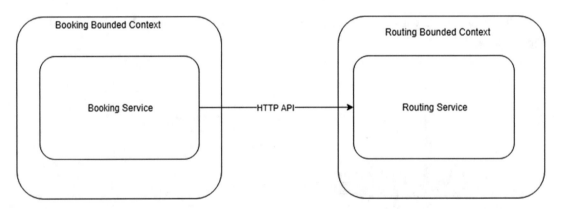

Figure 4-39. *HTTP invocation between two Bounded Contexts*

This however does pose a challenge in terms of the Domain Model. The Booking Bounded Context's Cargo aggregate has a representation of the Itinerary as a "***CargoItinerary***" object, while the Routing Bounded Context has a representation of the Itinerary as a "***TransitPath***" object. Thus, the invocation between the two Bounded Contexts will require a translation of sorts between their domain models.

This translation is typically done in the Anti-corruption Layer which acts as a bridge to communicate between two Bounded Contexts.

This is illustrated in Figure 4-40.

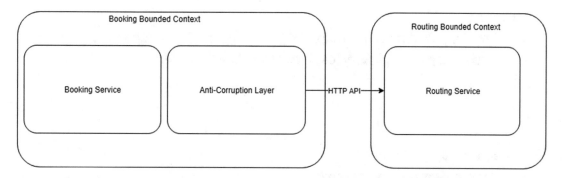

Figure 4-40. *Anti-corruption Layer between two Bounded Contexts*

The Booking Bounded Context relies on the MicroProfile Type Safe Rest Client capabilities provided by Helidon MP to invoke the Routing Service's REST API.

Let us walk through the complete implementation to understand the concept better:

- The first step is to implement the Routing Service REST API. This is done using the standard JAX-RS capabilities which we have implemented in the chapter before. Listing 4-27 demonstrates the Routing Service REST API implementation:

Listing 4-27. Cargo Routing controller implementation

```
package com.practicalddd.cargotracker.routingms.interfaces.rest;
import com.practicalddd.cargotracker.TransitPath;
import com.practicalddd.cargotracker.routingms.application.internal.
CargoRoutingService;
import javax.enterprise.context.ApplicationScoped;
import javax.inject.Inject;
import javax.ws.rs.*;
@Path("/cargoRouting")
@ApplicationScoped
public class CargoRoutingController {
    private CargoRoutingService cargoRoutingService; // Application Service
    Dependency

    /**
     * Provide the dependencies
     * @param cargoRoutingService
     */
```

```java
@Inject
public CargoRoutingController(CargoRoutingService cargoRoutingService){
    this.cargoRoutingService = cargoRoutingService;
}

/**
 *
 * @param originUnLocode
 * @param destinationUnLocode
 * @param deadline
 * @return TransitPath - The optimal route for a Route Specification
 */
@GET
@Path("/optimalRoute")
@Produces({"application/json"})
public TransitPath findOptimalRoute(
        @QueryParam("origin") String originUnLocode,
        @QueryParam("destination") String destinationUnLocode,
        @QueryParam("deadline") String deadline) {
    TransitPath transitPath = cargoRoutingService.findOptimalRoute
    (originUnLocode,destinationUnLocode,deadline);
    return transitPath;
}
}
```

The Routing Service implementation provides a REST API available at "/*optimalRoute*". It takes in a set of specifications - Origin Location, Destination Location, and Deadline. It then uses the Cargo Routing Application Services class to calculate the optimal route based on these specifications. The Domain model within the Routing Bounded Context represents the optimal route in terms of *Transit Paths (analogous to Itineraries)* and *Transit Edges (analogous to Legs)*.

Listing 4-28 demonstrates the Transit Path Domain Model class implementation:

Listing 4-28. Transit path model implementation

```java
import java.util.ArrayList;
import java.util.List;
/**
 * Domain Model representation of the Transit Path
 */
public class TransitPath {
    private List<TransitEdge> transitEdges;
    public TransitPath() {
        this.transitEdges = new ArrayList<>();
    }
    public TransitPath(List<TransitEdge> transitEdges) {
        this.transitEdges = transitEdges;
    }
    public List<TransitEdge> getTransitEdges() {
        return transitEdges;
    }
    public void setTransitEdges(List<TransitEdge> transitEdges) {
        this.transitEdges = transitEdges;
    }
    @Override
    public String toString() {
        return "TransitPath{" + "transitEdges=" + transitEdges + '}';
    }
}
```

Listing 4-29 demonstrates the Transit Edge Domain Model class implementation:

Listing 4-29. Transit Edge domain model implementation

```java
package com.practicalddd.cargotracker;

import java.io.Serializable;
import java.util.Date;

/**
 * Represents an edge in a path through a graph, describing the route of a
 * cargo.
 */
public class TransitEdge implements Serializable {

    private String voyageNumber;
    private String fromUnLocode;
    private String toUnLocode;
    private Date fromDate;
    private Date toDate;

    public TransitEdge() {    }

    public TransitEdge(String voyageNumber, String fromUnLocode,
            String toUnLocode, Date fromDate, Date toDate) {
        this.voyageNumber = voyageNumber;
        this.fromUnLocode = fromUnLocode;
        this.toUnLocode = toUnLocode;
        this.fromDate = fromDate;
        this.toDate = toDate;
    }

    public String getVoyageNumber() {
        return voyageNumber;
    }

    public void setVoyageNumber(String voyageNumber) {
        this.voyageNumber = voyageNumber;
    }
```

```java
public String getFromUnLocode() {
    return fromUnLocode;
}

public void setFromUnLocode(String fromUnLocode) {
    this.fromUnLocode = fromUnLocode;
}

public String getToUnLocode() {
    return toUnLocode;
}

public void setToUnLocode(String toUnLocode) {
    this.toUnLocode = toUnLocode;
}

public Date getFromDate() {
    return fromDate;
}

public void setFromDate(Date fromDate) {
    this.fromDate = fromDate;
}

public Date getToDate() {
    return toDate;
}

public void setToDate(Date toDate) {
    this.toDate = toDate;
}

@Override
public String toString() {
    return "TransitEdge{" + "voyageNumber=" + voyageNumber
            + ", fromUnLocode=" + fromUnLocode + ", toUnLocode="
            + toUnLocode + ", fromDate=" + fromDate
            + ", toDate=" + toDate + '}';
}
}
```

Figure 4-41 illustrates the class diagram for the implementation.

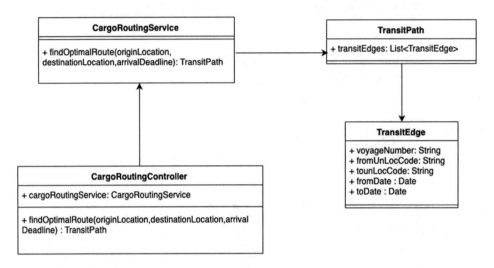

Figure 4-41. *Class diagram for the Outbound services*

The next step is to implement the client-side implementation for our Routing Rest service. The client is the ***CargoBookingCommandService*** class which is responsible for processing the "***Assign Route to Cargo***" command. As part of the processing of the command, this service class will need to invoke the Routing Service REST API to get the optimal route based on the cargo's Route Specification.

The CargoBookingCommandService makes use of an outbound service class – ***ExternalCargoRoutingService*** – to invoke the Routing Service REST API. The ***ExternalCargoRoutingService*** class also translates the data provided by the Routing Service's REST API into the format recognizable by the Booking Bounded Context's Domain Model.

Listing 4-30 demonstrates the method "***assignRouteToCargo***" within the ***CargoBookingCommandService.*** This service class is injected with the ***ExternalCargoRoutingService*** dependency which processes the request to invoke the Routing Service's REST API and returns the ***CargoItinerary*** object which is then assigned to the cargo:

Listing 4-30. Outbound service class dependency

```
@ApplicationScoped
public class CargoBookingCommandService {

    @Inject
    private ExternalCargoRoutingService externalCargoRoutingService;

    /**
      * Service Command method to assign a route to a Cargo
      * @param routeCargoCommand
      */
    @Transactional
    public void assignRouteToCargo(RouteCargoCommand routeCargoCommand){

        Cargo cargo = cargoRepository.find(new BookingId(routeCargoCommand.
        getCargoBookingId()));
        CargoItinerary cargoItinerary = externalCargoRoutingService.
        fetchRouteForSpecification(new RouteSpecification(
                new Location(routeCargoCommand.getOriginLocation()),
                new Location(routeCargoCommand.getDestinationLocation()),
                routeCargoCommand.getArrivalDeadline()
        ));

        cargo.assignToRoute(cargoItinerary);
        cargoRepository.store(cargo);

    }

    // All other implementations of Commands for the Booking Bounded Context

}
```

Listing 4-31 demonstrates the ExternalCargoRoutingService outbound service class. This class performs two things:

- It injects a Rest client "***ExternalCargoRoutingClient***" using the Type safe Rest client annotations (***@RestClient***) provided by MicroProfile. This client invokes the Routing Service's REST API using the ***RestClientBuilder*** API provided by MicroProfile.

- It also translates the Data provided by the Routing Service's Rest
  API (*TransitPath*, *TransitEdge*) to the Booking Bounded Context's
  Domain Model (*CargoItinerary*/*Leg*).

Listing 4-31. Outbound service class implementation

```
package com.practicalddd.cargotracker.bookingms.application.internal.
outboundservices.acl;

import com.practicalddd.cargotracker.TransitEdge;
import com.practicalddd.cargotracker.TransitPath;
import com.practicalddd.cargotracker.bookingms.domain.model.valueobjects.
CargoItinerary;
import com.practicalddd.cargotracker.bookingms.domain.model.valueobjects.Leg;
import com.practicalddd.cargotracker.bookingms.domain.model.valueobjects.
RouteSpecification;
import com.practicalddd.cargotracker.bookingms.infrastructure.services.
http.ExternalCargoRoutingClient;
import org.eclipse.microprofile.rest.client.RestClientBuilder;
import org.eclipse.microprofile.rest.client.inject.RestClient;

import javax.enterprise.context.ApplicationScoped;
import javax.inject.Inject;
import java.util.ArrayList;
import java.util.List;

/**
 * Anti Corruption Service Class
 */
@ApplicationScoped
public class ExternalCargoRoutingService {

    @Inject
    @RestClient // MicroProfile Type safe Rest Client API
    private ExternalCargoRoutingClient externalCargoRoutingClient;

    /**
     * The Booking Bounded Context makes an external call to the Routing
       Service of the Routing Bounded Context to
```

```
 * fetch the Optimal Itinerary for a Cargo based on the Route Specification
 * @param routeSpecification
 * @return
 */
public CargoItinerary fetchRouteForSpecification(RouteSpecification
routeSpecification){
    ExternalCargoRoutingClient cargoRoutingClient =
            RestClientBuilder
            .newBuilder().build(ExternalCargoRoutingClient.class);
            // MicroProfile Type safe Rest Client API

    TransitPath transitPath = cargoRoutingClient.findOptimalRoute(
            routeSpecification.getOrigin().getUnLocCode(),
            routeSpecification.getDestination().getUnLocCode(),
            routeSpecification.getArrivalDeadline().toString()
            ); // Invoke the Routing Service's API using the client

    List<Leg> legs = new ArrayList<Leg>(transitPath.getTransitEdges().
    size());
    for (TransitEdge edge : transitPath.getTransitEdges()) {
        legs.add(toLeg(edge));
    }

    return new CargoItinerary(legs);

}

/**
 * Anti-corruption layer conversion method from the routing service's
   domain model (TransitEdges)
 * to the domain model recognized by the Booking Bounded Context (Legs)
 * @param edge
 * @return
 */
private Leg toLeg(TransitEdge edge) {
    return new Leg(
            edge.getVoyageNumber(),
            edge.getFromUnLocode(),
```

```
                    edge.getToUnLocode(),
                    edge.getFromDate(),
                    edge.getToDate());
        }
}
```

Listing 4-32 demonstrates the ***ExternalCargoRoutingClient*** Type safe Rest client implementation. It is implemented as an ***interface*** and utilizes the ***@RegisterRestClient*** annotation to mark it as a Rest client. The method signature/method resource details should be exactly as the service whose API it is invoking (in this case the Routing Service's ***optimalRoute*** API):

Listing 4-32. ExternalCargoRoutingClient typesafe implementation

```
package com.practicalddd.cargotracker.bookingms.infrastructure.services.
http;

import javax.ws.rs.*;

import com.practicalddd.cargotracker.TransitPath;
import org.eclipse.microprofile.rest.client.inject.RegisterRestClient;

/**
 * Type safe Rest client for the Routing Service API
 */
@Path("cargoRouting")
@RegisterRestClient //Annotation to register this as a Rest client
public interface ExternalCargoRoutingClient {
    // The method signature / method resource details should be exactly as
    the calling service
    @GET
    @Path("/optimalRoute")
    @Produces({"application/json"})
    public TransitPath findOptimalRoute(
            @QueryParam("origin") String originUnLocode,
            @QueryParam("destination") String destinationUnLocode,
            @QueryParam("deadline") String deadline);
}
```

Figure 4-42 illustrates the class diagram for the implementation.

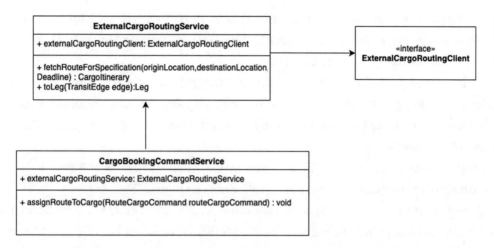

Figure 4-42. *Outbound Services (HTTP) implementation process class diagram*

All our Outbound Service implementations which require to communicate to other Bounded Contexts follow the same approach which is illustrated in Figure 4-43.

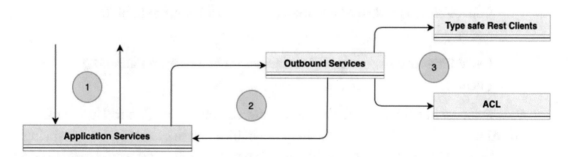

Figure 4-43. *Outbound Services (HTTP) implementation process*

1. Application Services classes receive Commands/Queries/Events.

2. As part of the processing, if it requires an interaction with another Bounded Context's API using REST, it makes use of an Outbound Service.

3. The Outbound service uses a Type safe Rest client to invoke the Bounded Context's API. It also performs the translation from the data format provided by that Bounded Context's API to the data model recognized by the current Bounded Context.

Outbound Services: Message Broker

The final type of outbound service that needs to be implemented is the interactions with Message Brokers. Message Brokers provide the necessary physical infrastructure for publishing/subscribing of Domain Events.

We have seen a couple of our Event classes *(CargoBooked, CargoRouted)* implemented using custom annotations. We have also seen the implementation of publishing them *(using the fire() method)* as well as subscribing them *(using the observes() method)*.

Let us look at an implementation of how we can enable the publishing and subscribing of these events from a RabbitMQ server's Queues/Exchanges.

Do note that neither the Eclipse MicroProfile platform nor Helidon MP's extensions provide capabilities to help CDI Events being published onto RabbitMQ, so we need to provide our own implementation for this. The source code of the chapter provides a separate project (*cargo-tracker-rabbimq-adaptor*). This project provides the following:

- Infrastructural capabilities (Connection Factories for RabbitMQ services, Managed Publishers, and Managed Consumers)

- Capabilities to publish AMQP messages for CDI Events to RabbitMQ exchanges

- Capabilities to consume AMQP messages for Events from RabbitMQ queues

We will not get into the detailed implementation of this project. We will just work with the APIs provided by this project to help us enable our use case of CDI Events being integrated with RabbitMQ Exchanges/Queues. To use this project, we would need to add the following dependency to each of our MicroProfile project's pom.xml dependency files:

```
<dependency>
    <groupId>com.practicalddd.cargotracker</groupId>
    <artifactId>cargo-tracker-rabbimq-adaptor</artifactId>
    <version>1.0.FINAL</version>
</dependency>
```

The first step in implementing the connectivity is to create a *"**Binder**"* class. The Binder class serves the following purposes:

- Bind CDI Events to Exchanges and Routing Keys

- Bind CDI Events to Queues

Listing 4-33 demonstrates the *"RoutedEventBinder"* which is responsible for binding of the *"**CargoRouted**"* CDI Event to the corresponding RabbitMQ exchange. It extends the *"**EventBinder**"* class provided by the adaptor project. We need to override the *"**bindEvents()**"* method where we perform all the bindings for **mapping CDI Events to Exchanges/Queues**. Also note that we perform the binding initialization in the **post-construct lifecycle method** provided by CDI:

Listing 4-33. RoutedEventBinder implementation class

```
package com.practicalddd.cargotracker.bookingms.infrastructure.brokers.
rabbitmq;
import javax.annotation.PostConstruct;
import javax.enterprise.context.ApplicationScoped;
import com.practicalddd.cargotracker.rabbitmqadaptor.EventBinder; //Adaptor
Class
/**
 * Component which initializes the Cargo Routed Events <-> Rabbit MQ bindings
 */
@ApplicationScoped
public class RoutedEventBinder extends EventBinder {
    /**
     * Method to bind the Cargo Routed Event class to the corresponding
       exchange in Rabbit MQ with
     * the corresponding Routing Key
     */
    @PostConstruct // CDI Annotation to initialize this in the post
    construct lifecycle method of this bean
```

```
public void bindEvents(){
    bind(CargoRoutedEvent.class)
            .toExchange("routed.exchange")
            .withPublisherConfirms()
            .withRoutingKey("routed.key");
    }
}
```

So every time you fire the Cargo Routed Event, it is delivered as an AMQP message to the corresponding exchange with the specified routing key.

The same mechanism applies to event subscriptions too. We "**bind**" CDI events to the corresponding RabbitMQ queues, and every time you observe a CDI Event, it is delivered as an AMQP Message from the corresponding queue.

The source code of the chapter has a complete implementation for Event Initializers for all the Bounded Contexts (see package com.practicalddd.cargotracker.<<bounded_context_name>>.infrastructure.brokers.rabbitmq).

Figure 4-44 illustrates the class diagram for the implementation.

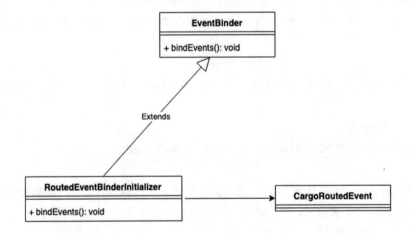

Figure 4-44. *Event Binder implementation*

This rounds off our DDD implementation of Cargo Tracker as a microservices application using the Eclipse MicroProfile Platform with Helidon MP providing the implementation.

Implementation Summary

We now have a complete DDD implementation of the Cargo Tracker application with the various DDD artifacts implemented using the corresponding specifications available within Eclipse MicroProfile.

The implementation summary is denoted in Figure 4-45.

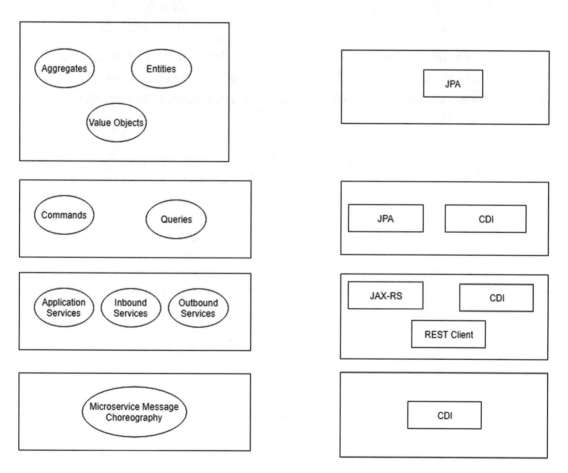

Figure 4-45. *DDD artifact implementation summary using Eclipse MicroProfile*

Summary

Summarizing our chapter

- We started by establishing the details about the Eclipse MicroProfile platform and the various capabilities it provides.

- We decided to use Helidon MP's implementation of the MicroProfile platform to help build Cargo Tracker as a microservices application.

- We rounded off by deep diving into the development of the various DDD artifacts – first the Domain Model and then the Domain Model Services using the technologies available on the Eclipse MicroProfile and Helidon MP.

CHAPTER 5

Cargo Tracker: Spring Platform

To quickly recap our journey until now

> We identified Cargo Tracking as the main problem space/core domain and the Cargo Tracker application as the solution to address this problem space.

> We identified the various sub-domains/bounded contexts for the Cargo Tracker application.

> We detailed out the domain model for each of our bounded contexts including identification of aggregates, entities, value objects, and domain rules.

> We identified the supporting domain services required within the bounded contexts.

> We identified the various operations within our bounded contexts (Commands, Queries, Events, and Sagas).

> We implemented a monolithic version of Cargo Tracker using Jakarta EE and a microservices version of Cargo Tracker using the Eclipse MicroProfile platform.

This chapter will detail the third DDD implementation of our Cargo Tracker application using the Spring platform. The Cargo Tracker application will again be designed using a microservices-based architecture, and as before we will map the DDD artifacts to the corresponding implementations available within the Spring Platform.

© Vijay Nair 2019
V. Nair, *Practical Domain-Driven Design in Enterprise Java*, https://doi.org/10.1007/978-1-4842-4543-9_5

As we progress through this implementation, there will be areas which will have a repetition from the previous chapters. This is to accommodate readers who might have an interest only in a specific implementation rather than going through all the implementations.

With that said, let us first go through an overview of the Spring Platform.

The Spring Platform

Originally released as an alternative to Java EE, the Spring Platform (`https://spring.io/`) has become the leading Java framework to build enterprise applications. The breadth of functionality offered via its project portfolio is extensive and covers almost every aspect required to build enterprise applications.

Unlike Jakarta EE or Eclipse MicroProfile wherein there are a set of specifications and multiple vendors providing implementations for the specifications, the Spring platform provides a portfolio of projects.

The project portfolio covers the following main areas:

- ***Core Infrastructure Projects*** which provide a foundational set of projects to build Spring-based applications

- ***Cloud-Native Projects*** which provide capabilities to build your Spring applications with cloud-native capabilities

- ***Data Management Projects*** which provide capabilities to manage any kind of data within Spring-based applications

The individual projects within the platform are listed in Figure 5-1.

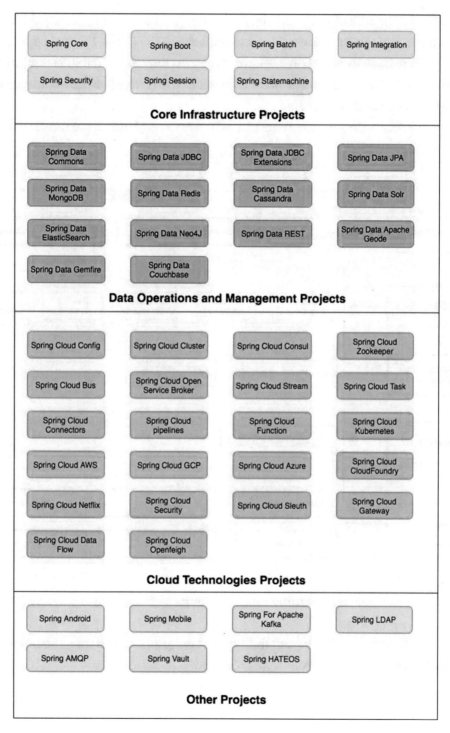

Figure 5-1. *Spring Platform projects*

As seen, the breadth of projects is large and provides a vast range of capabilities. To reiterate, the stated goal of this chapter is to implement the Cargo Tracker application utilizing DDD principles based on a microservices architecture. To that extent, we will just use a subset of the available projects *(Spring Boot, Spring Data, and Spring Cloud Stream)* to help us achieve our goal.

To quickly recap, the requirements of a Microservices platform are illustrated in Figure 5-2.

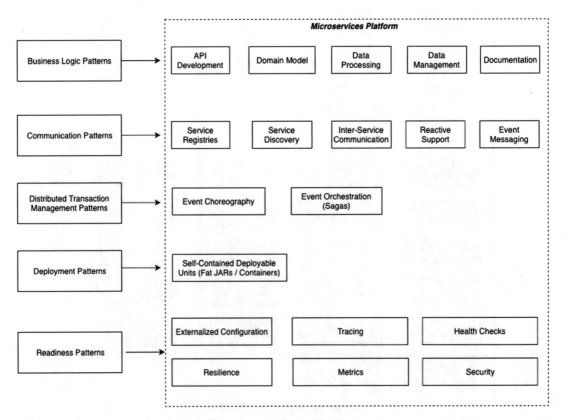

Figure 5-2. *Microservices platform requirements*

Let us briefly touch upon the capabilities of these projects and map them to the requirements illustrated earlier.

Spring Boot: Capabilities

Spring Boot acts as the foundational piece for any Spring-based microservices application. A highly opinionated platform, Spring Boot helps build microservices with REST, Data, and messaging capabilities using a uniform development experience. This is done by an abstraction/dependency management layer that Spring Boot implements on top of the actual projects that provide REST, Data, and Messaging capabilities. As a developer, you want to avoid the hassles of managing the dependencies as well as the configuration required when you build your microservices application. Spring Boot abstracts all of these for the developer by providing starter kits. The starter kits provide the required scaffolding to enable the developers to quickly start developing microservices which need to expose API(s), process data, and participate in event-driven architectures. In our implementation, we are going to be relying on three starter projects provided by Spring Boot (***spring-boot-starter-web, spring-boot-starter-data-jpa,*** and ***spring-cloud-starter-stream-rabbit***).

We will get into the details of these projects as we proceed with the implementation.

From a microservices requirements mapping perspective, the boxes in green as illustrated in Figure 5-3 are implemented with Spring Boot.

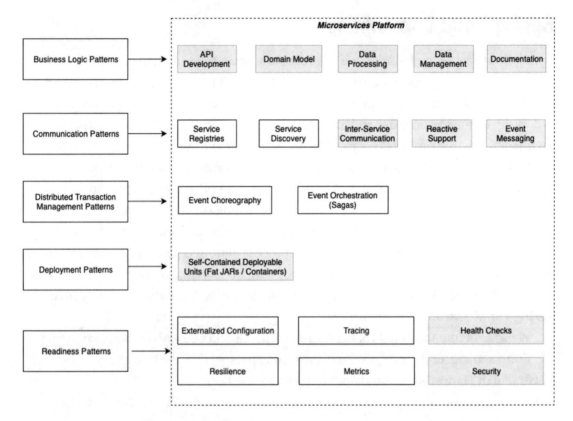

Figure 5-3. *Microservices platform components provided by Spring Boot*

Spring Cloud

While Boot provides the foundational technologies for building microservices applications, Spring Cloud helps implement the distributed systems patterns that Spring Boot–based microservices applications require. These include externalized configuration, service registration and discovery, messaging, distributed tracing, and API gateways. In addition, this project also provides projects to natively integrate with a third-party cloud provider like AWS/GCP/Azure.

From a microservices requirements mapping perspective, the boxes in orange as illustrated in Figure 5-4 are implemented with Spring Cloud.

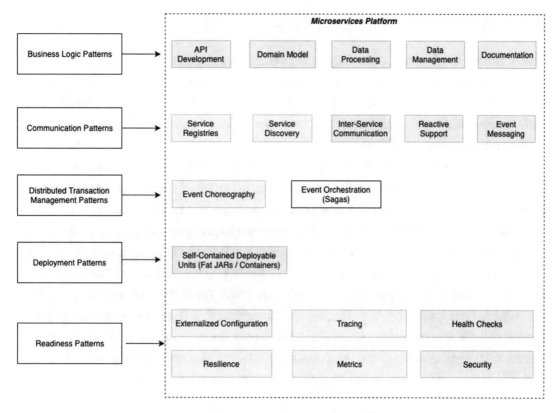

Figure 5-4. *Microservices platform components provided by Spring Cloud*

The Spring platform does not provide any out-of-the-box capabilities for Distributed Transaction management using orchestration-based sagas. We will implement ***Distributed Transactions using event choreography with a custom implementation*** utilizing Spring Boot and Spring Cloud Stream.

Spring Framework Summary

We now have a fair idea of what the Spring Platform provides to build microservices applications with the Spring Boot and the Spring Cloud projects.

Let us proceed to implement Cargo Tracker utilizing these technologies. As part of the implementation, there may be a fair bit of repetition since certain readers might be interested only in this implementation.

Bounded Context(s) with Spring Boot

The Bounded Context is the starting point of our solution phase for our DDD
implementation of the Cargo Tracker microservices application based on Spring. In
the microservices architectural style, each Bounded Context has to be a **self-contained
independent deployable unit** with no direct dependency on any other Bounded Context
within our problem space.

The pattern for splitting the Cargo Tracker application into multiple microservices
will be as before, that is, we split the core domain into a set of **Business Capabilities/
Sub-Domains** and **solution each of them as a separate Bounded Context.**

Implementing the Bounded Contexts involves a logical grouping of our DDD
artifacts into a single deployable artifact. Each of our Bounded Contexts within the Cargo
Tracker application is going to be built out as a Spring Boot Application. The resultant
artifact of a Spring Boot Application is a **self-contained fat JAR file** which contains all
the required dependencies (e.g., data access libraries, REST libraries) and configuration.
The fat JAR file also contains an embedded web container (in our case Tomcat) as the
runtime. This ensures that we do not need any external application server to run our fat
JAR. The anatomy of a Spring Boot application is illustrated in Figure 5-5.

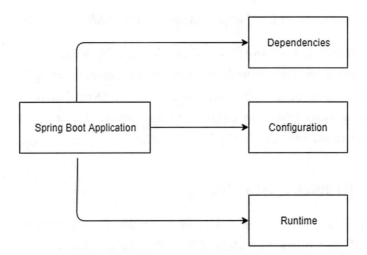

Figure 5-5. *Anatomy of a Spring Boot application*

From a deployment perspective as illustrated in Figure 5-6, each microservices is a separate self-contained deployable unit *(fat JAR file).*

Microservices will need a *DataStore* to store their state. We choose to adopt the *Database per service pattern,* that is, each of our microservices will have its own separate DataStore. Just like we have a polyglot choice of technology for our application tier, we have a polyglot choice for the DataStore too. We could choose to have a plain Relational Database (e.g., Oracle, MySQL, PostgreSQL), a NoSQL Database (e.g., MongoDB, Cassandra), or even an in-memory datastore (e.g., Redis). The choice depends primarily on the scalability requirements and the type of use case the microservices intends to cater to. For our implementation, we decide to go with MySQL as the choice of DataStore. The deployment architecture is illustrated in Figure 5-6.

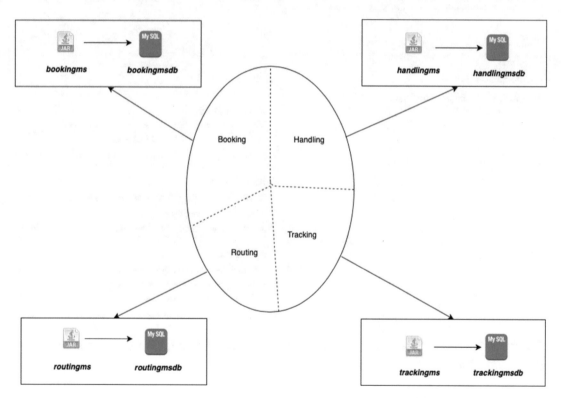

Figure 5-6. *Deployment Architecture for our Spring Boot-based microservices*

Bounded Contexts: Packaging

To get started with our packaging, the first step is to create a regular Spring Boot application. We will use the Spring Initializr tool (`https://start.spring.io/`), a browser-based tool which helps create Spring Boot applications easily. Figure 5-7 illustrates the creation of the Booking Microservices utilizing the Initializr tool.

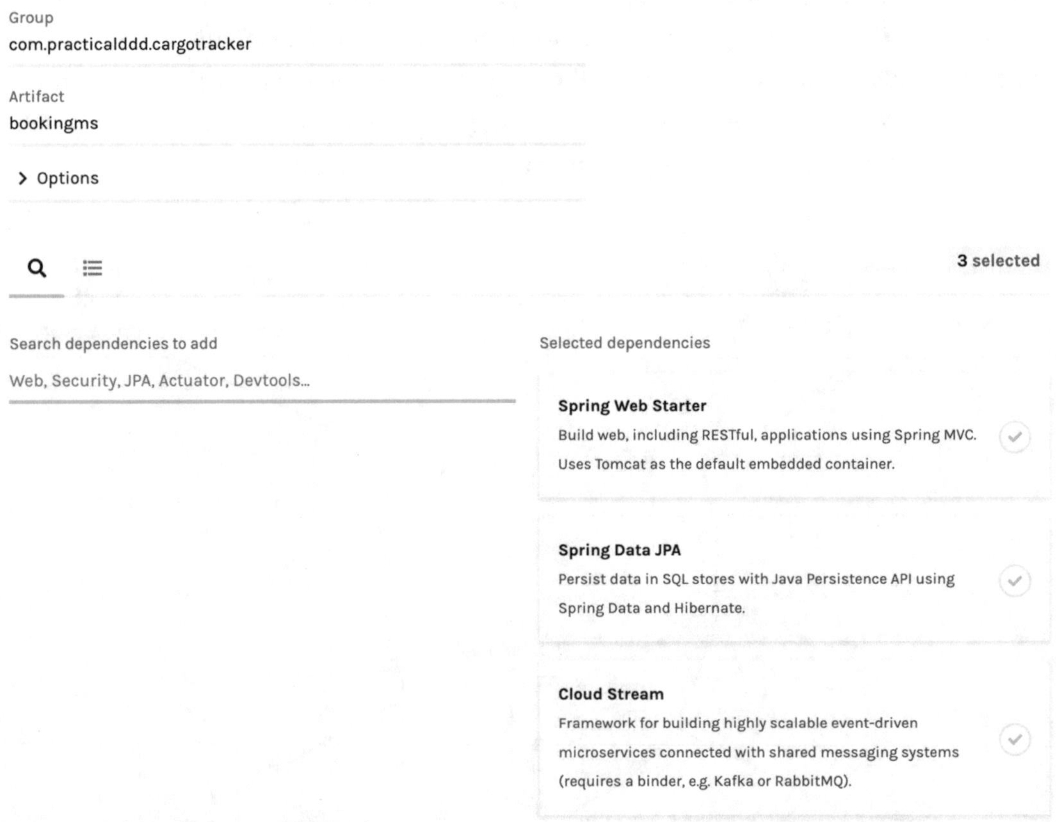

Figure 5-7. *Spring Initializr tool used for scaffolding Spring Boot projects with dependencies*

We have created the project with

- *Group* – com.practicalddd.cargotracker

- *Artifact* – bookingms

- *Dependencies* – Spring Web Starter, Spring Data JPA, and Spring Cloud Stream

Click the Generate Project icon. This will generate a ZIP file containing the Booking Spring Boot application with all the dependencies and the configuration made available.

The main application class for a Spring Boot application is annotated with the **@SpringBootApplication** annotation. It contains a public static void main method and is the entry point for the Spring Boot Application.

The **BookingmsApplication** class is the main class within our Booking Spring Boot Application. Listing 5-1 shows the BookingmsApplication class:

Listing 5-1. *Bookingms Application class*

```
package com.practicalddd.cargotracker.bookingms;
import org.springframework.boot.SpringApplication;
import org.springframework.boot.autoconfigure.SpringBootApplication;
@SpringBootApplication //Main class marker annotation
public class BookingmsApplication {
    public static void main(String[] args) {
        SpringApplication.run(BookingmsApplication.class, args);
    }
}
```

Building the project will result in a JAR file (***bookingms.jar***), and running it as a simple JAR file using the command "***java -jar bookingms.jar***" will bring up our Spring Boot application.

Bounded Contexts: Package Structure

With the packaging aspect decided, the next step is to decide the package structure of each of our Bounded Contexts, that is, to arrive at a logical grouping of the various DDD MicroProfile artifacts into a single deployable artifact. The logical grouping involves identifying a package structure where we place the various DD MicroProfile artifacts to achieve our overall solution for the Bounded Context.

The high-level package structure for any of our Bounded Context is illustrated in Figure 5-8.

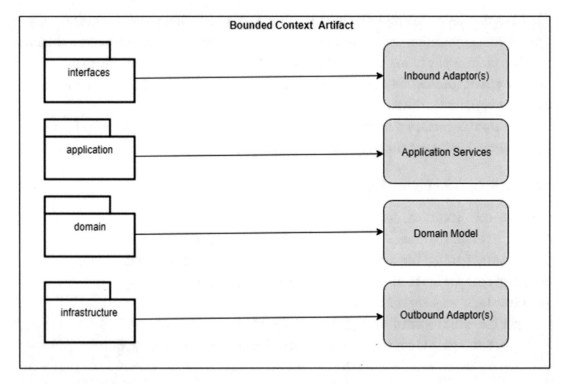

Figure 5-8. *Package structure for the Bounded Contexts*

Let us expand on the package structure a bit.

An example of the Booking Bounded Context Spring Boot Application's package structure is shown in Figure 5-9 with the `BookingmsApplication` as the main Spring Boot application class.

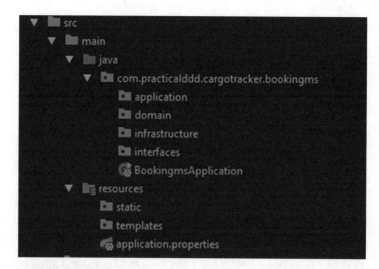

Figure 5-9. *Package structure for the Booking Bounded Context using Spring Boot*

Let us expand on the package structure.

interfaces

This package encloses all the inbound interfaces to our Bounded Context classified by the communication protocol. The main purpose of *interfaces* is to negotiate the protocol on behalf of the Domain Model (e.g., REST API(s), WebSocket(s), FTP(s), Custom Protocol).

As an example, the Booking Bounded Context provides REST APIs for sending *State Change Requests, that is, Commands,* to it (e.g., Book Cargo Command, Assign Route to Cargo Command). Similarly, the Booking Bounded Context provides REST APIs for sending *State Retrieval Requests, that is, Queries,* to it (e.g., Retrieve Cargo Booking Details, List all Cargos). This is grouped into the "*rest*" package.

It also has Event Handlers which subscribe to the various Events that are generated by other Bounded Contexts. All Event Handlers are grouped into the "*eventhandlers*" package. In addition to these two packages, the interface package also contains the "*transform*" package. This is used to translate the incoming API Resource/Event data to the corresponding Command/Query model required by the Domain Model.

Since we need to support REST, Events, and data transformation, the package structure is as illustrated in Figure 5-10.

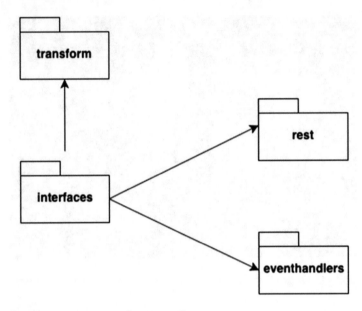

Figure 5-10. *Package structure for interfaces*

application

Application services act as the façade for the Bounded Context's Domain Model. They provide façade services to dispatch Commands/Queries to the underlying Domain Model. They are also the place where we place outbound calls to other Bounded Contexts as part of the processing of a Command/Query.

To summarize, Application Services

- Participate in Command and Query Dispatching

- Invoke infrastructural components where necessary as part of the Command/Query processing

- Provide Centralized concerns (e.g., Logging, Security, Metrics) for the underlying Domain Model

- Make callouts to other Bounded Contexts

The package structure is illustrated in Figure 5-11.

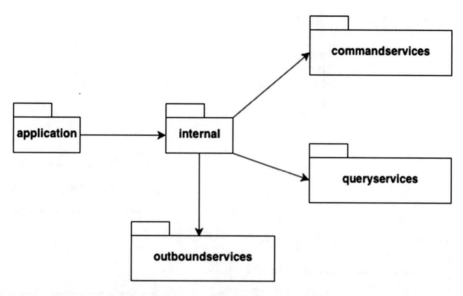

Figure 5-11. *Package structure for Application services*

domain

This package contains the Bounded Context's Domain Model. This is the heart of the Bounded Context's Domain Model which contains the implementation of the core Business Logic.

The core classes of our Bounded Contexts are as follows:

- Aggregates

- Entities

- Value Objects

- Commands

- Events

The package structure is illustrated in Figure 5-12.

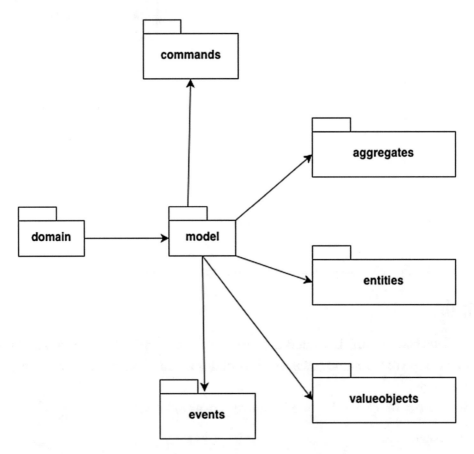

Figure 5-12. *Package structure for our domain model*

infrastructure

The infrastructure package serves three main purposes:

- When a Bounded Context receives an operation related to its state (Change of State, Retrieval of State), it ***needs an underlying repository to process the operation***; in our case, this repository is our MySQL Database instance(s). The infrastructure package contains all the necessary components required by the Bounded Context to communicate to the underlying repository. As part of our implementation, we intend to use either JPA or JDBC to implement these components.

- When a Bounded Context needs to communicate a state change event, it needs an underlying Event Infrastructure to publish the state change event. In our implementation, we intend to use a ***message broker as the underlying Event Infrastructure*** (RabbitMQ available for download at rabbitmq.com). The infrastructure package contains all the necessary components required by the Bounded Context to communicate to the underlying message broker.

- The final aspect that we include in the infrastructural layer is any kind of Spring Boot-specific configuration.

The package structure is illustrated in Figure 5-13.

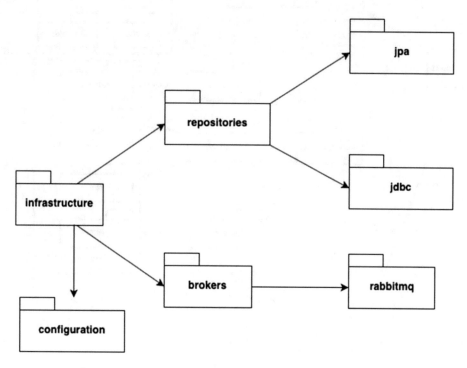

Figure 5-13. *Package structure for the infrastructure components*

A complete summary of the entire package structure for any of our Bounded Context is illustrated in Figure 5-14.

Figure 5-14. *Package structure for any of our Bounded Context*

This completes the implementation of the Bounded Contexts of our Cargo Tracker microservices application. Each of our Bounded Contexts is implemented as a Spring Boot application with a fat JAR as an artifact. The Bounded Contexts are neatly grouped by modules in a package structure with clearly separated concerns.

Let us step into the implementation of the Cargo Tracker Application.

Cargo Tracker Implementation

The next section of our chapter is going to detail the implementation of the Cargo Tracker application as a microservices application utilizing DDD and Spring Boot/ Spring Cloud. As stated before, some of these sections are a repeat of what we have already seen, but it would be helpful to go through it again to reinforce the concepts of DDD.

A high-level overview of the logical grouping of our various DDD artifacts is illustrated in Figure 5-15. As seen, we need to implement two groups of artifacts:

- The **Domain Model** which will contain our **Core Domain/Business Logic**

- The **Domain Model Services** which contain **supporting services for our Core Domain Model**

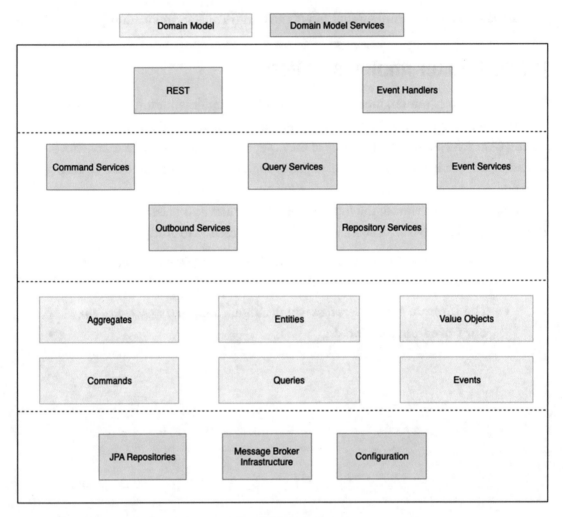

Figure 5-15. *Logical grouping of the DDD artifacts*

In terms of actual implementation of the Domain Model, this translates to the various *Commands, Queries, and Value Objects* of a specific Bounded Context/ Microservices.

In terms of actual implementation of the Domain Model Services, this translates to ***the Interfaces, Application Services, and Infrastructure*** that the Domain Model of the Bounded Context/Microservices requires.

Going back to our Cargo Tracker application, Figure 5-16 illustrates our microservices solution in terms of the various Bounded Contexts and the operations it supports. As seen, this contains the various ***Commands that each Bounded Context*** *will process*, the ***Queries that each Bounded Context will serve,*** and the ***Events that each Bounded Context will subscribe/publish***. Each of the microservices is a separate deployable artifact with its own storage.

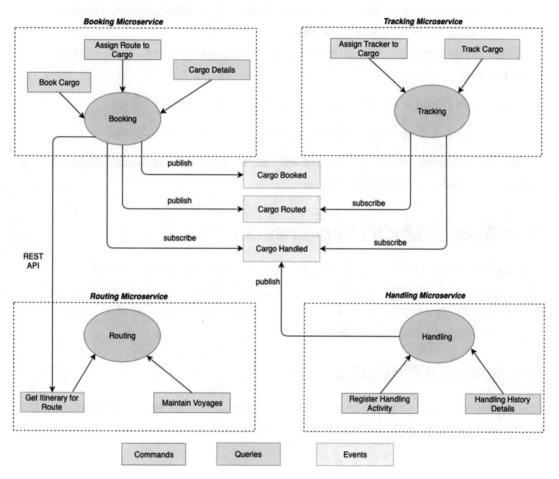

Figure 5-16. *Cargo Tracker Microservices solution*

Note   Certain code implementations will contain only summaries/snippets to help understand the implementation concepts. The source code for the chapter contains the full implementation of the concepts.

Domain Model: Implementation

Our Domain Model is the central feature of our Bounded Context and as stated earlier has a set of artifacts associated with it. Implementation of these artifacts is done with the help of the tools that Spring Boot provides.

To quickly summarize, the Domain Model artifacts that we need to implement are as follows:

- ***Core Domain Model*** – Aggregates, Entities, and Value Objects

- ***Domain Model Operations*** – Commands, Queries, and Events

Let's walk through each of these artifacts and see what corresponding tool(s) Spring Boot provides for us to implement these.

Core Domain Model: Implementation

The implementation of the Core Domain for any Bounded Context covers the identification of those artifacts that will express the business intent of the Bounded Context clearly. At a high level, this includes the identification and implementation of Aggregates, Entities, and Value Objects.

Aggregates/Entities/Value Objects

Aggregates are the centerpiece of our Domain Model. To recap, we have four aggregates within each of our Bounded Contexts as illustrated in Figure 5-17 below.

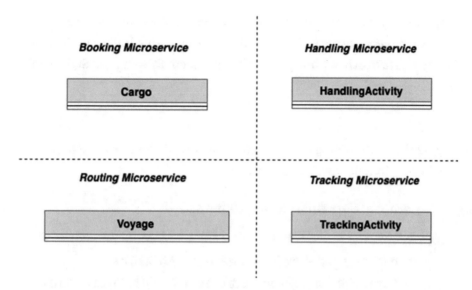

Figure 5-17. *Aggregates within our Bounded Context(s) / Microservices*

Implementation of an Aggregate covers the following aspects

- Aggregate Class Implementation

- Domain Richness via Business Attributes and finally

- Implementing Entities/Value Objects

Aggregate Class Implementation

Since we intend to use MySQL as our Datastore for each of our Bounded Contexts, we intend to use JPA (Java Persistence API) from the Java EE specification which provides a standard way of defining and implementing Entities/Services which interact with underlying SQL Datastores.

JPA Integration: Spring Data JPA

Spring Boot provides support for JPA by using the ***Spring Data JPA project*** (`https://` `spring.io/projects/spring-data-jpa`) which provides a sophisticated and easy mechanism to implement JPA-based repositories. Spring Boot provides a starter project (***spring-boot-starter-data-jpa***) which automatically configures a set of sensible defaults (e.g., Hibernate JPA Implementation, Tomcat connection pooling) for Spring Data JPA.

The dependency for the starter data JPA project is automatically added when we configure it as a dependency within the Initializr project. In addition to that, we need to add the MySQL Java driver library to enable connectivity to our MySQL Database instances:

pom.xml

Listing 5-2 shows the changes that need to be done in the ***pom.xml dependencies file*** that the Spring Initializr project generates:

Listing 5-2. pom.xml dependency maintainance

```
<dependency>
    <groupId>org.springframework.boot</groupId>
    <artifactId>spring-boot-starter-data-jpa</artifactId>
</dependency>
<dependency>
    <groupId>mysql</groupId>
    <artifactId>mysql-connector-java</artifactId>
</dependency>
```
application.properties

In addition to the dependencies, we also need to configure the connection properties for each of our MySQL Instances. This is done in the ***application.properties*** file provided by our Spring Boot application. Listing 5-3 demonstrates the configuration properties that need to be added. You would need to replace the values with your MySQL Instance(s) Details as necessary:

Listing 5-3. MySQL connection configuration

```
spring.datasource.url=jdbc:mysql://<<Machine-Name>>:<<Machine-
Port>>/<<MySQL-Database-Instance-Name>>
spring.datasource.username=<<MySQL-Database-Instance-UserID>>
spring.datasource.password==<<MySQL-Database-Instance-Password>>
```

These settings are enough to set up and implement JPA within our Spring Boot application. As stated before, the Spring Data JPA project configures a set of sensible defaults which enable us to get started with minimal effort. Unless stated otherwise, all our Aggregates within all our Bounded Contexts implement the same mechanism.

Each of our root aggregate classes is implemented as a JPA entity. There are no specific annotations that JPA provides to annotate a specific class as a root aggregate, so we take a regular POJO and use the JPA-provided standard annotation *@Entity*. Taking the Booking Bounded Context as an example which has Cargo as the root Aggregate, Listing 5-4 shows the minimalistic code required for a JPA Entity:

Listing 5-4. Cargo root aggregate as a JPA Entity

```
package com.practicalddd.cargotracker.bookingms.domain.model.aggregates;
import javax.persistence.*;
@Entity //JPA Entity Marker
public class Cargo {
}
```

Every JPA Entity requires an identifier. For our Aggregate Identifier implementation, we choose to have a ***technical/surrogate identifier (Primary Key)*** for our Cargo Aggregate derived from a MySQL sequence. In addition to the technical identifier, we also choose to have a ***Business Key***.

The Business key conveys the business intent of the aggregate identifier clear, that is, Booking Identifier of a newly booked cargo, and is the key that is exposed to external consumers of the Domain Model (more on this later). The technical key on the other hand is a pure internal representation of the aggregate identifier and is useful to maintain relationships ***within a Bounded Context*** between the Aggregates and its Dependent Objects (see Value Objects/Entities in the following).

Continuing with our example of the Cargo Aggregate within the Booking Bounded Context, we add the Technical/Business Keys to the Class implementation until now.

Listing 5-5 demonstrates this. The *"@Id"* annotation identifies the primary key on our Cargo Aggregate. There is no specific annotation to identify the Business Key, so we just implement it as a regular POJO (***BookingId***) and ***embed*** it within our Aggregate using the "*@Embedded*" annotation provided by JPA:

Listing 5-5. Identifier for the Cargo root aggregate

```
package com.practicalddd.cargotracker.bookingms.domain.model.aggregates;
import javax.persistence.*;
@Entity
public class Cargo {
```

```
    @Id //Identifier Annotation provided by JPA
    @GeneratedValue(strategy = GenerationType.IDENTITY) // Rely on a MySQL
    generated sequence
    private Long id;
    @Embedded //Annotation which enables usage of Business Objects instead
    of primitive types
    private BookingId bookingId; // Business Identifier
}
```

Listing 5-6 shows the implementation of the BookingId Business Key Class:

Listing 5-6. Business key implementation for the Cargo root aggregate

```
package com.practicalddd.cargotracker.bookingms.domain.model.aggregates;
import javax.persistence.*;
import java.io.Serializable;
/**
 * Business Key Identifier for the Cargo Aggregate
 */
@Embeddable
public class BookingId implements Serializable {
    @Column(name="booking_id")
    private String bookingId;
    public BookingId(){}
    public BookingId(String bookingId){this.bookingId = bookingId;}
    public String getBookingId(){return this.bookingId;}
}
```

We now have a bare-bones implementation of an Aggregate (Cargo) using JPA. The other aggregates have the same mechanism of implementation barring the Handling Activity Bounded Context. Since it is an event log, we decide to implement only one key for the Aggregate, that is, the Activity Id.

Figure 5-18 summarizes our bare-bones implementation of all our Aggregates.

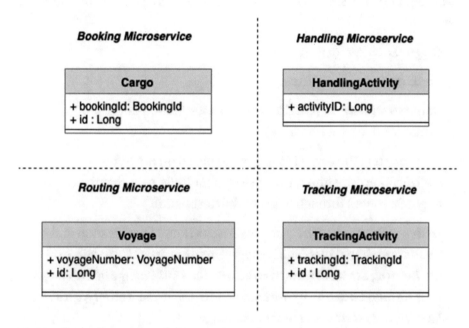

Figure 5-18. *Bare-Bones implementation of our Aggregates*

Domain Richness: Business Attributes

With the bare-bones implementation ready, let us move onto the meat of the Aggregate – Domain richness. ***The Aggregate of any Bounded Context should be able to express the Business Language of the Bounded Context clearly***. Essentially, what it means in pure technical terms is that our Aggregate should not be anemic, that is, only containing getter/setter methods.

An ***anemic aggregate*** goes against the fundamental principle of DDD since it essentially would mean ***the Business Language being expressed in multiple layers of an application*** which in turn leads to an unmaintainable piece of software in the long run.

So how do we implement a Domain-Rich Aggregate? The short answer is ***Business Attributes and Business Methods.*** Our focus in this section is going to be on the Business Attributes aspect while we will cover the Business Methods part as part of the Domain Model Operations implementation.

Business Attributes of an Aggregate capture the state of an Aggregate as attributes depicted using Business Terms rather than Technical Terms.

Let us walk through the example of our Cargo aggregate.

Translating state to business concepts, the Cargo Aggregate has the following attributes:

- **Origin Location** of the cargo

- **Booking Amount** of the cargo

- **Route specification** (Origin Location, Destination Location, Destination Arrival Deadline)

- **Itinerary** that the cargo is assigned to based on the Route Specification. The Itinerary consists of multiple **Legs** that the cargo might be routed through to get to the destination

- **Delivery Progress** of the cargo against its Route Specification and Itinerary assigned to it. The Delivery Progress provides details on the **Routing Status, Transport Status, Current Voyage of the cargo, Last Known Location of the cargo, Next Expected Activity, and the Last Activity that occurred on the cargo.**

Figure 5-19 illustrates the Cargo Aggregate and its relationships with its dependent objects. Notice how we are able to clearly represent the Cargo Aggregate in *pure Business Terms.*

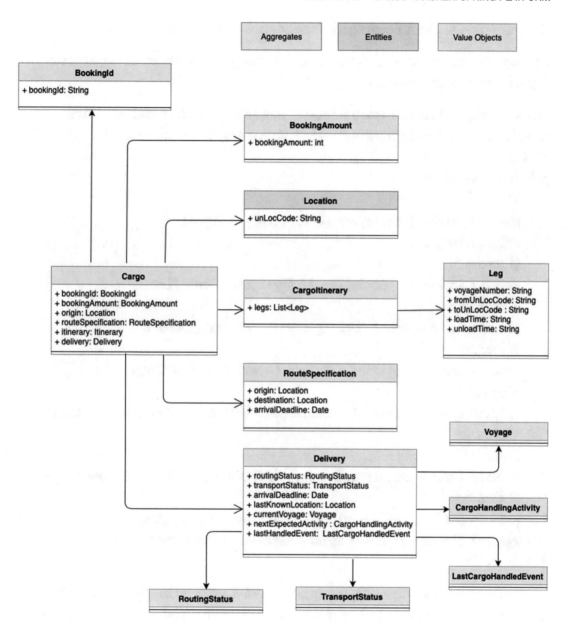

Figure 5-19. *Cargo Aggregate and its dependent associations*

JPA provides us a set of annotations (***@Embedded, @Embeddable***) to help implement our Aggregate class using Business Objects.

Listing 5-7 shows the example of our Cargo Aggregate with all the ***Dependencies modeled as Business Objects:***

Listing 5-7. Cargo root aggregate dependencies as business objects

```
package com.practicalddd.cargotracker.bookingms.domain.model.aggregates;
import javax.persistence.*;

import com.practicalddd.cargotracker.bookingms.domain.model.entities.*;
import com.practicalddd.cargotracker.bookingms.domain.model.valueobjects.*;
@Entity
public class Cargo {
    @Id
    @GeneratedValue(strategy = GenerationType.IDENTITY)
    private Long id;
    @Embedded
    private BookingId bookingId; // Aggregate Identifier
    @Embedded
    private BookingAmount bookingAmount; //Booking Amount
    @Embedded
    private Location origin; //Origin Location of the Cargo
    @Embedded
    private RouteSpecification routeSpecification; //Route Specification of
    the Cargo
    @Embedded
    private CargoItinerary itinerary; //Itinerary Assigned to the Cargo
    @Embedded
    private Delivery delivery; // Checks the delivery progress of the cargo
    against the actual Route Specification and Itinerary
}
```

Dependent classes for an Aggregate are ***modeled either as Entity Objects or Value Objects***. To recap, Entity Objects within a Bounded Context have an identity of their own but always exist within a root aggregate, that is, they cannot exist independently, and they never change during the complete lifecycle of the aggregate. Value Objects on the other hand have no identity of their own and are easily replaceable in any instance of an aggregate

Continuing with our example, within the Cargo Aggregate, we have the following:

- **"Origin"** of the cargo as an **Entity Object** (Location). This cannot change within a Cargo Aggregate Instance and hence is modeled as an Entity Object.

- **Booking Amount** of the cargo, **Route Specification** of the cargo, **Cargo Itinerary** assigned to the cargo, and the **Delivery of the cargo** as Value Objects. These objects are replaceable in any Cargo Aggregate Instance and hence are modeled as Value Objects.

Let us walk through the scenarios and the rationale why we have these as value objects and not as entities because it is an **important domain modeling decision**:

- When a new cargo is booked, we will have **a new Route Specification**, **an empty Cargo Itinerary,** and **no delivery progress**.

- As the cargo is assigned an itinerary, the **empty Cargo Itinerary** is replaced by an **allocated Cargo Itinerary.**

- As the cargo progresses through multiple ports as part of its itinerary, the **Delivery** progress is updated and replaced within the root aggregate.

- Finally, if the customer chooses to change the delivery location of the cargo or the deadline for delivery, the **Route Specification changes**, a **new Cargo Itinerary** will be assigned, the **Delivery is recalculated,** and the **Booking Amount changes.**

They are **all replaceable and hence modeled as Value Objects.** That is the **thumb rule for modeling Entities and Value Objects within an Aggregate.**

Implementing Entity Objects/Value Objects

Entity Objects/Value Objects are implemented as JPA Embeddable objects using the **"@Embeddable"** annotation provided by JPA. They are then embedded into the Aggregate using the "**@Embedded**" annotation.

Listing 5-8 shows the mechanism of embedding into the Aggregate class.

Let us look at the implementation of the Cargo Aggregate's Entity Objects/Value Objects.

Listing 5-8 demonstrates the ***Location Entity Object***. Notice the package name (***grouped under model.entities***):

Listing 5-8. Location entity object

```
package com.practicalddd.cargotracker.bookingms.domain.model.entities;
import javax.persistence.Column;
import javax.persistence.Embeddable;
/**
 * Location Entity class represented by a unique 5-digit UN Location code.
 */
@Embeddable
public class Location {
    @Column(name = "origin_id")
    private String unLocCode;
    public Location(){}
    public Location(String unLocCode){this.unLocCode = unLocCode;}
    public void setUnLocCode(String unLocCode){this.unLocCode = unLocCode;}
    public String getUnLocCode(){return this.unLocCode;}
}
```

Listing 5-9 demonstrates examples of the ***Booking Amount/Route Specification Value Object(s)***. Notice the package name (***grouped under model.valueobjects***):

Listing 5-9. Booking Amount value object implementation

```
package com.practicalddd.cargotracker.bookingms.domain.model.valueobjects;
import javax.persistence.Column;
import javax.persistence.Embeddable;
/**
 * Domain model representation of the Booking Amount for a new Cargo.
 * Contains the Booking Amount of the Cargo
 */
@Embeddable
public class BookingAmount {
    @Column(name = "booking_amount", unique = true, updatable= false)
    private Integer bookingAmount;
```

```
    public BookingAmount(){}
    public BookingAmount(Integer bookingAmount){this.bookingAmount =
    bookingAmount;}
    public void setBookingAmount(Integer bookingAmount){this.bookingAmount =
    bookingAmount;}
    public Integer getBookingAmount(){return this.bookingAmount;}
}
```

Listing 5-10 demonstrates the ***Route Specification Value Object***:

Listing 5-10. Route Specification value object implementation

```
package com.practicalddd.cargotracker.bookingms.domain.model.valueobjects;
import com.practicalddd.cargotracker.bookingms.domain.model.entities.
Location;
import javax.persistence.*;
import javax.validation.constraints.NotNull;
import java.util.Date;
/**
 * Route Specification of the Booked Cargo
 */
@Embeddable
public class RouteSpecification {
    private static final long serialVersionUID = 1L;
    @Embedded
    @AttributeOverride(name = "unLocCode", column = @Column(name = "spec_
    origin_id"))
    private Location origin;
    @Embedded
    @AttributeOverride(name = "unLocCode", column = @Column(name = "spec_
    destination_id"))
    private Location destination;
    @Temporal(TemporalType.DATE)
    @Column(name = "spec_arrival_deadline")
    @NotNull
    private Date arrivalDeadline;
    public RouteSpecification() { }
```

```
/**
 * @param origin origin location
 * @param destination destination location
 * @param arrivalDeadline arrival deadline
 */
public RouteSpecification(Location origin, Location destination,
                        Date arrivalDeadline) {
    this.origin = origin;
    this.destination = destination;
    this.arrivalDeadline = (Date) arrivalDeadline.clone();
}
public Location getOrigin() {
    return origin;
}
public Location getDestination() {
    return destination;
}

public Date getArrivalDeadline() {
    return new Date(arrivalDeadline.getTime());
}
}
```

The remaining Value Objects (*RouteSpecification, CargoItinerary, and Delivery*) are implemented in the same way using the "*@Embeddable*" annotation and embedded into the Cargo Aggregate using the "*@Embedded*" annotation.

Note   Please refer to the chapter's source code for the complete implementation.

Let us look at abbreviated class diagrams for the other Aggregates (HandlingActivity, Voyage, and Tracking). Figures 5-20, 5-21, and 5-22 illustrate this.

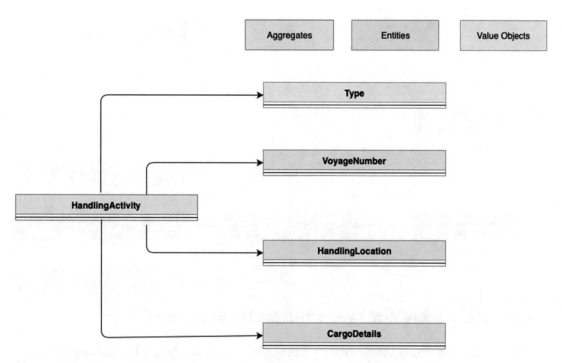

Figure 5-20. *Handling Activity and its dependent associations*

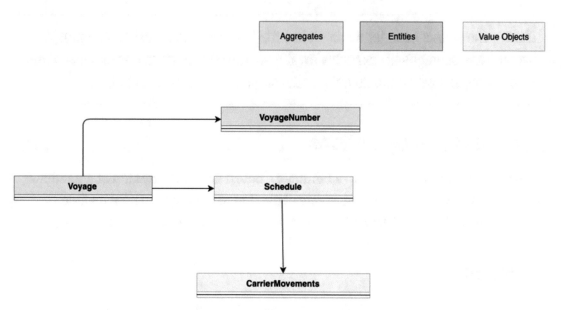

Figure 5-21. *Voyage and its dependent associations*

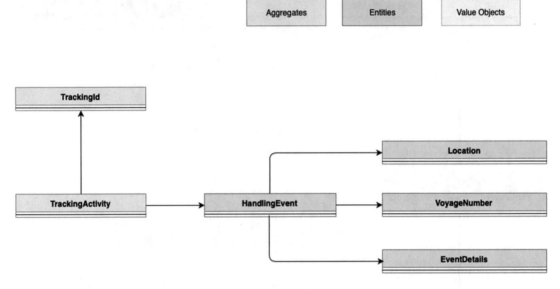

Figure 5-22. Tracking Activity and its dependent associations

This completes the implementation of the Core Domain Model. Let us look at the implementation of the Domain model operations next.

Note   The source code for the book has the Core Domain Model demonstrated via package segregation. You can view the source code to get a clearer view of the types of objects within the domain model at github.com/practicalddd.

Domain Model Operations

Domain Model operations within a Bounded Context deal with any kind of operations associated with the state of the Aggregate of the Bounded Context. These include *inbound operations (Commands/Queries) and outbound operations (Events).*

Commands

Commands are responsible for changing the state of the Aggregate within a Bounded Context.

Implementation of Commands within a Bounded Context involves the following steps:

- Identification/implementation of Commands

- Identification/implementation of Command Handlers to process Commands

Identification of Commands

Identification of Commands revolves around identifying any operation that affects the state of the Aggregate. For example, the Booking Command Bounded Context has the following operations or commands:

- Book a Cargo

- Route a Cargo

Both these operations result in a change of state of the Cargo Aggregate within the Bounded Context and are hence identified as Commands.

Implementation of Commands

Once identified, implementing the identified Commands within the Spring Boot implementation is done using regular POJOs. Listing 5-11 demonstrates the implementation of the BookCargoCommand class for the Book Cargo Command:

Listing 5-11. BookCargoCommand class implementation

```
package com.practicalddd.cargotracker.bookingms.domain.model.commands;
import java.util.Date;
/**
* Book Cargo Command class
*/
public class BookCargoCommand {

    private String bookingId;
    private int bookingAmount;
    private String originLocation;
    private String destLocation;
    private Date destArrivalDeadline;

    public BookCargoCommand(){}

    public BookCargoCommand(int bookingAmount,
```

```
                    String originLocation, String destLocation,
                    Date destArrivalDeadline){

    this.bookingAmount = bookingAmount;
    this.originLocation = originLocation;
    this.destLocation = destLocation;
    this.destArrivalDeadline = destArrivalDeadline;
}

public void setBookingId(String bookingId){this.bookingId = bookingId;}

public String getBookingId(){return this.bookingId;}

public void setBookingAmount(int bookingAmount){
    this.bookingAmount = bookingAmount;
}

public int getBookingAmount(){
    return this.bookingAmount;
}

public String getOriginLocation() {return originLocation; }

public void setOriginLocation(String originLocation) {this.
originLocation = originLocation; }

public String getDestLocation() { return destLocation; }

public void setDestLocation(String destLocation) { this.destLocation =
destLocation; }

public Date getDestArrivalDeadline() { return destArrivalDeadline; }

public void setDestArrivalDeadline(Date destArrivalDeadline) { this.
destArrivalDeadline = destArrivalDeadline; }
}
```

Identification of Command Handlers

Every Command will have a corresponding Command Handler. The purpose of the Command Handler is **to process the input command and set the state of the Aggregate**. Command Handlers are **the only place within the Domain Model where Aggregate** *state is set*. This is a strict rule that needs to be followed to help implement a rich Domain Model.

Implementation of Command Handlers

Since the Spring Framework does not provide any out-of-the box capabilities to implement Command Handlers, our methodology of implementation will be to just *identify the routines on the Aggregates which can be denoted as Command Handlers*. For our first command **Book Cargo,** we identify the constructor of the Aggregate as our Command Handler; and for our second command **Route Cargo,** we create a new routine "***assignToRoute()***" which acts as our Command Handler.

Listing 5-12 shows the snippet of code of the constructor of the Cargo Aggregate. The constructor accepts the ***BookCargoCommand*** as an input parameter and sets the corresponding state of the Aggregate:

Listing 5-12. Command handler for the BookCargo command

```
/**
 * Constructor Command Handler for a new Cargo booking
 */
public Cargo(BookCargoCommand bookCargoCommand){
    this.bookingId = new BookingId(bookCargoCommand.getBookingId());
    this.routeSpecification = new RouteSpecification(
                new Location(bookCargoCommand.getOriginLocation()),
                new Location(bookCargoCommand.getDestLocation()),
                bookCargoCommand.getDestArrivalDeadline()
        );
    this.origin = routeSpecification.getOrigin();
    this.itinerary = CargoItinerary.EMPTY_ITINERARY; //Empty Itinerary
    since the Cargo has not been routed yet
    this.bookingAmount = bookingAmount;
    this.delivery = Delivery.derivedFrom(this.routeSpecification,
            this.itinerary, LastCargoHandledEvent.EMPTY);
}
```

Listing 5-13 shows the snippet of code for the ***assignToRoute()*** Command Handler. It accepts the ***RouteCargoCommand*** class as input and sets the state of the Aggregate:

Listing 5-13. Command handler for the route assignment command

```
/**
 * Command Handler for the Route Cargo Command. Sets the state of the
 Aggregate and registers the
 * Cargo routed event
 * @param routeCargoCommand
 */
public void assignToRoute(RouteCargoCommand routeCargoCommand) {
    this.itinerary = routeCargoCommand.getCargoItinerary();
    // Handling consistency within the Cargo aggregate synchronously
    this.delivery = delivery.updateOnRouting(this.routeSpecification,
            this.itinerary);

}
```

In summary, Command Handlers play a very important role of managing the Aggregate state within a Bounded Context. The actual invocation of Command Handlers happens via Application Services which we shall see in the sections that follow.

Figure 5-23 illustrates the class diagram for our Command Handler implementation.

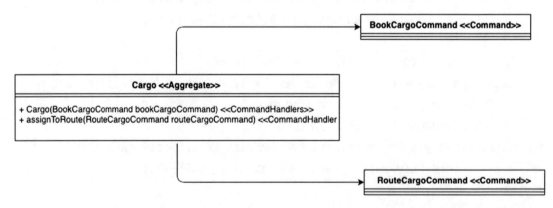

Figure 5-23. *Class diagram for the Command Handler implementation*

This completes the implementation of Commands within the Domain Model. We shall now see how to implement Queries.

Queries

Queries within the Bounded Context are responsible for *providing the state of the Bounded Context's Aggregate* to external consumers.

To implement Queries, we utilize *JPA Named Queries,* that is, queries that can be defined on an Aggregate to retrieve state in various forms. Listing 5-14 demonstrates the snippet of code from the Cargo Aggregate that defines the queries that need to be made available. In this case, we have three queries – *Find All Cargos, Find a Cargo by its Booking Identifier, and Final Booking Identifiers for all Cargos:*

Listing 5-14. Named queries within the Cargo root aggregate

```
@NamedQueries({
        @NamedQuery(name = "Cargo.findAll",
                query = "Select c from Cargo c"),
        @NamedQuery(name = "Cargo.findByBookingId",
                query = "Select c from Cargo c where c.bookingId = :bookingId"),
        @NamedQuery(name = "Cargo.findAllBookingIds",
                query = "Select c.bookingId from Cargo c") })
public class Cargo{}
```

In summary, Query Handlers play the role of presenting the Aggregate state within a Bounded Context. The actual invocation and execution of these queries happens via Application Services and Repository classes which we shall see in the sections that follow.

This completes the implementation of Queries within the Domain Model. We shall now see how to implement Events.

Domain Events

An event within a Bounded Context is any operation that *publishes the Bounded Context's Aggregate State Changes as Events*. Since Commands change the state of an Aggregate, it is safe to assume that any Command operation within a Bounded Context will result in a corresponding Event.

Domain Events play a central role within a microservices architecture, and it is critical to implement them in a robust manner. The distributed nature of a microservices architecture mandates the usage of Events via a *choreography mechanism* to *maintain state and transactional consistency* between the various Bounded Contexts of a microservices-based application.

Figure 5-24 illustrates examples of the events that flow between the various Bounded Contexts of the Cargo Tracker Application.

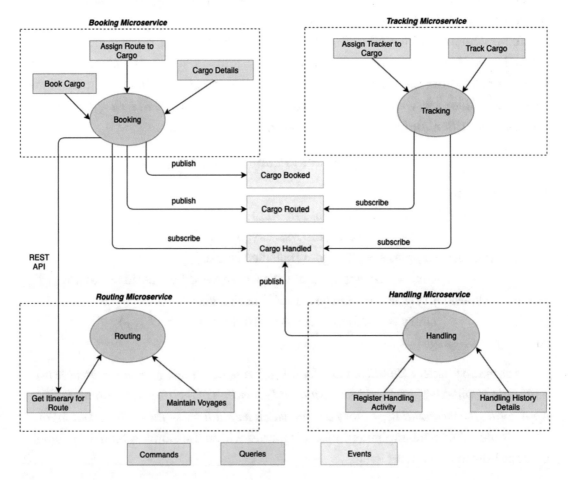

Figure 5-24. *Flow of Events in a Microservices architecture*

Let us explain this a bit more using an example Business case.

When a cargo is assigned a route, this means that the cargo can now be tracked which requires a Tracking Identifier to be issued to the cargo. The assigning of route to the cargo is handled within the Booking Bounded Context, while issuing the tracking identifier is handled within the Tracking Bounded Context. In the monolithic way of doing things, the process of assigning a route to the cargo and issuing the tracking identifier happens together since ***we can maintain the same transactional context across multiple Bounded Contexts due to the shared model for processes, runtimes, and Datastores***.

However, in a microservices architecture, it is not possible to achieve the same since it is *a shared nothing architecture*. When a cargo is assigned a route, the Booking Bounded Context is only responsible for ensuring that the Cargo Aggregate's state reflects the new route. The Tracking Bounded Context needs to know about this change of state so that it can issue the Tracking Identifier accordingly to **complete the business use case**. This is where **Domain Events and Event Choreography** play an important role. If the Cargo Bounded Context can raise the event that the Cargo Aggregate has been assigned a Route, the Tracking Bounded Context can subscribe to that specific event and issue the tracking identifier to complete this business use case. The mechanism of **raising events** and **delivering events** to various Bounded Contexts to complete a business use case is the **event choreography pattern.**

There are four stages to the implementation of a robust event-driven choreography architecture:

- **Register** the Domain Events that need to be raised from a Bounded Context.

- **Raise** the Domain Events that need to be published from a Bounded Context.

- **Publish** the Events that are raised from a Bounded Context.

- **Subscribe** to the Events that have been published from other Bounded Contexts.

Considering the complexity of this architecture, the implementation is split across multiple areas:

- Registration of Domain Events is implemented **by the Aggregate.**

- Raising/publishing of Events is implemented **by the Outbound Services.**

- Subscribing to Events is handled **by the Interface/Inbound services.**

The only area that we will cover in this section, since we are in the phase of implementing the Domain Model, is the registration of events by the Aggregate. The subsequent sections of the chapter will deal with each of the other aspects (Outbound services will cover the implementation of the raising/publishing of Events, and Inbound Services will cover the implementation of subscribing to the Events).

Registration of Events

To help implement this, we will utilize the template class "*AbstractAggregateRoot*" provided by Spring Data. This template class provides the capability to register events that occur.

Let us take an example to walk us through the implementation. Listing 5-15 shows the Cargo Aggregate class which extends the AbstractAggregateRoot Template class:

Listing 5-15. AbstractAggregateRoot template class

```
package com.practicalddd.cargotracker.bookingms.domain.model.aggregates;
import javax.persistence.*;
import org.springframework.data.domain.AbstractAggregateRoot;
@Entity
public class Cargo extends AbstractAggregateRoot<Cargo> {
}
```

The next step is to *implement the registered Aggregate events* whenever the *state of the Aggregate changes*. As we have stated and seen earlier, *Command Operations on Aggregates change state* and are *the most likely place where we would like to register Aggregate Events*. Within the Cargo Aggregate, we have two Command Operations: the first one when a new cargo is booked and the second one when the cargo is routed. The Aggregate state changes are placed within the Command Handlers of the Aggregate, the Cargo Booking within the *Constructor method of the Cargo Aggregate,* and the Cargo Routing within the *assignToRoute method of the Cargo Aggregate.* We will implement the registration and raising of the Aggregate Events within these two methods using the *registerEvent()* method provided by the AbstractAggregateRoot template class.

Listing 5-16 shows the implementation of the Registration of Aggregate Events within the *Command Handler methods* of the Cargo Aggregate. We add a new method within the Aggregate "*addDomainEvent()*" which is an encapsulation of the "*registerEvent()*". It takes as an input parameter a *Generic Event Object which is the event that needs to be registered.* Within the constructor and the assignToRoute() method, we invoke the addDomainEvent() method with the corresponding Events that need to be registered, that is, *CargoBookedEvent* and *CargoRoutedEvent:*

Listing 5-16. Event registration within the Cargo root aggregate

```
package com.practicalddd.cargotracker.bookingms.domain.model.aggregates;
import javax.persistence.*;
import org.springframework.data.domain.AbstractAggregateRoot;
@Entity
public class Cargo extends AbstractAggregateRoot<Cargo> {
/**
* Constructor - Used for a new Cargo booking. Registers the Cargo Booked Event
* @param bookingId - Booking Identifier for the new Cargo
* @param routeSpecification - Route Specification for the new Cargo
*/
    /**
    * Constructor Command Handler for a new Cargo booking. Sets the state
    * of the Aggregate and registers the Cargo Booked Event
    *
    */
    public Cargo(BookCargoCommand bookCargoCommand){
        this.bookingId = new BookingId(bookCargoCommand.getBookingId());
        this.routeSpecification = new RouteSpecification(
                new Location(bookCargoCommand.getOriginLocation()),
                new Location(bookCargoCommand.getDestLocation()),
                bookCargoCommand.getDestArrivalDeadline()
            );
        this.origin = routeSpecification.getOrigin();
        this.itinerary = CargoItinerary.EMPTY_ITINERARY; //Empty Itinerary
        since the Cargo has not been routed yet
        this.bookingAmount = bookingAmount;
        this.delivery = Delivery.derivedFrom(this.routeSpecification,
                this.itinerary, LastCargoHandledEvent.EMPTY);

        //Add this domain event which needs to be fired when the new cargo
        is saved
        addDomainEvent(new
                CargoBookedEvent(
                        new CargoBookedEventData(bookingId.getBookingId())));
```

```
    }
    /**
     * Assigns route to the Cargo. Registers the Cargo Routed Event
     * @param itinerary
     */
       /**
     * Command Handler for the Route Cargo Command. Sets the state of the
     * Aggregate and registers the Cargo routed event
     * @param routeCargoCommand
     */

    public void assignToRoute(RouteCargoCommand routeCargoCommand) {
        this.itinerary = routeCargoCommand.getCargoItinerary();
        // Handling consistency within the Cargo aggregate synchronously
        this.delivery = delivery.updateOnRouting(this.routeSpecification,
                this.itinerary);

        //Add this domain event which needs to be fired when the new cargo
        is saved
        addDomainEvent(new
                CargoRoutedEvent(
                new CargoRoutedEventData(bookingId.getBookingId())));
    }
/**
     * Method to register the event
     * @param event
     */
    public void addDomainEvent(Object event){
        registerEvent(event);
    }
}
```

Listing 5-17 shows the implementation of the ***CargoBookedEvent*** class. It is a regular POJO which encapsulates the Event Data, that is, ***CargoBookedEventData:***

Listing 5-17. CargoBookedEvent implementation class

```
/**
 * Event Class for the Cargo Booked Event. Wraps up the Cargo Booked Event
Data
 */
public class CargoBookedEvent {
    CargoBookedEventData cargoBookedEventData;
    public CargoBookedEvent(CargoBookedEventData cargoBookedEventData){
        this.cargoBookedEventData = cargoBookedEventData;
    }
    public CargoBookedEventData getCargoBookedEventData(){
        return cargoBookedEventData;
    }
}
```

Listing 5-18 shows the implementation of the CargoBookedEventData class. This is again a regular POJO and contains the Event Data, in this case just the Booking Id:

Listing 5-18. CargoBookedEventData implementation class

```
/**
 * Event Data for the Cargo Booked Event
 */
public class CargoBookedEventData {
    private String bookingId;
    public CargoBookedEventData(String bookingId){
        this.bookingId = bookingId;
    }
    public String getBookingId(){return this.bookingId;}
}
```

The ***CargoRoutedEvent*** and the ***CargoRoutedEventData*** implementations follow the same approach as earlier.

Figure 5-25 illustrates the class diagram for our implementation.

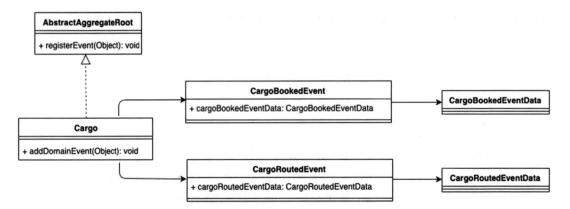

Figure 5-25. *Class diagram for the Aggregate Event Registration implementation*

In summary, Aggregates register Domain Events after the processing of a Command. The registration of these events is always implemented within the Command Handler methods of the Aggregates.

This completes the implementation of the Domain Model. We shall now proceed to implement the Domain Model Services for the Domain Model.

Domain Model Services

Domain Model Services are used for two primary reasons. The first is to enable the Bounded Context's state to be ***made available to external parties*** through ***well-defined Interfaces.*** The second is ***interacting with external parties*** be it to persist the Bounded Context's state to ***Datastores*** (Databases), publish the Bounded Context's state change events to external ***Message Brokers,*** or to ***communicate with other Bounded Contexts.***

There are three types of Domain Model Services for any Bounded Context:

- ***Inbound Services*** where we implement well-defined interfaces which enable external parties to interact with the Domain Model

- ***Outbound Services*** where we implement all interactions with External Repositories/other Bounded Contexts

- ***Application Services*** which act as the façade layer between the Domain Model and both Inbound and Outbound services

Figure 5-26 illustrates the Domain Model Services implementation.

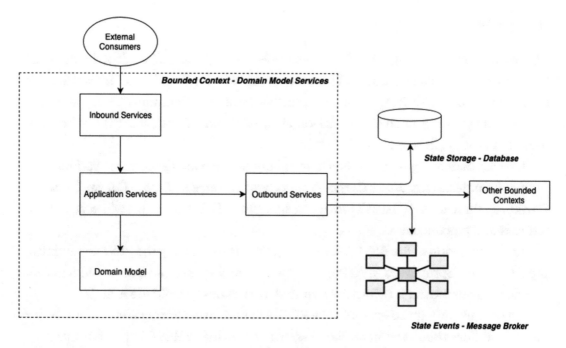

Figure 5-26. *Domain Model Services implementation summary*

Inbound Services

Inbound services (or Inbound Adaptors as denoted in the Hexagonal Architectural Pattern) act as the outermost gateway for our Core Domain Model. As stated, it involves the implementation of well-defined interfaces which enable external consumers to interact with the core domain model.

The type of inbound services ***depends upon the types of operations*** we need to expose to ***enable the external consumers of the Domain Model.***

Considering that we are implementing the microservices architectural pattern for our Cargo Tracker application, we provide two types of Inbound Services:

- ***An API Layer based on REST*** which is used by external consumers to invoke operations on the Bounded Context (***Commands/Queries***)

- ***An Event Handling Layer based on Spring Cloud Stream*** which consumes Events from the Message Broker and processes them

REST API

The responsibility of the REST API is to receive HTTP requests on behalf of the Bounded Context from external consumers. This request could be for Commands or Queries. The responsibility of the REST API layer is to translate it into the Command/Query Model recognized by the Bounded Context's Domain Model and delegate it to the Application Services Layer to further process it.

Looking back at Figure 4-5 which detailed out all the operations for the various Bounded Contexts *(e.g., Book Cargo, Assign Route to Cargo, Handle Cargo, Track Cargo),* all these operations will have corresponding REST APIs which will accept these requests and process them.

Implementation of the REST API in Spring Boot is by utilizing the REST capabilities provided by the Spring Web MVC Project. The *spring-boot-starter-web* dependency that we added to our project provides the required capabilities to build the API(s).

Let us walk through an example of a REST API built using Spring Web. Listing 5-19 depicts the *CargoBookingController class* which provides a REST API for our *Cargo Booking Command*:

- The REST API is available at the URL "/*cargobooking*".

- It has a single POST method that accepts a BookCargoResource which is the input payload to the API. This is marked with the annotation "*@RequestBody*".

- It has a dependency on the CargoBookingCommandService which is an Application services which acts as a façade (see implementation in the following). This dependency is injected into the API class utilizing a Constructor-based Dependency Injection.

- It transforms the Resource Data (*BookCargoResource*) to the Command Model (*BookCargoCommand*) using an Assembler utility class (*BookCargoCommandDTOAssembler*).

- After transforming, it delegates the process to the CargoBookingCommandService for further processing.

- It returns back a Response to the external consumer with the Booking Identifier of the newly booked cargo.

Listing 5-19. CargoBookingController implementation class

```
package com.practicalddd.cargotracker.bookingms.interfaces.rest;
import com.practicalddd.cargotracker.bookingms.application.internal.
commandservices.CargoBookingCommandService;
import com.practicalddd.cargotracker.bookingms.domain.model.aggregates.
BookingId;
import com.practicalddd.cargotracker.bookingms.interfaces.rest.dto.
BookCargoResource;
import com.practicalddd.cargotracker.bookingms.interfaces.rest.transform.
BookCargoCommandDTOAssembler;

import org.springframework.stereotype.Controller;
import org.springframework.web.bind.annotation.*;

@Controller     // This means that this class is a Controller
@RequestMapping("/cargobooking") // The URI of the API
public class CargoBookingController {
    private CargoBookingCommandService cargoBookingCommandService;
    // Application Service Dependency
    /**
     * Provide the dependencies
     * @param cargoBookingCommandService
     */
    public CargoBookingController(CargoBookingCommandService
    cargoBookingCommandService){
        this.cargoBookingCommandService = cargoBookingCommandService;
    }
    /**
     * POST method to book a cargo
     * @param bookCargoResource
     */
    @PostMapping
    @ResponseBody
    public BookingId bookCargo(@RequestBody  BookCargoResource
    bookCargoResource){
        BookingId bookingId  = cargoBookingCommandService.bookCargo(
```

```
                    BookCargoCommandDTOAssembler.toCommandFromDTO(bookCargo
                    Resource));
        return bookingId;
    }
}
```

Listing 5-20 shows the implementation for the ***BookCargoResource*** class:

Listing 5-20. CargoBookingResource implementation class

```
package com.practicalddd.cargotracker.bookingms.interfaces.rest.dto;

import java.time.LocalDate;

/**
 * Resource class for the Book Cargo Command API
 */
public class BookCargoResource {

    private int bookingAmount;
    private String originLocation;
    private String destLocation;
    private LocalDate destArrivalDeadline;

    public BookCargoResource(){}

    public BookCargoResource(int bookingAmount,
                            String originLocation, String destLocation,
                            LocalDate destArrivalDeadline){

        this.bookingAmount = bookingAmount;
        this.originLocation = originLocation;
        this.destLocation = destLocation;
        this.destArrivalDeadline = destArrivalDeadline;
    }

    public void setBookingAmount(int bookingAmount){
        this.bookingAmount = bookingAmount;
    }
```

```
public int getBookingAmount(){
    return this.bookingAmount;
}

public String getOriginLocation() {return originLocation; }

public void setOriginLocation(String originLocation) {this.
originLocation = originLocation; }

public String getDestLocation() { return destLocation; }

public void setDestLocation(String destLocation) { this.destLocation =
destLocation; }


public LocalDate getDestArrivalDeadline() { return destArrivalDeadline; }

public void setDestArrivalDeadline(LocalDate destArrivalDeadline) {
this.destArrivalDeadline = destArrivalDeadline; }
}
```

Listing 5-21 shows the implementation for the **_BookCargoCommandDTOAssembler_**
class:

Listing 5-21. DTOAssembler implementation class

```
package com.practicalddd.cargotracker.bookingms.interfaces.rest.transform;

import com.practicalddd.cargotracker.bookingms.domain.model.commands.
BookCargoCommand;
import com.practicalddd.cargotracker.bookingms.interfaces.rest.dto.
BookCargoResource;

/**
 * Assembler class to convert the Book Cargo Resource Data to the Book
Cargo Model
 */
public class BookCargoCommandDTOAssembler {
```

```
/**
 * Static method within the Assembler class
 * @param bookCargoResource
 * @return BookCargoCommand Model
 */
public static BookCargoCommand toCommandFromDTO(BookCargoResource
bookCargoResource){

    return new BookCargoCommand(
                            bookCargoResource.getBookingAmount(),
                            bookCargoResource.getOriginLocation(),
                            bookCargoResource.getDestLocation(),
                            java.sql.Date.valueOf(bookCargoResource.
                            getDestArrivalDeadline()));
}
}
```

Listing 5-22 shows the implementation for the ***BookCargoCommand*** class:

Listing 5-22. BookCargoCommand implementation class

```
package com.practicalddd.cargotracker.bookingms.domain.model.commands;

import java.util.Date;

/**
 * Book Cargo Command class
 */
public class BookCargoCommand {

    private int bookingAmount;
    private String originLocation;
    private String destLocation;
    private Date destArrivalDeadline;

    public BookCargoCommand(){}

    public BookCargoCommand(int bookingAmount,
```

```
                    String originLocation, String destLocation,
                    Date destArrivalDeadline){

    this.bookingAmount = bookingAmount;
    this.originLocation = originLocation;
    this.destLocation = destLocation;
    this.destArrivalDeadline = destArrivalDeadline;
}

public void setBookingAmount(int bookingAmount){
    this.bookingAmount = bookingAmount;
}

public int getBookingAmount(){
    return this.bookingAmount;
}

public String getOriginLocation() {return originLocation; }

public void setOriginLocation(String originLocation) {this.
originLocation = originLocation; }

public String getDestLocation() { return destLocation; }

public void setDestLocation(String destLocation) { this.destLocation =
destLocation; }

public Date getDestArrivalDeadline() { return destArrivalDeadline; }

public void setDestArrivalDeadline(Date destArrivalDeadline) { this.
destArrivalDeadline = destArrivalDeadline; }
}
```

Figure 5-27 demonstrates the class diagram for our implementation.

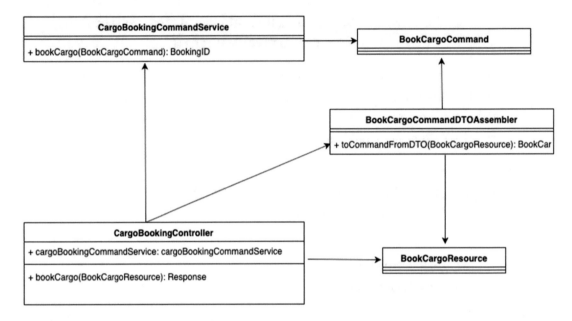

Figure 5-27. *Class diagram for the REST API implementation*

All our inbound REST API implementations follow the same approach which is illustrated in Figure 5-28.

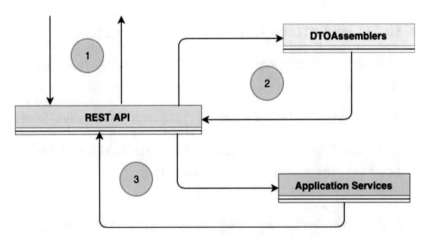

Figure 5-28. *Inbound Services implementation process summary*

1.   The inbound request for a Command/Query comes to the REST
     API. API classes are implemented using the Spring Web MVC
     project which gets configured when we add the *spring-boot-
     starter-web* dependency to the project.

2.   The REST API class uses a utility Assembler component to convert
     the Resource Data format to the Command/Query Data format
     required by the Domain Model.

3.   The Command/Query Data is sent to the Application Services for
     further processing.

Event Handlers

The other type of interfaces that exist within our Bounded Contexts are the Event
Handlers. Within a Bounded Context, Event Handlers are responsible for processing
Events that the Bounded Context is interested in. These Events are raised by other
Bounded Contexts within the application. These "*EventHandlers*" are created within
the subscribing Bounded Context which resides within the *inbound/interface* layer. The
Event Handlers receive the Event along with the Event payload data and process them as
a regular Command operation.

Implementation of the Event Handlers will be done utilizing the capabilities
provided by Spring Cloud Stream. Our message broker will be RabbitMQ, so our
implementation will assume that we have a RabbitMQ instance up and running. We do
not need to create any specific exchanges, destinations, or queues within RabbitMQ.

We will use the example of the Tracking Bounded Context interested in the
"*CargoRouted*" event which the Booking Bounded Context publishes after the
processing of the Route Cargo command:

1.   The first step is to *implement the Handler Class*. The handler
     class is implemented as a regular service class with *"@Service"*
     stereotype annotation. We bind the service class to the channel
     connection for the message broker using the *"@EnableBinding"*
     annotation. Finally, we mark the event handler method within the
     Handler class with the *"@StreamListener"* annotation with the
     target destination details. The annotation marks the method to
     receive the stream of events being published onto the destination
     that the Handler is interested in.

Listing 5-23 demonstrates the implementation of the
CargoRoutedEventHandler class:

Listing 5-23. CargoRoutedEvent handler implementation class

```
package com.practicalddd.cargotracker.trackingms.interfaces.events;

import com.practicalddd.cargotracker.shareddomain.events.CargoRoutedEvent;
import org.springframework.cloud.stream.annotation.EnableBinding;
import org.springframework.cloud.stream.annotation.StreamListener;
import org.springframework.cloud.stream.messaging.Sink;
import org.springframework.stereotype.Service;

/**
 * Event Handler for the Cargo Routed Event that the Tracking Bounded
Context is interested in
 */
@Service
@EnableBinding(Sink.class) //Bind to the channel connection for the message
broker
public class CargoRoutedEventHandler {

    @StreamListener(target = Sink.INPUT) //Listen to the stream of messages
    on the destination
    public void receiveEvent(CargoRoutedEvent cargoRoutedEvent) {
        //Process the Event
    }
}
```

2. We also need to implement broker configuration such as the
   ***broker connection details and the broker target/destination
   mappings***. Listing 5-24 demonstrates the configuration that needs
   to be implemented in the *application.properties* file of the Spring
   Boot application. The properties for the broker configuration have
   the default values set by RabbitMQ when we first install it:

Listing 5-24. RabbitMQ configuration properties

```
spring.rabbitmq.host=localhost
spring.rabbitmq.port=5672
spring.rabbitmq.username=guest
spring.rabbitmq.password=guest
spring.cloud.stream.bindings.input.destination=cargoRoutings
spring.cloud.stream.bindings.input.group=cargoRoutingsQueue
```

The ***destination is configured with the same value*** that is used when we publish the "CargoRouted" event in the Booking Bounded Context (see section on Outbound Services).

Figure 5-29 demonstrates the class diagram for our implementation.

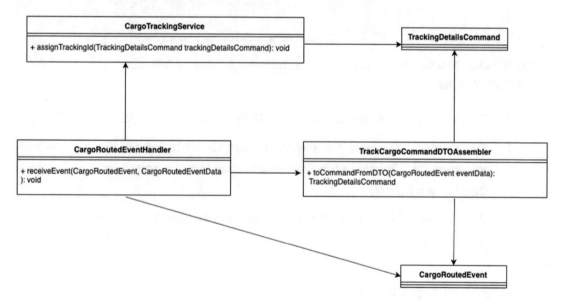

Figure 5-29. *Class diagram for our Event Handler implementation*

All our Event Handler implementations follow the same approach as illustrated in Figure 5-30.

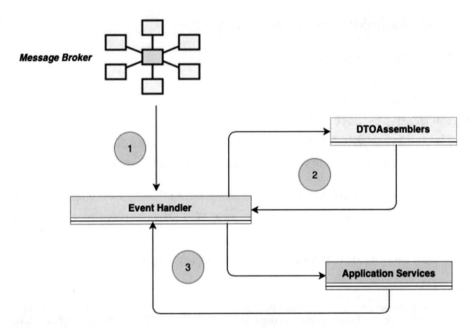

Figure 5-30. *Implementation process summary for Event Handler implementations*

1. Event Handlers receive inbound events from a Message Broker.

2. Event Handlers use a utility Assembler component to convert the Resource Data format to the Command Data format required by the Domain Model.

3. The Command Data is sent to the Application Services for further processing.

Application Services

Application Services act as a façade or a port between the Inbound/Outbound Services and the Core Domain Model within a Bounded Context.

Within a Bounded Context, Application services are responsible for ***receiving requests from the Inbound Services*** and ***delegating them to the corresponding services,*** that is, Commands are delegated to ***Command Services*** and Queries are delegated to ***Query Services.*** As part of a ***command delegation process***, Application services are responsible for persisting the Aggregate state in the underlying datastore. As part of a query delegation process, Application services are responsible for retrieving the Aggregate state from the underlying datastore.

As part of these responsibilities, Application services rely on **outbound services** to complete these tasks. Outbound services provide the necessary infrastructural components required to connect to the physical datastores. We will deep dive into the outbound services implementation separately (***see section on Outbound Services***).

Figure 5-31 illustrates the responsibilities of the Application Services.

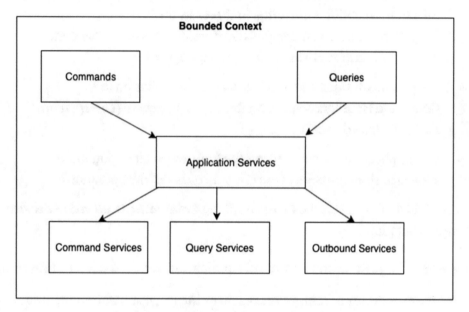

Figure 5-31. *Responsibilities of the Application Services*

Application Services: Command/Query Delegation

As part of this responsibility, Application services within a Bounded Context receive requests for processing Commands/Queries. These requests come in typically from the Inbound Services (API Layer). As part of the processing, Application services first utilize the ***CommandHandlers/QueryHandlers*** (see section on Domain Model) of the Domain model to set state or query state. They then utilize the Outbound Services to persist state or execute queries on the state of the Aggregate.

Let us first walk through an example of a Command Delegator Application Services Class, the ***Cargo Booking Command Application Services Class***. This class has two routines - "***bookCargo()***" and "***assignRouteToCargo()***" which handle the ***Cargo Booking Command*** and the ***Route Cargo Command:***

- The Application services class is implemented as a regular Spring Managed Bean with an "**@Service**" marker annotation attached to it which indicates that it is a Service class.

- The Application services class is provided with the necessary dependencies via the Constructor Dependency Injection capabilities of Spring. In this case, the CargoBookingCommandApplicationService class has dependencies on an **outbound repository class** (**CargoRepository**).

- In both the routines, the Application services relies on the Command Handlers defined on the Cargo Aggregate **(Constructor, assignToRoute)** to set its state.

- The Application services utilizes the CargoRepository outbound service to store the state of the Cargo in either of the operations.

Listing 5-25 demonstrates the **Cargo Booking Command Application Services Class** implementation:

Listing 5-25. CargoBookingCommand Application services class implementation

```
package com.practicalddd.cargotracker.bookingms.application.internal.
commandservices;

import com.practicalddd.cargotracker.bookingms.application.internal.
outboundservices.acl.ExternalCargoRoutingService;
import com.practicalddd.cargotracker.bookingms.domain.model.aggregates.
BookingId;
import com.practicalddd.cargotracker.bookingms.domain.model.aggregates.Cargo;
import com.practicalddd.cargotracker.bookingms.domain.model.commands.
BookCargoCommand;
import com.practicalddd.cargotracker.bookingms.domain.model.commands.
RouteCargoCommand;
import com.practicalddd.cargotracker.bookingms.domain.model.entities.Location;
import com.practicalddd.cargotracker.bookingms.domain.model.valueobjects.
CargoItinerary;
import com.practicalddd.cargotracker.bookingms.domain.model.valueobjects.
RouteSpecification;
```

```
import com.practicalddd.cargotracker.bookingms.infrastructure.repositories.
CargoRepository;
import org.springframework.stereotype.Service;

import java.util.UUID;
/**
 * Application Service class for the Cargo Booking Commands
 */

@Service
public class CargoBookingCommandService {

    private CargoRepository cargoRepository;
    private ExternalCargoRoutingService externalCargoRoutingService;

    public CargoBookingCommandService(CargoRepository cargoRepository){

        this.cargoRepository = cargoRepository;
        this.externalCargoRoutingService = externalCargoRoutingService;
    }

    /**
     * Service Command method to book a new Cargo
     * @return BookingId of the Cargo
     */

    public BookingId bookCargo(BookCargoCommand bookCargoCommand){

        String random = UUID.randomUUID().toString().toUpperCase();
        bookCargoCommand.setBookingId(random);
        Cargo cargo = new Cargo(bookCargoCommand);
        cargoRepository.save(cargo);
        return new BookingId(random);
    }

    /**
     * Service Command method to assign a route to a Cargo
     * @param routeCargoCommand
     */
```

```
public void assignRouteToCargo(RouteCargoCommand routeCargoCommand){

    Cargo cargo = cargoRepository.findByBookingId(routeCargoCommand.
    getCargoBookingId());
    CargoItinerary cargoItinerary = externalCargoRoutingService.
    fetchRouteForSpecification(new RouteSpecification(
            new Location(routeCargoCommand.getOriginLocation()),
            new Location(routeCargoCommand.getDestinationLocation()),
            routeCargoCommand.getArrivalDeadline()
    ));
    routeCargoCommand.setCargoItinerary(cargoItinerary);
    cargo.assignToRoute(routeCargoCommand);
    cargoRepository.save(cargo);

}

}
```

Listing 5-26 demonstrates the ***Cargo Booking Query Application Services Class*** implementation which serves all queries related to the Booking Bounded Context:

Listing 5-26. CargoBookingQuery Application services implementation

```
package com.practicalddd.cargotracker.bookingms.application.internal.
queryservices;

import com.practicalddd.cargotracker.bookingms.domain.model.aggregates.
BookingId;
import com.practicalddd.cargotracker.bookingms.domain.model.aggregates.Cargo;
import com.practicalddd.cargotracker.bookingms.infrastructure.repositories.
CargoRepository;
import org.springframework.stereotype.Service;

import java.util.List;

/**
 * Application Service which caters to all queries related to the Booking
Bounded Context
 */
```

```java
@Service
public class CargoBookingQueryService {

    private CargoRepository cargoRepository; // Inject Dependencies

    /**
     * Find all Cargos
     * @return List<Cargo>
     */

    public List<Cargo> findAll(){
        return cargoRepository.findAll();
    }

    /**
     * List All Booking Identifiers
     * @return List<BookingId>
     */
    public List<BookingId> getAllBookingIds(){

        return cargoRepository.findAllBookingIds();
    }

    /**
     * Find a specific Cargo based on its Booking Id
     * @param bookingId
     * @return Cargo
     */
    public Cargo find(String bookingId){
        return cargoRepository.findByBookingId(bookingId);
    }
}
```

Figure 5-32 illustrates the class diagram for our implementation.

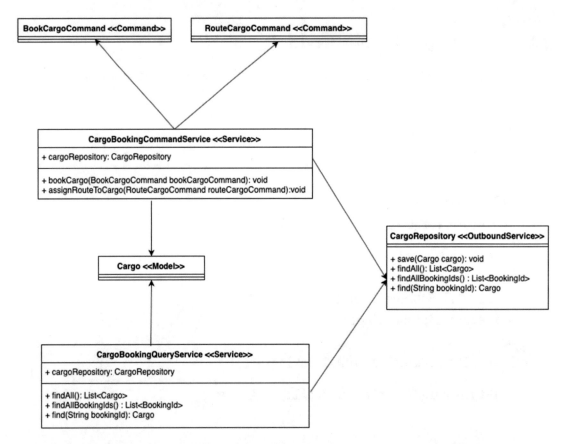

Figure 5-32. *Class diagram for our Application Services Command/Query delegation*

All our Application Services implementations which are responsible for Command/Query delegations follow the same approach which is illustrated in Figure 5-33.

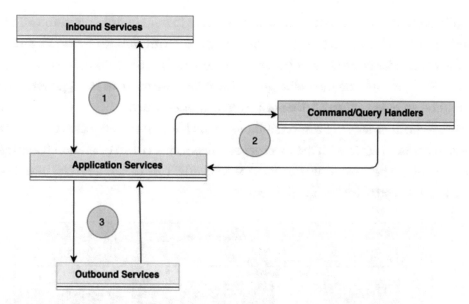

Figure 5-33. *Application Services implementation process summary*

1. The request for a Command/Query operation comes to the
    Application Services of a Bounded Context typically from the Inbound
    Services layer. Application Services Classes are ***implemented as
    Spring Managed Beans*** with the ***@Service*** marker annotation, and
    they have all their ***dependencies injected via the Constructor.***

2. Application Services rely on ***CommandHandlers/QueryHandlers***
    defined within the Domain Model to set/query Aggregate state.

3. Application Services utilize ***Outbound Services*** (e.g.,
    Repositories) to persist the state of the Aggregate or execute the
    query on the Aggregate.

Outbound Services

As we have seen in the Application Services implementation earlier, during the
processing of a Command/Query, Application services might be required to
communicate with ***external services*** such as the following:

- ***Repositories*** *to store/retrieve state of the Bounded Context*

- ***Message Brokers*** *to communicate state change of the Bounded Context*

- ***Other Bounded Contexts***

Application Services rely on **Outbound Services** to help in this communication.

Outbound Services provide capabilities to interact with **these external services**. The **external service could be the Datastore** where we store the Bounded Context's Aggregate State, it could be the **message broker where we publish the Aggregate state,** or it could be an **interaction with another Bounded Context.**

Figure 5-34 illustrates the responsibilities of the Outbound Services. They receive requests to communicate with the external services as part of an operation (Commands, Queries, Events). They use APIs (Persistence APIs, REST APIs, Broker APIs) based on the external service type to interact with them.

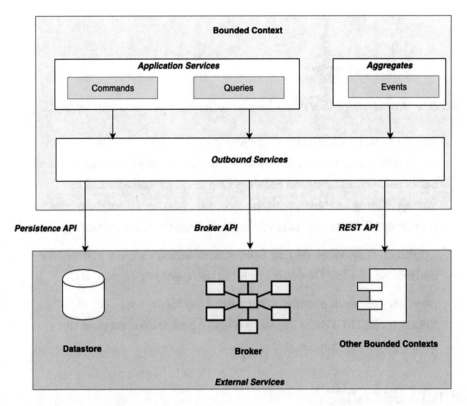

Figure 5-34. *Outbound Services*

Let us look at implementing these Outbound Service types.

Outbound Services: Repository Classes

The outbound services for Database access are implemented as *"Repository" classes.*
A repository class is built around a specific aggregate and deals with all database
operations for that aggregate including the following:

- Persistence of a new aggregate and its associations

- Update of an aggregate and its associations

- Querying the aggregate and its associations

Spring Data JPA helps us implement JPA repository classes with ease. Let us walk
through an example of a Repository class, the ***Cargo Repository Class,*** which handles all
Database operations related to the ***Cargo Aggregate:***

- The Cargo Repository is implemented as an interface extending the
  JpaRepository<T,ID> interface.

- Spring Data JPA automatically implements the default CRUD
  operations required for the Cargo Aggregate.

- We just add the methods required for any kind of custom queries
  which are mapped to the corresponding named queries defined
  within the Cargo Aggregate.

Listing 5-27 demonstrates the implementation of the Cargo Repository class:

Listing 5-27. CargoRepository JPA interface

```
package com.practicalddd.cargotracker.bookingms.infrastructure.repositories;

import com.practicalddd.cargotracker.bookingms.domain.model.aggregates.
BookingId;
import com.practicalddd.cargotracker.bookingms.domain.model.aggregates.Cargo;
import org.springframework.data.jpa.repository.JpaRepository;

import java.util.List;
/**
 * Repository class for the Cargo Aggregate
 */
public interface CargoRepository extends JpaRepository<Cargo, Long> {
```

```
    Cargo findByBookingId(String BookingId);

    List<BookingId> findAllBookingIds();

    List<Cargo> findAll();

}
```

Figure 5-35 illustrates the class diagram for our implementation.

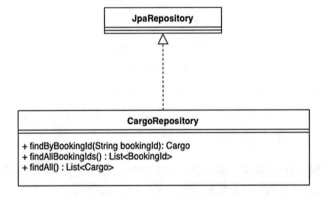

Figure 5-35. *Outbound Services – Repository implementation*

All our Repository implementations follow the same approach.

Outbound Services: Rest API(s)

Usage of REST API(s) as a mode of communication between microservices is quite a common requirement. While we have seen event choreography as one mechanism to do it, sometimes a direct call between Bounded Contexts might be a requirement too.

Let us explain this through an example. As part of the Cargo Booking process, we need to allocate the cargo an itinerary depending upon the route specification. The data required to generate an optimal itinerary is maintained as part of the Routing Bounded Context which maintains vessel movements, itineraries, and schedules. This requires the Booking Bounded Context's Booking Service to make an outbound call to the Routing Bounded Context's Routing Service which provides a REST API to retrieve all possible itineraries depending upon the cargo's Route Specification.

This is illustrated in Figure 5-36.

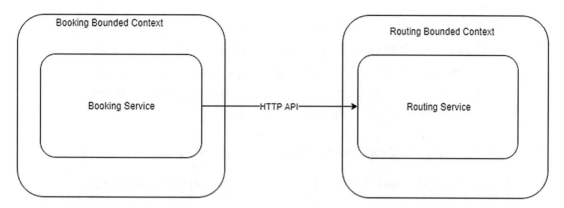

Figure 5-36. *HTTP invocation between two Bounded Contexts*

This however does pose a challenge in terms of the Domain Model. The Booking Bounded Context's Cargo aggregate has a representation of the Itinerary as a "***CargoItinerary***" object, while the Routing Bounded Context has a representation of the Itinerary as a "***TransitPath***" object. Thus, the invocation between the two Bounded Contexts will require a translation of sorts between their domain models.

This translation is typically done in the Anti-corruption Layer which acts as a bridge to communicate between two Bounded Contexts.

This is illustrated in Figure 5-37.

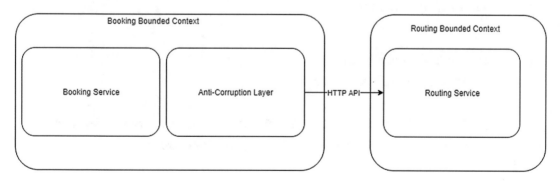

Figure 5-37. *Anti-corruption Layer between two Bounded Contexts*

The Booking Bounded Context relies on the Rest Template capabilities provided by Spring Web to invoke the Routing Service's REST API.

Let us walk through the complete implementation to understand the concept better:

- The first step is to implement the Routing Service REST API. This is done using the standard Spring Web capabilities which we have implemented in the chapter before. Listing 5-28 demonstrates the Routing Service REST API implementation:

Listing 5-28. CargoRoutingController implementation class

```
package com.practicalddd.cargotracker.routingms.interfaces.rest;

import com.practicalddd.cargotracker.TransitPath;
import com.practicalddd.cargotracker.routingms.application.internal.
CargoRoutingService;
import org.springframework.stereotype.Controller;
import org.springframework.web.bind.annotation.*;

@Controller    // This means that this class is a Controller
@RequestMapping("/cargorouting")
public class CargoRoutingController {

    private CargoRoutingService cargoRoutingService;
    // Application Service Dependency

    /**
     * Provide the dependencies
     * @param cargoRoutingService
     */
    public CargoRoutingController(CargoRoutingService cargoRoutingService){
        this.cargoRoutingService = cargoRoutingService;
    }

    /**
     *
     * @param originUnLocode
     * @param destinationUnLocode
     * @param deadline
     * @return TransitPath - The optimal route for a Route Specification
     */
```

```
@GetMapping(path = "/optimalRoute")
@ResponseBody
public TransitPath findOptimalRoute(
        @PathVariable("origin") String originUnLocode,
        @PathVariable("destination") String destinationUnLocode,
        @PathVariable("deadline") String deadline) {

    TransitPath transitPath = cargoRoutingService.findOptimalRoute
    (originUnLocode,destinationUnLocode,deadline);

    return transitPath;

}
}
```

The Routing Service implementation provides a REST API available at
"/*optimalRoute*". It takes in a set of specifications - Origin Location, Destination
Location, and Deadline. It then uses the Cargo Routing Application Services class to
calculate the optimal route based on these specifications. The Domain model within
the Routing Bounded Context represents the optimal route in terms of *Transit Paths
(analogous to Itineraries)* and *Transit Edges (analogous to Legs).*

Listing 5-29 demonstrates the Transit Path Domain Model class implementation:

Listing 5-29. TransitPath Domain model class implementation

```
import java.util.ArrayList;
import java.util.List;
/**
 * Domain Model representation of the Transit Path
 */
public class TransitPath {
    private List<TransitEdge> transitEdges;
    public TransitPath() {
        this.transitEdges = new ArrayList<>();
    }
    public TransitPath(List<TransitEdge> transitEdges) {
        this.transitEdges = transitEdges;
    }
```

```java
    public List<TransitEdge> getTransitEdges() {
        return transitEdges;
    }
    public void setTransitEdges(List<TransitEdge> transitEdges) {
        this.transitEdges = transitEdges;
    }
    @Override
    public String toString() {
        return "TransitPath{" + "transitEdges=" + transitEdges + '}';
    }
}
```

Listing 5-30 demonstrates the Transit Edge Domain Model class implementation:

Listing 5-30. TransitEdge Domain model class implementation

```java
package com.practicalddd.cargotracker;

import java.io.Serializable;
import java.util.Date;

/**
 * Represents an edge in a path through a graph, describing the route of a
 * cargo.
 */
public class TransitEdge implements Serializable {

    private String voyageNumber;
    private String fromUnLocode;
    private String toUnLocode;
    private Date fromDate;
    private Date toDate;

    public TransitEdge() {    }

    public TransitEdge(String voyageNumber, String fromUnLocode,
            String toUnLocode, Date fromDate, Date toDate) {
        this.voyageNumber = voyageNumber;
        this.fromUnLocode = fromUnLocode;
```

```java
        this.toUnLocode = toUnLocode;
        this.fromDate = fromDate;
        this.toDate = toDate;
    }

    public String getVoyageNumber() {
        return voyageNumber;
    }

    public void setVoyageNumber(String voyageNumber) {
        this.voyageNumber = voyageNumber;
    }

    public String getFromUnLocode() {
        return fromUnLocode;
    }

    public void setFromUnLocode(String fromUnLocode) {
        this.fromUnLocode = fromUnLocode;
    }

    public String getToUnLocode() {
        return toUnLocode;
    }

    public void setToUnLocode(String toUnLocode) {
        this.toUnLocode = toUnLocode;
    }

    public Date getFromDate() {
        return fromDate;
    }

    public void setFromDate(Date fromDate) {
        this.fromDate = fromDate;
    }

    public Date getToDate() {
        return toDate;
    }
```

```java
public void setToDate(Date toDate) {
    this.toDate = toDate;
}

@Override
public String toString() {
    return "TransitEdge{" + "voyageNumber=" + voyageNumber
            + ", fromUnLocode=" + fromUnLocode + ", toUnLocode="
            + toUnLocode + ", fromDate=" + fromDate
            + ", toDate=" + toDate + '}';
}
}
```

Figure 5-38 illustrates the class diagram for the implementation.

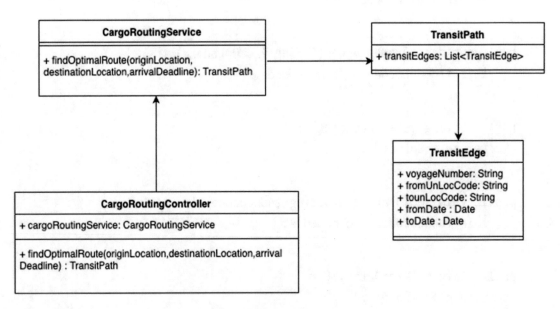

Figure 5-38. *Class diagram for the REST API*

- The next step is to implement the client-side implementation
  for our Routing Rest service. The client is the
  CargoBookingCommandService class which is responsible for
  processing the "***Assign Route to Cargo***" command. As part of the
  processing of the command, this service class will need to invoke
  the Routing Service REST API to get the optimal route based on the
  cargo's Route Specification.

  The CargoBookingCommandService makes use of an outbound service
  class – ***ExternalCargoRoutingService*** – to invoke the Routing Service
  REST API. The ***ExternalCargoRoutingService*** class also translates
  the data provided by the Routing Service's REST API into the format
  recognizable by the Booking Bounded Context's Domain Model.

  Listing 5-31 demonstrates the method "***assignRouteToCargo***" within
  the ***CargoBookingCommandService.*** This service class is injected
  with the ***ExternalCargoRoutingService*** dependency which processes
  the request to invoke the Routing Service's REST API and returns the
  CargoItinerary object which is then assigned to the cargo:

Listing 5-31. Dependencies for outbound services

```
@ApplicationScoped
public class CargoBookingCommandService {

    @Inject
    private ExternalCargoRoutingService externalCargoRoutingService;

    /**
     * Service Command method to assign a route to a Cargo
     * @param routeCargoCommand
     */
    @Transactional
    public void assignRouteToCargo(RouteCargoCommand routeCargoCommand){
```

```
        Cargo cargo = cargoRepository.find(new BookingId(routeCargoCommand.
        getCargoBookingId()));
        CargoItinerary cargoItinerary = externalCargoRoutingService.
        fetchRouteForSpecification(new RouteSpecification(
                new Location(routeCargoCommand.getOriginLocation()),
                new Location(routeCargoCommand.getDestinationLocation()),
                routeCargoCommand.getArrivalDeadline()
        ));

        cargo.assignToRoute(cargoItinerary);
        cargoRepository.store(cargo);

    }

    // All other implementations of Commands for the Booking Bounded Context

}
```

Listing 5-32 demonstrates the ExternalCargoRoutingService outbound service class. This class performs two things:

- It makes use of the **RestTemplate** class provided by the Spring Web project which helps build Rest clients.

- It also translates the Data provided by the Routing Service's Rest API (**TransitPath**, **TransitEdge**) to the Booking Bounded Context's Domain Model (**CargoItinerary**/**Leg**).

Listing 5-32. Outbound service implementation class

```
package com.practicalddd.cargotracker.bookingms.application.internal.
outboundservices.acl;

import com.practicalddd.cargotracker.bookingms.domain.model.valueobjects.
CargoItinerary;
import com.practicalddd.cargotracker.bookingms.domain.model.valueobjects.Leg;
import com.practicalddd.cargotracker.bookingms.domain.model.valueobjects.
RouteSpecification;
```

```
import com.practicalddd.cargotracker.shareddomain.TransitEdge;
import com.practicalddd.cargotracker.shareddomain.TransitPath;
import org.springframework.stereotype.Service;
import org.springframework.web.client.RestTemplate;

import java.util.ArrayList;
import java.util.HashMap;
import java.util.List;
import java.util.Map;

/**
 * Anti Corruption Service Class
 */

@Service
public class ExternalCargoRoutingService {

    /**
     * The Booking Bounded Context makes an external call to the Routing
     * Service of the Routing Bounded Context to fetch the Optimal
     * Itinerary for a Cargo based on the Route Specification
     * @param routeSpecification
     * @return
     */
    public CargoItinerary fetchRouteForSpecification(RouteSpecification
    routeSpecification){

        RestTemplate restTemplate = new RestTemplate();
        Map<String,Object> params = new HashMap<>();
        params.put("origin",routeSpecification.getOrigin().getUnLocCode());
        params.put("destination",routeSpecification.getDestination().
        getUnLocCode());
        params.put("arrivalDeadline",routeSpecification.
        getArrivalDeadline().toString());

        TransitPath transitPath = restTemplate.getForObject("<<ROUTING_
        SERVICE_URL>>/cargorouting/",
                    TransitPath.class,params);
```

```java
        List<Leg> legs = new ArrayList<>(transitPath.getTransitEdges().
        size());
        for (TransitEdge edge : transitPath.getTransitEdges()) {
            legs.add(toLeg(edge));
        }

        return new CargoItinerary(legs);

    }

    /**
     * Anti-corruption layer conversion method from the routing service's
     * domain model (TransitEdges) to the domain model recognized by the
     * Booking Bounded Context (Legs)
     * @param edge
     * @return
     */
    private Leg toLeg(TransitEdge edge) {
        return new Leg(
                edge.getVoyageNumber(),
                edge.getFromUnLocode(),
                edge.getToUnLocode(),
                edge.getFromDate(),
                edge.getToDate());

    }
}
```

Figure 5-39 illustrates the class diagram for the implementation.

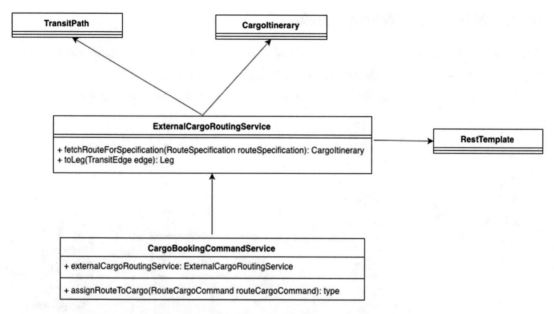

Figure 5-39. *Outbound Services – REST API implementation*

All our Outbound Service implementations which require to communicate to other Bounded Contexts follow the same approach which is illustrated in Figure 5-40.

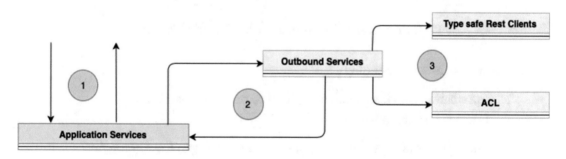

Figure 5-40. *Outbound Services (HTTP) implementation process*

1. Application Services classes receive Commands/Queries/Events.

2. As part of the processing, if it requires an interaction with another Bounded Context's API using REST, it makes use of an Outbound Service.

3. The Outbound service uses the ***RestTemplate class*** to create a Rest client to invoke the Bounded Context's API. It also performs the translation from the data format provided by that Bounded Context's API to the data model recognized by the current Bounded Context.

269

Outbound Services: Message Broker

The final responsibility of outbound services is to raise and publish the Domain Events registered by the Aggregate during the processing of a Command.

Figure 5-41 illustrates the entire mechanism of the event flow within a Bounded Context.

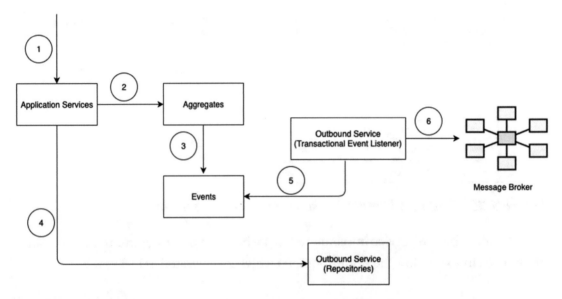

Figure 5-41. *Event flow mechanism within a Bounded Context*

Let us walk through the sequence of events:

1. Application Services receive requests to process a particular Command (e.g., Book Cargo, Route Cargo).

2. The Application services delegates the processing to the Aggregate Command Handlers.

3. Command Handlers register the event (e.g., Cargo Booked, Cargo routed) that needs to be published.

4. The Application services persists the aggregate state utilizing the Repositories of the Outbound Services.

5. ***The repository operation triggers Event Listeners within Outbound services***. The Event Listeners ***collect all pending registered Domain Events*** that need to be published.

6. The Event Listeners publish the Domain Events to the external Message Broker (i.e., RabbitMQ) ***within the same transaction.***

Implementation of the Event Listeners will be done utilizing the capabilities provided by Spring Cloud Stream. Our message broker will be RabbitMQ, so our implementation will assume that we have a RabbitMQ instance up and running. We do not need to create any specific exchanges, destinations, or queues within RabbitMQ.

We will continue with our example of the Booking Bounded Context where we need to publish the "***Cargo Booked Event***" and the "***Cargo Routed Event***" at the end of the "***Book Cargo Command***" and the "***Route Cargo Command***":

1. The first step is to ***implement the event source***. The event source contains the details of the output channels (***logical connections***) for our Events.

   Listing 5-33 demonstrates the implementation of the ***CargoEventSource.*** We have created two Output Messaging Channels (***cargoBookingChannel, cargoRoutingChannel***):

Listing 5-33. Event source class implementation

```
package com.practicalddd.cargotracker.bookingms.infrastructure.brokers.
rabbitmq;
import org.springframework.cloud.stream.annotation.Output;
import org.springframework.messaging.MessageChannel;
/**
 * Interface depicting all output channels
 */
public interface CargoEventSource {
    @Output("cargoBookingChannel")
    MessageChannel cargoBooking();
    @Output("cargoRoutingChannel")
    MessageChannel cargoRouting();
}
```

2. The next step is to **implement the event listener.** The event source contains the details of the output channels (**logical connections**) for our Events.

Listing 5-34 demonstrates the implementation of the **CargoEventPublisherService.** This is the event listener for all Domain Events registered by the Cargo Aggregate and publishing them to the Message Broker.

Implementing the event listener involves the following steps:

- The event listener is implemented as a regular Spring Managed bean with the stereotype **@Service** annotation. Listing 5-34 demonstrates the implementation.

- We **bind** the event listener to the event source that we created in the first step using the **@EnableBinding** annotation.

- For every Domain Event type that is registered by the Cargo Aggregate, we have a corresponding handling routine within the listener, for example, the CargoBookedEvent will have a handleCargoBooked() routine and similarly the CargoRoutedEvent will have a handleCargoRouted() routine. These routines take in the registered Event as the input parameter.

- These routines are marked with the @TransactionalEventListener annotation to indicate that it should be part of the same transaction of the repository operation.

- Finally within the routine, we publish the registered Event to the corresponding channel of the message broker.

Listing 5-34. Event listener class implementation

```
package com.practicalddd.cargotracker.bookingms.application.internal.
outboundservices;

import com.practicalddd.cargotracker.bookingms.infrastructure.brokers.
rabbitmq.CargoEventSource;
import com.practicalddd.cargotracker.shareddomain.events.CargoBookedEvent;
import com.practicalddd.cargotracker.shareddomain.events.CargoRoutedEvent;
import org.springframework.cloud.stream.annotation.EnableBinding;
```

```java
import org.springframework.messaging.support.MessageBuilder;
import org.springframework.stereotype.Service;
import org.springframework.transaction.event.TransactionalEventListener;

/**
 * Transactional Event Listener for all Cargo Aggregate Events
 */
@Service
@EnableBinding(CargoEventSource.class) //Bind to the Event Source
public class CargoEventPublisherService {

    CargoEventSource cargoEventSource;

    public CargoEventPublisherService(CargoEventSource cargoEventSource){
        this.cargoEventSource = cargoEventSource;
    }

    @TransactionalEventListener //Attach it to the transaction of the
    repository operation
    public void handleCargoBookedEvent(CargoBookedEvent cargoBookedEvent){
        cargoEventSource.cargoBooking().send(MessageBuilder.
        withPayload(cargoBookedEvent).build()); //Publish the event
    }

    @TransactionalEventListener
    public void handleCargoRoutedEvent(CargoRoutedEvent cargoRoutedEvent){
        cargoEventSource.cargoRouting().send(MessageBuilder.
        withPayload(cargoRoutedEvent).build());
    }
}
```

3. In addition to code implementation, we also need to implement broker configuration such as the ***broker connection details and the broker channel/exchange mappings***. Listing 5-35 demonstrates the configuration that needs to be implemented in the *application.properties* file of the Spring Boot application. The properties for the broker configuration have the default values set by RabbitMQ when we first install it:

Listing 5-35. RabbitMQ configuration details

```
spring.rabbitmq.host=localhost
spring.rabbitmq.port=5672
spring.rabbitmq.username=guest
spring.rabbitmq.password=guest
spring.cloud.stream.bindings.cargoBookingChannel.destination=cargoBookings
spring.cloud.stream.bindings.cargoRoutingChannel.destination=cargoRoutings
```

All outbound services that need to publish Domain Events follow the same approach as listed earlier.

Figure 5-42 illustrates the class diagram for our implementation.

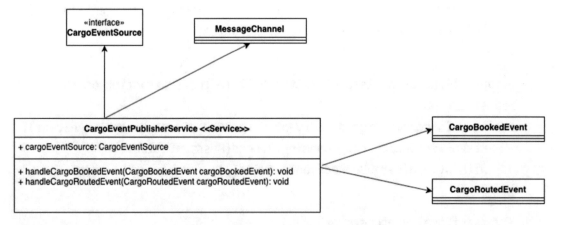

Figure 5-42. *Class diagram for the Event Publisher implementation*

This completes the implementation of the Outbound services, Domain Model Services, and the Cargo Tracker application as a microservices application utilizing DDD principles and the Spring platform.

Implementation Summary

We now have a complete DDD implementation of the Cargo Tracker microservices application with the various DDD artifacts implemented using the corresponding projects available within the Spring platform.

The implementation summary is denoted in Figure 5-43.

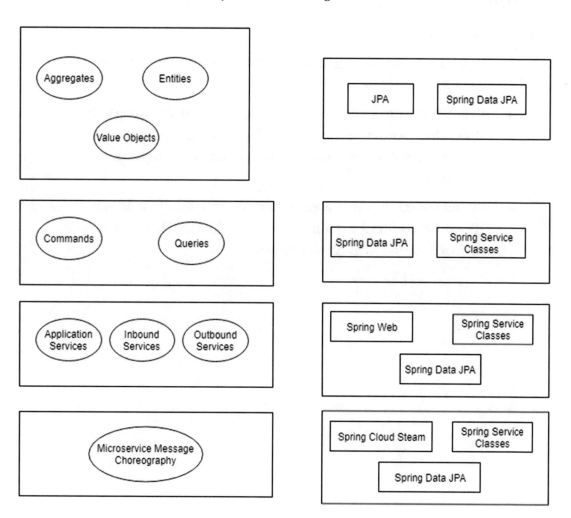

Figure 5-43. *DDD artifact implementation summary using Spring Boot*

Summary

Summarizing our chapter

- We started by establishing the details about the Spring platform and the various capabilities it provides.

- We decided to use a subset of the projects (Spring Boot, Spring Web, Spring Cloud Stream, and Spring Data) from the Spring Platform's complete portfolio to help build Cargo Tracker as a microservices application.

- We rounded off by deep diving into the development of the various DDD artifacts – first the Domain Model and then the Domain Model Services using the technologies chosen.

CHAPTER 6

Cargo Tracker: Axon Framework

We have now implemented three variations of the Cargo Tracker:

> *A DDD implementation based on a monolithic architecture using Jakarta EE*

> *A DDD implementation based on a microservices architecture using Eclipse MicroProfile*

> *A DDD implementation based on a microservices architecture using Spring Boot*

Our final DDD implementation is going to be based on an event-driven microservices architectural pattern using the following:

> *A pure **ES (Event Sourcing) framework***

> *A pure **CQRS (Command/Query Responsibility Segregation)** approach*

We shall implement this with the Axon Framework. Axon is one of the few frameworks available within the Enterprise Java space that offers an out-of-the-box, stable, complete, and feature-rich solution to implement a CQRS/ES-based architecture.

Using a pure play CQRS/ES framework like Axon requires a fundamental change in our thought process on building applications. Every aspect of the state of an application, be it State Construction, State Change, and State Queries, revolves around Events, which is fundamentally different from traditional applications. The primary entity that represents the state of the various Bounded Contexts of the application is its Aggregate, so our conversation will primarily revolve around Aggregate State.

Before we get into the implementation, let us talk a bit more about the Event Sourcing/CQRS patterns and approaches to building applications. We shall also examine the differences with our previous implementations of these patterns.

© Vijay Nair 2019
V. Nair, *Practical Domain-Driven Design in Enterprise Java*, https://doi.org/10.1007/978-1-4842-4543-9_6

Event Sourcing

The Event Sourcing pattern adopts a different approach in storing application state, retrieving application state, and publishing application state changes within the various Bounded Contexts of an application.

Before we get into the details of event sourcing, let us look at the traditional approach of state maintenance.

Traditional applications use *"Domain Sourcing or State Sourcing"* to store/retrieve Aggregate state. The concept of domain sourcing is that we construct, modify, or query Aggregate state using a traditional data storage mechanism (e.g., Relational Databases, NoSQL Database). Only once the Aggregate state has been persisted do we publish the event onto a message broker. Our previous implementations have all been based on *"Domain Sourcing."*

This is illustrated in Figure 6-1.

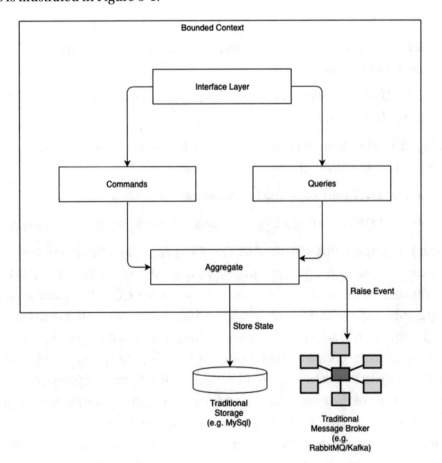

Figure 6-1. *Domain-sourced applications with storage of application state in traditional datastores*

Domain-sourced applications are fairly straightforward in usage since they use the traditional mechanisms of storing and retrieving state. The state of an Aggregate within the various Bounded Contexts is **stored as is** whenever there is an operation on the Aggregate, for example, when we **Book a New Cargo**, a new cargo is created, and the details of the new cargo are stored in the corresponding CARGO table in the database (in our case a Database Schema within the Booking Bounded Context). We raise a **New Cargo Booked Event** which is pushed onto a traditional message broker which can be subscribed by any other bounded context. We use a **dedicated message broker** onto which these events are published.

On the other hand, **Event Sourcing** works exclusively with events that occur on Aggregates. Every change of state of an Aggregate is captured as an event, and only the event is persisted instead of the whole Aggregate Instance with payload as the Aggregate Instance.

> **Again to reemphasize, we only store the event and not the aggregate as a whole.**

Let us walk through an example to explain this as illustrated in Figure 6-2.

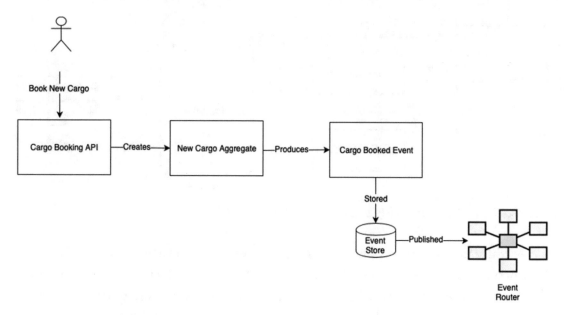

Figure 6-2. *Cargo Booking use case using Event Sourcing*

As depicted, at the end of the "Book New Cargo" operation, we persist only the "Cargo Booked Event" and not the Cargo Aggregate Instance. The event is persisted in a **specialized purpose-built Event Store**. The event store in addition to acting as the persistence store for events also needs to **double up as an Event Router,** that is, it should make the persisted event available to interested subscribers.

Similarly, when the state of the Aggregate needs to be updated, we utilize a very different approach. The steps are outlined as follows:

- We need to load the set of events that occurred on that particular Aggregate instance from the event store.

- We replay it on the Aggregate instance to get to the current state.

- We update (not persist) the Aggregate State based on the operation.

- We persist only the updated event.

Let us walk through an example again to explain this as illustrated in Figure 6-3.

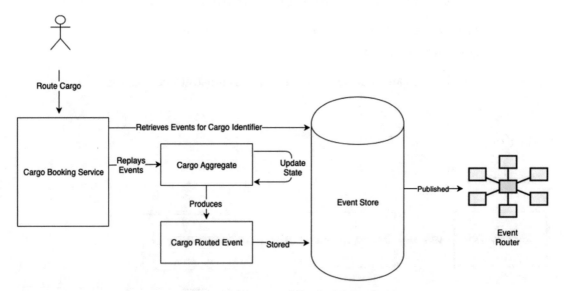

Figure 6-3. *Cargo Routing use case using Event Sourcing*

As illustrated, when we want to route a cargo, we first retrieve the set of events that have occurred for a specific cargo based on its identifier (Booking Id), replay the events that have occurred till date on that specific Cargo Aggregate instance, update the Cargo Aggregate with the route that it is supposed to take, and finally publish only the Cargo Routed Event. Again, this is quite a different approach from how traditional applications would deal with modification of state.

Figure 6-4 depicts the records of the Event store at the end of the two operations on the Cargo Aggregate.

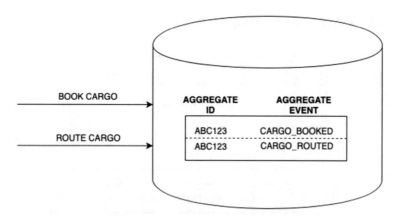

Figure 6-4. *Event Store data after two operations on the Cargo Aggregate*

The Event Sourcing pattern advocates a radical way of managing Aggregate state within a Bounded Context using a purely Event-based approach.

So then, how do we generate these Events? If we only persist Events, how do we get the state of the Aggregate? That is where the ***CQRS (Command/Query Responsibility Segregation) principle*** comes into play.

Event Sourcing is primarily used in conjunction with CQRS with the ***Command Side*** used to generate Aggregate Events and ***the Query Side*** used to query Aggregate State.

CQRS

The Command/Query Responsibility Segregation principle is essentially an application development pattern that exhorts the segregation between operations that update state and operations that query state.

Essentially, CQRS advocates usage of

> ***Commands*** *to update the state of various application objects*
> *(Aggregate within a Bounded Context)*

> ***Queries*** *to query the state of the various application objects*
> *(Aggregate within a Bounded Context)*

We have already implemented variations of the CQRS pattern in our previous chapters utilizing Jakarta EE, Spring Boot, and Eclipse MicroProfile.

Figure 6-5 depicts our previous implementations of CQRS.

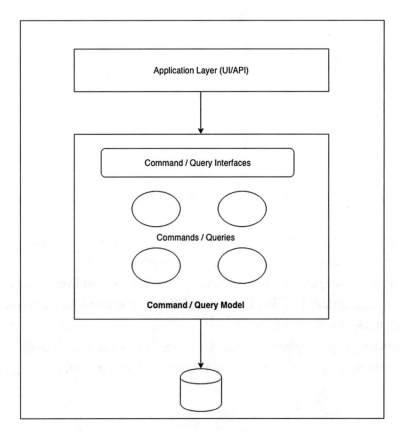

Figure 6-5. *Our previous CQRS implementations*

The implementations were based on a shared approach, that is, Commands and Queries had a shared model (e.g., the Cargo Aggregate itself processed Commands and served Queries). We utilized Domain Sourcing, that is, state was persisted and retrieved as is within a traditional database.

When we need to use CQRS along with Event Sourcing, things get a bit different. In this approach, Commands and Queries will have

- Separate models
- Separate code flows
- Separate interfaces
- Separate logical processes
- Separate persistent storage

This is depicted in Figure 6-6.

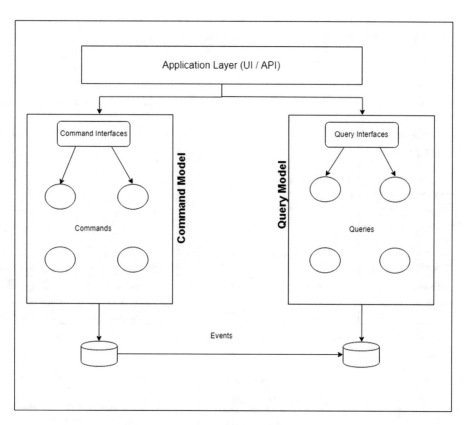

Figure 6-6. *CQRS with ES segregated model*

As seen in the illustration, within a Bounded Context, Commands/Queries have their own set of interfaces, models, processes, and storage. The Command side ***processes Commands*** to modify Aggregate State. This ***results in Events*** which are persisted and subscribed by the Query Side to update a ***Read Model***. The Read Model is a projection of the state of the Application, targeted at a specific audience, with a specific information requirement. These Events can be subscribed to by other Bounded Contexts.

Figure 6-7 brings CQRS and ES together.

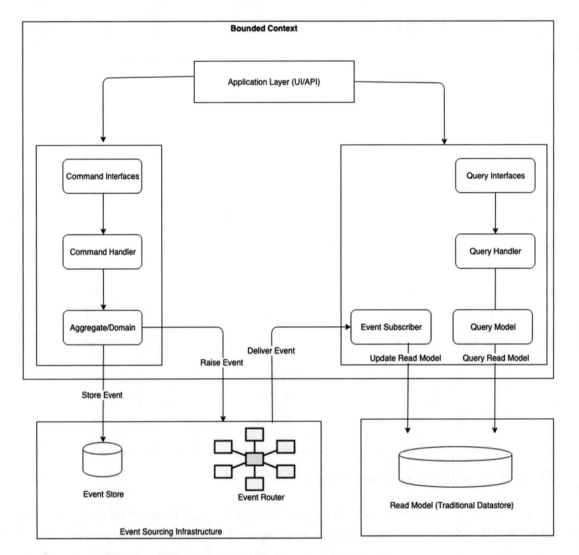

Figure 6-7. *CQRS with Event Sourcing*

To summarize, applications built using Event Sourcing and CQRS

- Have **Events** as first-class citizens

- Use a **Command Model** which updates the state of Aggregates and generates Events

- Store Events rather than direct application state in a purpose-built **Event Store**.

The event store also doubles up as an ***Event Router*** which makes the persisted events available to interested subscribers

- Provide a ***Read Model/Projection*** of the Aggregate state via ***a Query Model*** which is updated by subscribing to state change events.

Applications utilizing this pattern are tailor-made for building event-driven microservices applications.

Before we embark on the implementation, here is an introduction to the Axon Framework.

The Axon Framework

The framework was first released in 2010 as a pure open source CQRS/ES framework.

The framework has significantly evolved over the past years and in addition to the core framework offers a server option which includes an Event Store and an Event Router. Axon's core framework coupled with the server abstracts the complex infrastructural concerns required in implementing CQRS/ES patterns and helps enterprise developers focus only on the business logic.

Implementing an architecture based on Event Sourcing is extremely complex and difficult to achieve. There seems to be a growing tendency to implement event stores utilizing streaming platforms (e.g., Kafka). The downside to this is the significant custom effort involved in implementing event sourcing features which these streaming platforms do not provide (they were meant to be streaming platforms after all, not event sourcing platforms!). Axon shines in this area, and its feature set helps applications adopt CQRS/ES patterns with ease.

The icing on the cake is that it adopts DDD as the fundamental building block for building out applications. With the recent push among enterprises to adopt a microservices architectural style, Axon with its approach of combining DDD and CQRS/ES patterns provides a robust and feature-complete solution for customers to build event-driven microservices.

Axon Components

At a high level, Axon provides the following components:

- ***Axon Framework, Domain Model*** - A core framework that helps you build a domain model centered on DDD, Event Sourcing, and CQRS patterns

- ***Axon Framework, Dispatch Model*** – Logical infrastructure to support the domain model mentioned earlier, that is, the routing and coordination of commands and queries that deal with the state of the Domain Model

- ***Axon Server*** – Physical infrastructure to support the Domain/ Dispatch Model mentioned earlier.

This is illustrated in Figure 6-8.

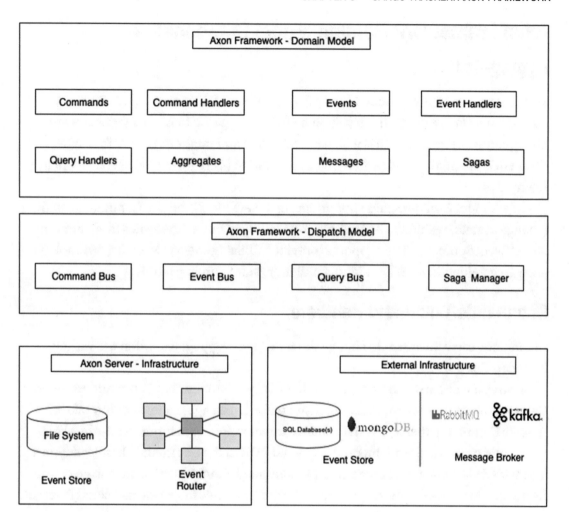

Figure 6-8. *Axon Framework components*

We could always choose an external infrastructure in place of Axon server as depicted above, but this would mean implementing a set of features that are available out of the box with Axon server.

We will take a whirlwind tour of the Axon Framework components in the following. As part of the implementation of the Domain Model for Cargo Tracker, we will be deep diving into them again, so for now just read through the section to get a broad idea of these components.

Axon Framework Domain Model Components

Aggregates

The centerpiece of any Bounded Context's domain model, Axon provides first-class support for defining and developing DDD Aggregates. In Axon, Aggregates are implemented as regular POJOs which contain state and methods to alter that state. The POJOs are marked with a Stereotype Annotation (@Aggregate) to specify them as Aggregates.

In addition, Axon provides support for Aggregate Identification/Command Handling (change of state) within the Aggregates and loading of these Aggregates from an Event Store (Event Sourcing). The support is provided utilizing specific Stereotype Annotations (@AggregateIdentifier, @CommandHandler, @EventSourcingHandler).

Commands/Command Handlers

Commands carry the intent to change the state of the Aggregates within the various Bounded Contexts.

Axon provides first-class support for handling Commands via Command Handlers. Command Handlers are routines which are placed in an aggregate; and they take a specific Command, that is, the state change intent as the main input. While the actual Command classes are implemented as regular POJOs, the Command Handler support is provided via stereotype annotations (@CommandHandler) which are placed on the Aggregate. Axon also supports placing of these commands in an external class (External Command Handler) in case it is required. Command Handlers are also responsible for raising the domain events and delegating these events to the event store/router infrastructure of Axon.

Events/Event Handlers

The processing of Commands on Aggregates always results in the generation of Events. Events notify the change of state of an Aggregate within the Bounded Context to interested subscribers. Event classes themselves are implemented as regular POJOs with no specific annotations required. Aggregates use lifecycle methods that Axon provides to push the events out to the event store and subsequently the event router after the processing of a Command.

Consumption of Events is handled via "Event Handlers" that subscribe to the events they are interested in. Axon provides a stereotype annotation "@EventHandler" which is placed on routines within regular POJOs which enables the consumption and subsequent processing of events.

Query Handlers

Queries carry the intent to retrieve the state of aggregates within our Bounded Contexts. Queries in Axon are handled by Query Handlers via the @QueryHandler annotation which is placed on regular POJOs. Query Handlers rely on the Read Model/Projection data storage to retrieve Aggregate state. They use traditional frameworks (e.g., Spring Data, JPA) to execute the Query requests.

Sagas

The Axon Framework provides first-class support for both ***Choreography-Based Sagas and Orchestration-based Sagas***. To quickly recap, choreography-based sagas rely on Events being raised and subscribed by the various Bounded Contexts that participate in a Saga. On the other hand, orchestration-based Sagas rely on a central component that is responsible for event coordination among the various Bounded Contexts that participate in a Saga. Choreography-based sagas are achieved through regular Event Handlers provided by the Axon Framework. The Axon Framework provides a comprehensive implementation to support Orchestration-based Sagas.

This includes the following:

- Lifecycle Management (Start/End Sagas via corresponding annotations, Saga Managers)

- Event Handling (via @SagaEventHandler annotation)

- Saga state storage with support for multiple implementations (JDBC, Mongo, etc.)

- Association Management across multiple services

- Deadline Handling

This completes the Domain Model components available within the Axon Framework. Let us talk a bit about the Dispatch Model components available within Axon.

Axon Dispatch Model Components

The Dispatch Model of Axon is important to understand while building Axon-based applications. To recap, any Bounded Context participates in four types of operations:

- Handle Commands to change state

- Handle Queries to retrieve state

- Publish Events/consume Events

- Saga(s)

Axon's dispatch model provides the necessary infrastructure to enable Bounded Contexts to participate in these operations, for example, when a command is sent to a Bounded Context, it is the dispatch model that ensures that the Command is routed correctly to the corresponding Command Handler within that Bounded Context.

Let us walk through the Dispatch Model in more detail.

Command Bus

Commands which are sent to the Bounded Context need to be processed by Command Handlers. The Command Bus/Command Gateway helps in dispatching of Commands to their corresponding Command Handlers for processing.

To expand

- ***CommandBus*** – An Axon infrastructure component which routes the Command to the corresponding `CommandHandler`.

- ***CommandGateway*** – An Axon infrastructure utility component which is a wrapper around the `CommandBus`. Utilizing the `CommandBus` requires us to create repeatable code for every command dispatching (e.g., `CommandMessage` creation, `CommandCallback` routines). Using the CommandGateway helps in eliminating a lot of the boilerplate code. We will come back to the implementation in the subsequent sections of this book.

Axon provides multiple implementations of the CommandBus:

- SimpleCommandBus

- AxonServerCommandBus

- AsynchronousCommandBus

- DisruptorCommmandBus

- DistributedCommandBus

- RecordingCommandBus

For our implementation, we shall use AxonServerCommandBus, an implementation which utilizes Axon Server as the dispatching mechanism for the various commands.

A summary of the implementation is shown in Figure 6-9.

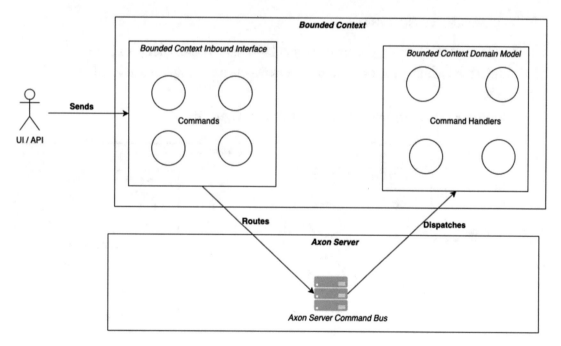

Figure 6-9. *Axon Server Command Bus implementation*

291

Query Bus

Similar to Commands, Queries which are sent to the Bounded Context need to be processed by Query Handlers. The Query Bus/Query Gateway helps in dispatching of Queries to their corresponding Query Handlers for processing:

- **QueryBus** – An Axon infrastructure component which routes the Query to the corresponding QueryHandler.

- **QueryGateway** – An Axon infrastructure utility component which is a wrapper around the QueryBus. Utilizing the QueryGateway eliminates the boilerplate code.

Axon provides multiple implementations of the Query Bus:

- SimpleQueryBus

- AxonServerQueryBus

For our implementation purpose, we shall use AxonServerQueryBus, an implementation which utilizes Axon Server as the dispatching mechanism for the various Queries.

A summary of the implementation is shown in Figure 6-10.

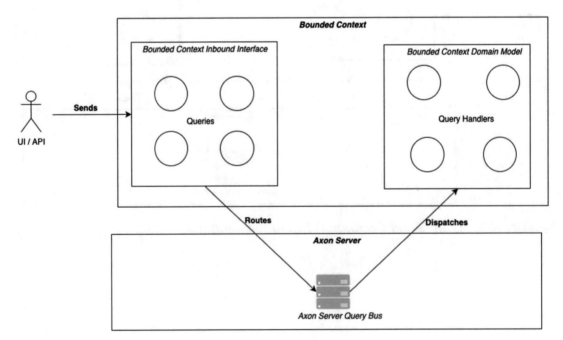

Figure 6-10. *Axon Server Query Bus implementation*

Event Bus

Event Bus is the mechanism that receives events from Command Handlers and dispatches them to the corresponding Event Handlers which could be any other Bounded Context interested in that event. Axon provides three implementations of the Event Bus:

- AxonServerEventStore

- EmbeddedEventStore

- SimpleEventBus

For our implementation, we will utilize the AxonServerEventStore. Figure 6-11 depicts the Event Bus mechanism within Axon.

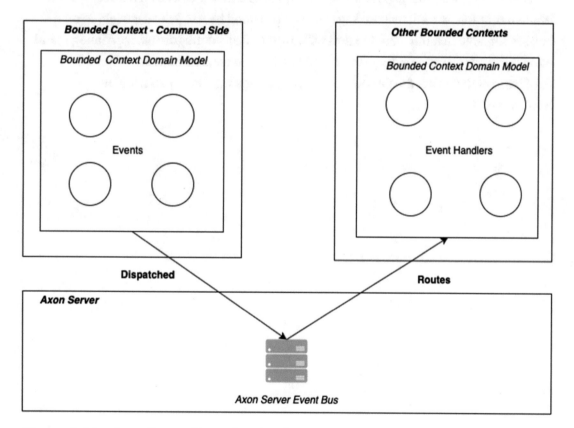

Figure 6-11. *Axon Server Event Bus implementation*

Sagas

As stated earlier, Axon Framework **provides support for** both *orchestration*-*based and **choreography**-based Sagas.* Implementation of choreography-based sagas is straightforward in the sense that Bounded Contexts participating in a particular Saga will raise and subscribe to events directly similar to regular event processing.

On the other hand, in orchestration-based Sagas, the lifecycle coordination happens through a central component. This central component is responsible for Saga creation, coordination of the flow across the various Bounded Contexts participating in the Saga, and finally the Saga Termination itself. The Axon Framework provides a component **SagaManager** for this. Similarly, orchestration-based sagas require state storage to store and retrieve Saga instances. There are various storage implementations that the Axon Framework supports (JPA, In-Memory, JDBC and Mongo, Axon Server). For our implementation, we will use the Saga storage provided by Axon Server itself. Axon applies sensible defaults here too and will automatically configure a Saga Manager and Axon Server as the state storage mechanism when we create a Saga.

Figure 6-12 depicts the Orchestration-Based Saga mechanism within our implementation.

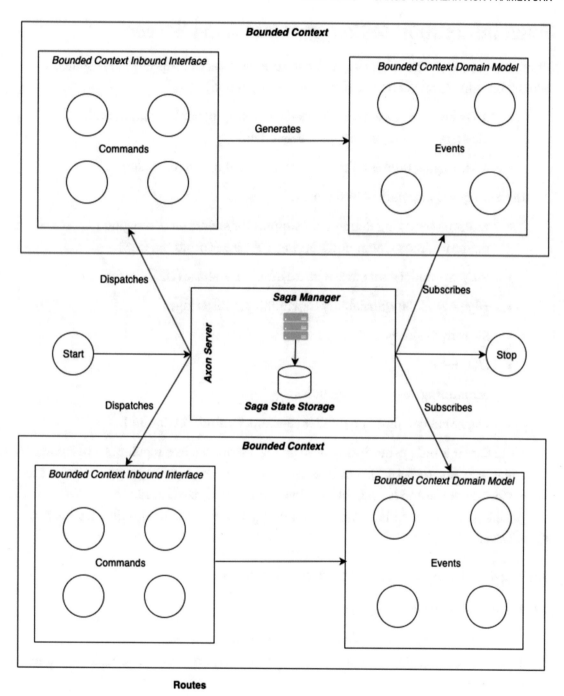

Figure 6-12. *Axon's Orchestration based saga approach*

Axon Infrastructure Components: Axon Server

Axon Server provides the physical infrastructure necessary to support the Dispatch Model. Broadly, Axon Server has two main components:

- An Event Store based on H2 (used for storage of configuration) and a file system (used for storage of event data)

- A Messaging Router for the Events flowing through the system

Here is a quick summary of its features:

- Built-in Messaging Router with support for advanced messaging patterns (Sticky Command Routing, Message Throttling, QoS)

- Purpose-built Event Store with an inbuilt Database (H2)

- High Availability/Scalability Capabilities (Clustering)

- Security Controls

- UI Console

- Monitoring/Metrics Capabilities

- Data Management Capabilities (Backup, Tuning, Versioning)

Axon Server is built using Spring Boot and is distributed as a regular JAR file (current version is at axonserver-4.1.2). It utilizes its own file-system based storage engine as the event store database and is available for download at `www.axoniq.io`.

Bringing up the server is as simple as running it as a traditional JAR file. Listing 6-1 demonstrates this:

Listing 6-1. Command to bring up the Axon server

```
java -jar axonserver-4.1.2.jar
```

This brings up Axon Server, and its console can be accessed at `http://localhost:8024`. Figure 6-13 depicts the Dashboard as part of the UI console provided by Axon Server.

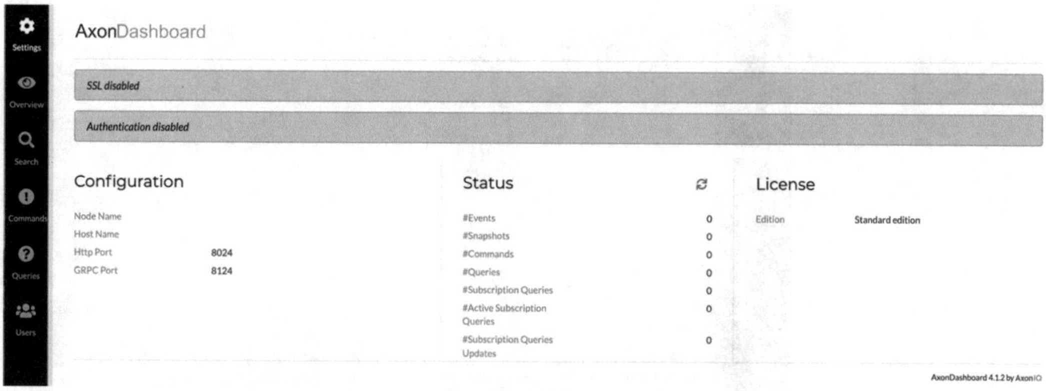

Figure 6-13. *Axon Server Console*

The Console provides capabilities to monitor and manage your Axon Server. Let us go through a quick overview of these. As we progress through the implementation, we will start seeing these in more detail.

Settings – This is the landing page of the Server Dashboard. It contains all the details of the Configurations, Status of the various operations, and License/Security Details. A short note here: Axon supports both HTTP and gRPC as inbound protocols.

Overview – This page provides a visual graphic of Axon Server and the application instances that connect to it. As of now, since we have not built any applications yet, it depicts only the main server as illustrated in Figure 6-14.

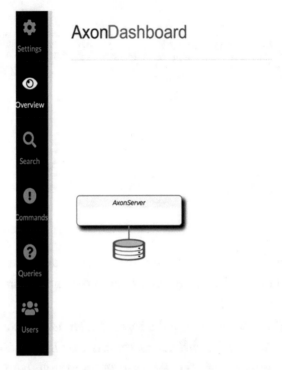

Figure 6-14. *Axon Server visual display*

Search – This page provides a visual representation of the underlying Event Store. Axon also provides a query language to help query the Event Store. Figure 6-15 depicts this.

Figure 6-15. *Axon Query Console along with a Query DSL*

Results of searching are depicted in Figure 6-16.

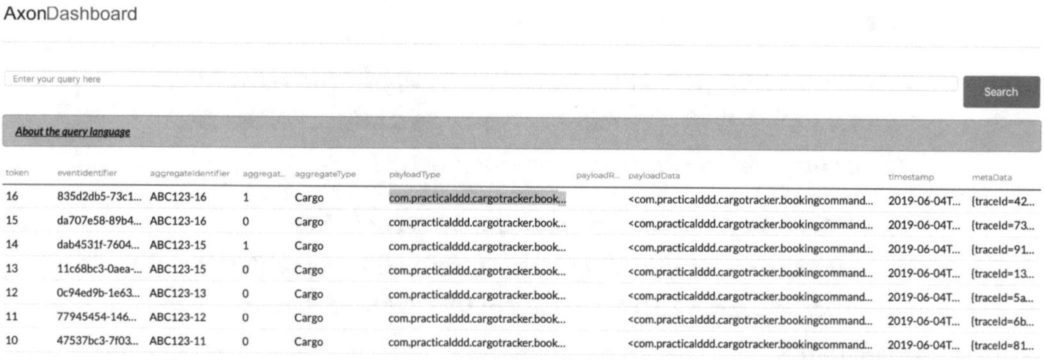
AxonDashboard
Enter your query here
Search
About the query language
token | eventIdentifier | aggregateIdentifier | aggregat... | aggregateType | payloadType | payloadR... | payloadData | timestamp | metaData
16 | 835d2db5-73c1... | ABC123-16 | 1 | Cargo | com.practicalddd.cargotracker.book... | | <com.practicalddd.cargotracker.bookingcommand... | 2019-06-04T... | {traceId=42...
15 | da707e58-89b4... | ABC123-16 | 0 | Cargo | com.practicalddd.cargotracker.book... | | <com.practicalddd.cargotracker.bookingcommand... | 2019-06-04T... | {traceId=73...
14 | dab4531f-7604... | ABC123-15 | 1 | Cargo | com.practicalddd.cargotracker.book... | | <com.practicalddd.cargotracker.bookingcommand... | 2019-06-04T... | {traceId=91...
13 | 11c68bc3-0aea-... | ABC123-15 | 0 | Cargo | com.practicalddd.cargotracker.book... | | <com.practicalddd.cargotracker.bookingcommand... | 2019-06-04T... | {traceId=13...
12 | 0c94ed9b-1e63... | ABC123-13 | 0 | Cargo | com.practicalddd.cargotracker.book... | | <com.practicalddd.cargotracker.bookingcommand... | 2019-06-04T... | {traceId=5a...
11 | 77945454-146... | ABC123-12 | 0 | Cargo | com.practicalddd.cargotracker.book... | | <com.practicalddd.cargotracker.bookingcommand... | 2019-06-04T... | {traceId=6b...
10 | 47537bc3-7f03... | ABC123-11 | 0 | Cargo | com.practicalddd.cargotracker.book... | | <com.practicalddd.cargotracker.bookingcommand... | 2019-06-04T... | {traceId=81...

Figure 6-16. *Axon Query Console search results*

Users – This page provides the capability to add/delete users along with their corresponding roles (ADMIN/USER) to access Axon server. This is depicted in Figure 6-17.

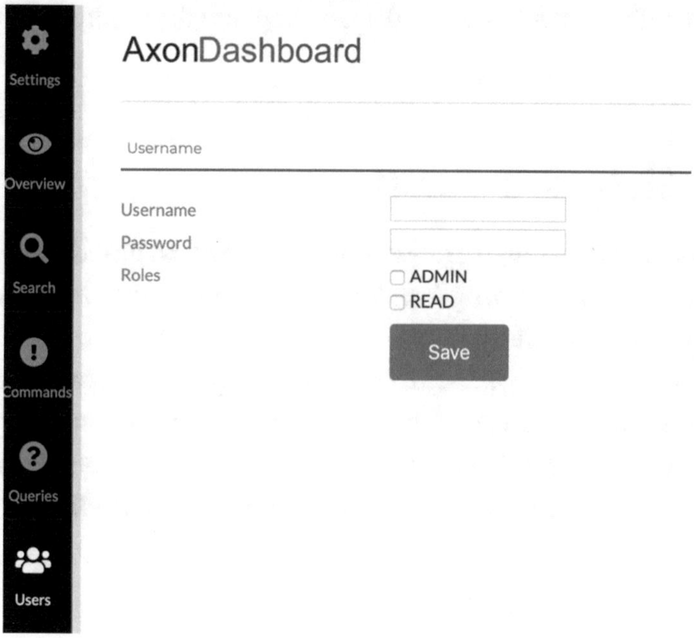
Settings
Overview
Search
Commands
Queries
Users
AxonDashboard
Username
Username
Password
Roles
ADMIN
READ
Save

Figure 6-17. *Axon Query user administration*

To summarize

Axon offers a pure play implementation for applications wanting to utilize CQRS/Event Sourcing, Event-Driven Microservices, and DDD as the fundamental architectural patterns.

Axon provides a Domain Model/Dispatch Model (Axon Framework) and a supporting event store/messaging router infrastructure (Axon Server) to help build CQRS/ES-based applications.

Axon puts events and event sourcing as the fundamental blocks for building event-driven microservices applications utilizing CQRS/ES.

Axon provides an Administrative console to Query, Secure, and Administer Event Data.

With the capabilities of Axon covered, let us step into the implementation details of Cargo Tracker.

Cargo Tracker with Axon

Our implementation of the Cargo Tracker Application will be based on an event-driven microservices architecture utilizing Axon's core framework (Axon Framework) and Axon's infrastructure (Axon Server).

Axon Framework provides ***first-class support for Spring Boot*** as the underlying technology to build and run the various Axon artifacts. While it is not necessary to use Spring Boot, with the support that Axon provides, it becomes extremely easy to configure the components using ***Spring Boot's auto-configuration capabilities.***

Bounded Contexts with Axon

For our microservices implementations, we adopt the approach of splitting the Cargo Tracker application into four Bounded Contexts with each Bounded Context containing a set of microservices. We adopt the same approach for splitting the Application within the Axon implementation too.

Figure 6-18 depicts our four Bounded Contexts.

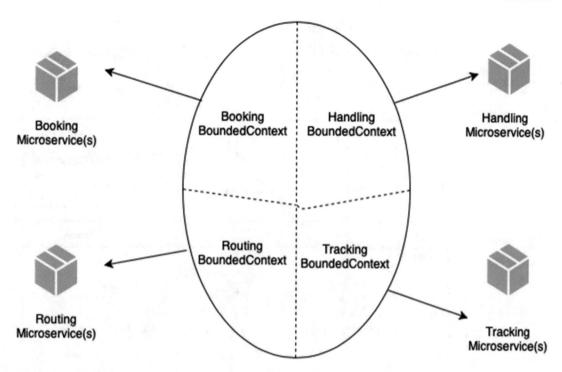

Figure 6-18. *The Bounded Contexts within the Cargo Tracker Application*

While the approach of splitting is the same as our previous microservices implementations, we are going to implement a lot of aspects very differently than what we have done before. Each of our Bounded Contexts is going to split into a Command Side and a Query Side. The Command side of a Bounded Context handles any state change requests for the Aggregate of the Bounded Context. The Command side also generates and publishes the Aggregate state changes as Events. The Query side of each Bounded Context provides a Read Model/Projection of the Aggregate's current state utilizing a separate persistence storage. This Read Model/Projection is updated by the Query side by subscribing to the state change events.

An overall summary is depicted in Figure 6-19.

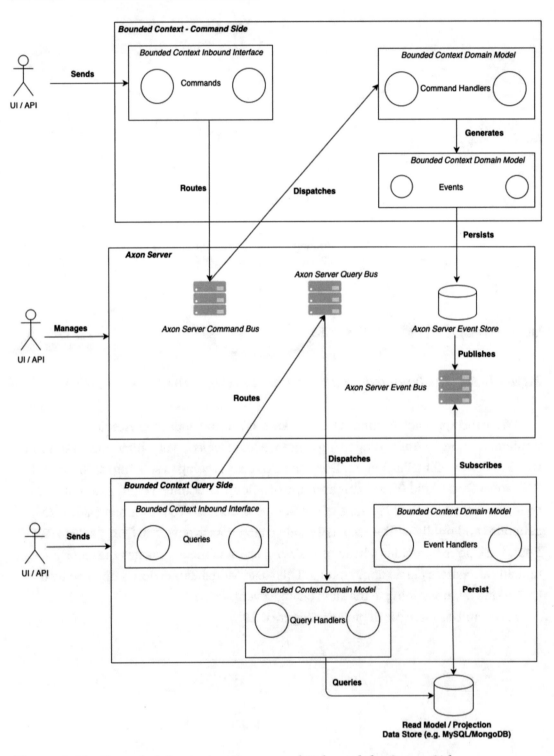

Figure 6-19. *Bounded Contexts – Command Side and the Query Side*

Bounded Contexts: Artifact Creation

Each Bounded Context has its own deployable artifact. Each of these Bounded Contexts contain a set of microservice(s) which can be developed, deployed, and scaled independently. Each artifact is built as an Axon + Spring Boot fat JAR file which has all the required dependencies and the runtime required for it to run independently.

The artifact summary is depicted in Figure 6-20.

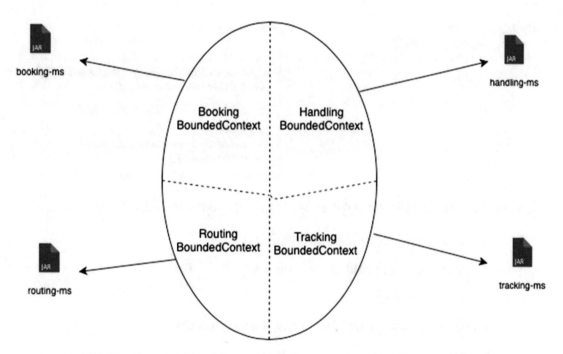

Figure 6-20. *Bounded Contexts – mapped to their microservices artifacts*

To get started with Axon, the first step is to create a regular Spring Boot application with the following dependencies: spring-web and spring-data-jpa.

Figure 6-21 depicts the creation of the booking microservices utilizing the Initializr project from Spring Boot (***start.spring.io***).

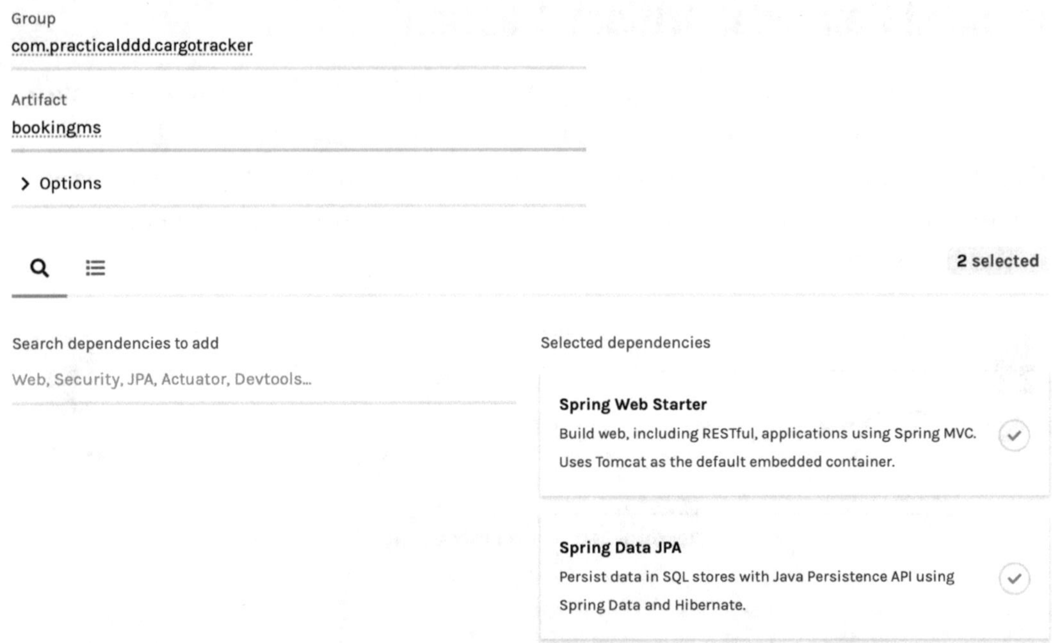

Group
com.practicalddd.cargotracker

Artifact
bookingms

> Options

Q   ☰   2 selected

Search dependencies to add   Selected dependencies

Web, Security, JPA, Actuator, Devtools...

Spring Web Starter
Build web, including RESTful, applications using Spring MVC.   ✓
Uses Tomcat as the default embedded container.

Spring Data JPA
Persist data in SQL stores with Java Persistence API using   ✓
Spring Data and Hibernate.

Figure 6-21. *Booking Microservices Spring Boot Project with its dependencies*

We have created the project with the following:

- Group – com.practicalddd.cargotracker

- Artifact – bookingms

- Dependencies – Spring Web Starter, Spring Data JPA

Axon leverages Spring Boot's auto-configuration capabilities to configure its components. To enable this integration, we simply add the dependency of "***axon-spring-boot-starter***" to our Boot project's pom file. Once this dependency is available, the *axon-spring-boot-starter* will ***automatically configure the dispatch model*** (Command Bus, Query Bus, Event Bus) and the ***Event Store***.

The dependency is illustrated in Listing 6-2:

Listing 6-2. Dependencies for Axon spring boot starter

```
<dependency>
      <groupId>org.axonframework</groupId>
      <artifactId>axon-spring-boot-starter</artifactId>
      <version>4.1.1</version>
</dependency>
```

Axon uses sensible defaults to configure Axon Server as the dispatch model infrastructure and the event store. This does not need to be explicitly included in any of our Spring Boot configuration or source files. Just adding the dependency mentioned in Listing 6-2 *auto-configures Axon Server* as the implementation for the dispatch model infrastructure in addition to it being the event store.

The anatomy of an Axon Spring Boot application is summarized in Figure 6-22.

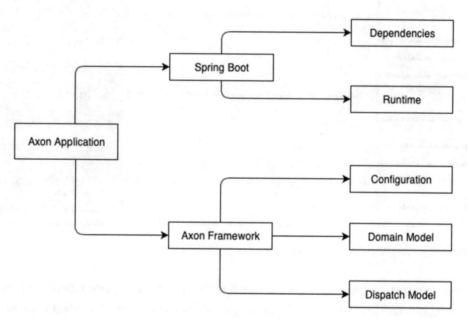

Figure 6-22. *Anatomy of a Spring Boot application*

Bounded Contexts: Package Structure

The first step in implementing the Bounded Contexts is to arrive at a logical grouping of the various Axon artifacts into a deployable artifact. The logical grouping involves identifying a package structure where we place the various Axon artifacts to achieve our overall solution for the Bounded Context.

The high-level package structure for any of our Bounded Context (Command Side, Query Side) is depicted in Figure 6-23. As seen, there is no change from our previous implementations as the CQRS/ES pattern fits in beautifully with the hexagonal architecture that we laid out in Chapter 2 (Figure 2-9).

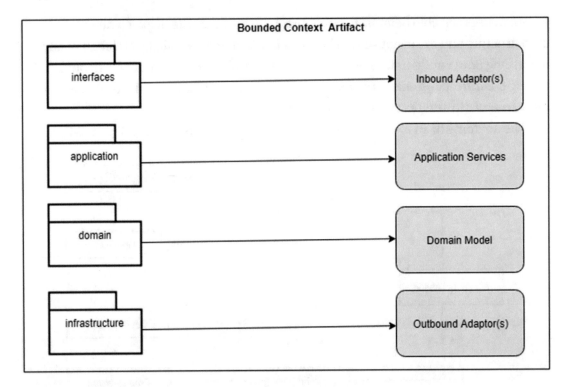

Figure 6-23. *Bounded Contexts – Package Structure*

Let us expand the package structure a bit taking our Booking Bounded Contexts (Booking Command Side Bounded Context, Booking Query Side Bounded Context) as examples.

interfaces

This package encloses all the inbound interfaces to our bounded context classified by the communication protocol. The main purpose of interfaces is to negotiate the protocol on behalf of the Domain Model (e.g., REST API(s), WebSocket(s), FTP(s), Custom Protocol).

As an example, the Booking Command Bounded Context provides REST APIs for sending Commands to it (e.g., Book Cargo Command, Update Cargo Command). Similarly, the Booking Query Bounded Context provides REST APIs for sending Queries to it (e.g., Retrieve Cargo Booking Details, List all Cargos). This is grouped into the "***rest***" package. It also has Event Handlers which subscribe to the various Events that are generated by Axon. All Event Handlers are grouped into the "***eventhandlers***" package.

In addition to these two packages, the interface package also contains the "**transform**" package. This is used to translate the incoming API Resource/Event data to the corresponding Command/Query model.

The Interface package structure is illustrated in Figure 6-24. It is the same irrespective of whether it is a Command or Query project.

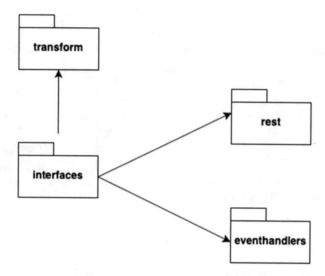

Figure 6-24. *Interface Package Structure*

application

To quickly recap, Application services act as the façade for the Bounded Context's domain model. In addition to acting as the façade, within the CQRS/ES pattern, Application services are responsible for delegating to Axon's Dispatch Model (Command Gateway, Query Gateway) invoking the Dispatch Model.

To summarize, Application Services

- Participate in Command Dispatching, Query Dispatching, and Saga(s)

- Provide Centralized concerns (e.g., Logging, Security, Metrics) for the underlying domain model

- Make callouts to other Bounded Contexts

The Application package structure is illustrated in Figure 6-25.

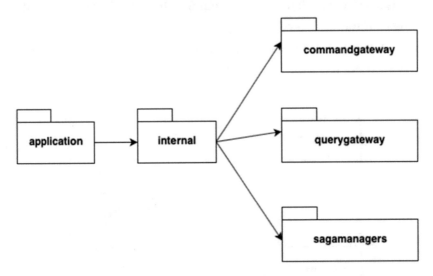

Figure 6-25. *Application package Structure*

domain

This package contains the Bounded Context's domain model.

The domain model consists of the following:

- Aggregate(s)

- Aggregate Projections (Read Model)

- Commands

- Queries

- Events

- Query Handlers

The Domain package structure is depicted in Figure 6-26.

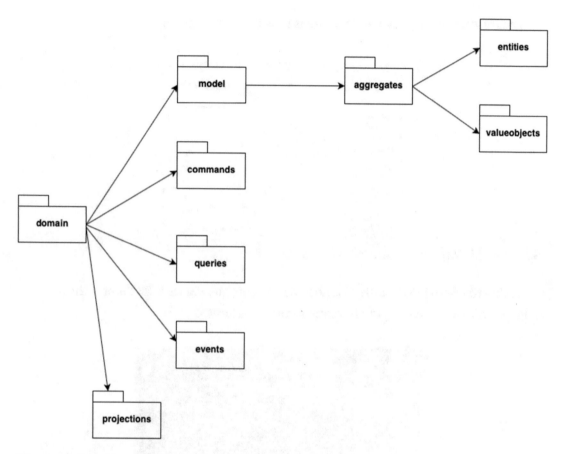

Figure 6-26. *Domain model package Structure*

infrastructure

The infrastructure package serves two main purposes:

- Infrastructural components required by the Bounded Context's Domain model to communicate to any external repositories, for example, Query Side Bounded Context communicating to the underlying Read Model repository like a MySQL Database or a MongoDB Document Store.

- Any Axon-specific configuration, for example, for a quick test, we might want to use an Embedded Event Store rather than Axon Server's Event Store. That configuration would be put in the infrastructure package classes.

The infrastructure package structure is illustrated in Figure 6-27.

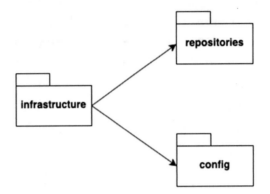

Figure 6-27. *Infrastructure package Structure*

Taking the Booking Bounded Context as an example, Figure 6-28 depicts the layout of the package structure for the Booking Bounded Context.

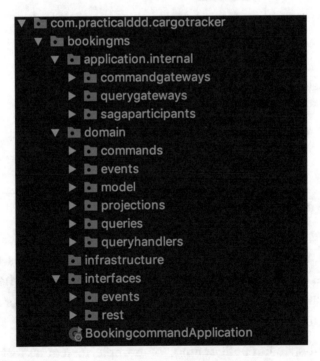

Figure 6-28. *Booking Bounded Context Package Structure*

Building the Booking Bounded Context application results in a Spring Boot JAR file (bookingms-1.0.jar). To bring up the Booking Bounded Context Application, we first bring up Axon Server. We then run the Booking Bounded Context as a regular Spring Boot JAR file. This is illustrated in Listing 6-3:

Listing 6-3. Command to bring up the Booking Bounded Context as a spring boot application

```
java -jar bookingqueryms-1.0.jar
```

The axon-spring-boot dependency within will automatically look for the running Axon server and automatically connect to it. Figure 6-29 depicts the Axon dashboard showing the Booking Microservices connected to the running Axon server.

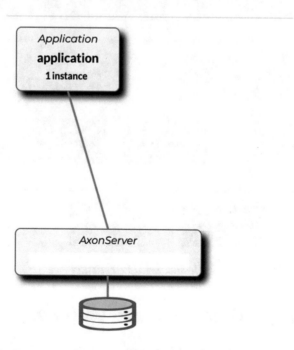

Figure 6-29. *Booking Microservices connected to Axon Server and ready to process Commands/Queries*

This completes the implementation of the Bounded Contexts of our Cargo Tracker Application based on Microservices and based on the CQRS/ES patterns utilizing the Axon Framework. Each of our Bounded Contexts is implemented as an Axon Spring Boot application. The Bounded Contexts are neatly grouped by modules in a package structure with clearly separated concerns.

The next two sections of this chapter will deal with the implementation of the Axon Framework–based DDD artifacts of the Cargo Tracker Application – *the Domain Model* and *the Domain Model Services*. The overall layout of the DDD artifacts is depicted in Figure 6-30.

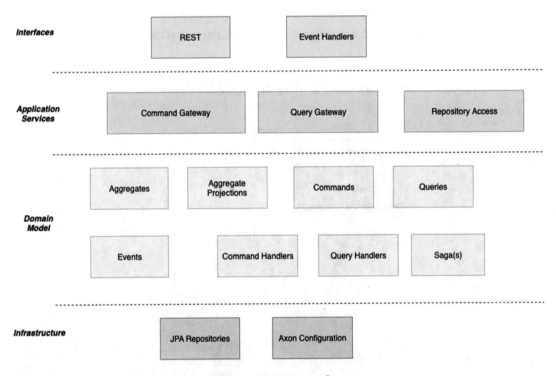

Figure 6-30. *Axon Framework–based DDD artifacts*

Implementing the Domain Model with Axon

The domain model is the centerpiece of each of our Bounded Contexts representing the core business functionality. Our implementation of the Domain Model with Axon is going to be radically different than our previous implementation considering that Axon follows the DDD/CQRS/ES doctrine very strictly.

We are going to implement the following set of artifacts for our Domain Model:

- Aggregates/Commands

- Aggregate Projections (Read Model)/Queries

- Events

- Sagas

Aggregates

Aggregates are the centerpiece of our Domain Model within a Bounded Context. In our implementation since we have adopted the CQRS pattern, we have two Bounded Contexts per sub-domain, one for the Command Side and one for the Query Side. We are going to primarily have **Aggregates** for the Command Side Bounded Context, while we will maintain **Aggregate Projections** for the Query Side Bounded Context.

Figure 6-31 depicts the Aggregates for each of our Command Side Bounded Contexts.

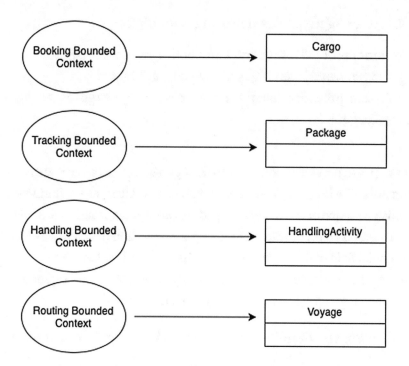

Figure 6-31. *Aggregates for each of our Command Side Bounded Contexts*

Implementation of an Aggregate Class covers the following aspects:

- Aggregate Class Implementation

- State

- Command Handling

- Event Publishing

- State Maintenance

Axon provides first-class support for building Aggregate classes using **Stereotype Annotations**. The first step in implementing the Aggregate is to take a regular POJO and mark it with the Axon-provided **@Aggregate** Annotation. This annotation indicates to the framework that it is the Aggregate class within the Bounded Context.

As before, we will walk through the implementation of the Cargo Aggregate which is the Aggregate for the Booking Command Side Bounded Context example.

Listing 6-4 shows the first step of implementing the Cargo Aggregate:

Listing 6-4. Cargo Aggregate using Axon annotations

```
package com.practicalddd.cargotracker.bookingms.domain.model;
import org.axonframework.spring.stereotype.Aggregate;
@Aggregate //Axon provided annotation for marking Cargo as an Aggregate
public class Cargo {
}
```

The next step is to provide uniqueness to the Aggregate, that is, the key to identify the Aggregate instance. Having an Aggregate Identifier is mandatory as the framework utilizes it to identify which instance of an Aggregate needs to be targeted when a particular Command needs to be processed. Axon provides a Stereotype Annotation (**@AggregateIdentifier**) to identify a particular field of the Aggregate as the Aggregate Identifier.

Continuing with our example of the Cargo Aggregate, the Booking Identifier (or BookingId) is our Aggregate Identifier as depicted in Listing 6-5:

Listing 6-5. Aggregate Identifier implementation using Axon annotations

```
package com.practicalddd.cargotracker.bookingms.domain.model;
import org.axonframework.spring.stereotype.Aggregate;
import org.axonframework.modelling.command.AggregateIdentifier;
```

```
@Aggregate //Axon provided annotation for marking Cargo as an Aggregate
public class Cargo {
    @AggregateIdentifier //Axon provided annotation for marking the
    Booking ID as the Aggregate Identifier
  private String bookingId;
}
```

The final step in the implementation is to provide a no-args constructor. This is required by the framework primarily during operations to update the Aggregate. Axon will use the no-args constructor to create an empty Aggregate Instance and then play all the past events that occurred on that Aggregate instance to arrive at the current and latest state. We will touch upon this topic in detail later in the section on State Maintenance. For now, let us place it in the Aggregate implementation.

Listing 6-6 demonstrates the addition of the no-args constructor to the Aggregate implementation:

Listing 6-6. Cargo Aggregate constructor

```
package com.practicalddd.cargotracker.bookingms.domain.model;
import org.axonframework.spring.stereotype.Aggregate;
import org.axonframework.modelling.command.AggregateIdentifier;
import org.slf4j.Logger;
import org.slf4j.LoggerFactory;
import java.lang.invoke.MethodHandles;
@Aggregate //Axon provided annotation for marking Cargo as an Aggregate
public class Cargo {
    private final static Logger logger = LoggerFactory.
    getLogger(MethodHandles.lookup().lookupClass());
      @AggregateIdentifier //Axon provided annotation for marking the
      Booking ID as the Aggregate Identifier
    private String bookingId;

    protected Cargo() { //Empty no-args constructor
      logger.info("Empty Cargo created.");
    }
}
```

The Aggregate class implementation is depicted in Figure 6-32. The next step is to ***Add State***.

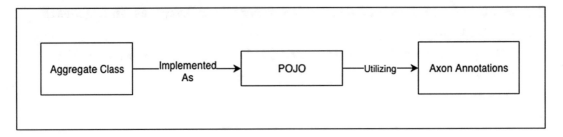

Figure 6-32. *Aggregate Class implementation*

State

We discussed about Domain-Rich Aggregates vs. Anemic aggregates in our Jakarta EE implementation in Chapter 3. DDD recommends having Domain-Rich Aggregates, which convey the state of the bounded context using ***Business Concepts***.

Let us walk through the case of our Cargo root aggregate class within the Booking Command Bounded Context. The essence of DDD is to capture the state of an Aggregate as attributes depicted using Business Terms rather than Technical Terms.

Translating state to business concepts, the Cargo Aggregate has the following attributes:

- ***Origin Location*** of the cargo

- ***Booking Amount***

- ***Route specification*** (Origin Location, Destination Location, Destination Arrival Deadline)

- ***Itinerary*** that the cargo is assigned to based on the Route Specification. The Itinerary consists of multiple ***Legs*** that the cargo might be routed through to get to the destination.

Figure 6-33 depicts the UML class diagram for the Cargo Aggregate with its corresponding associations.

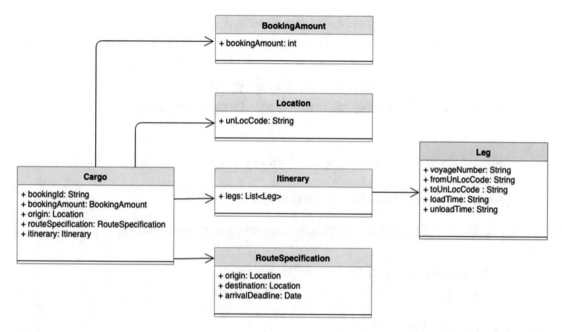

Figure 6-33. *Class diagram for the Cargo Aggregate*

Let us include these attributes in the Cargo Aggregate. These attributes are implemented as regular POJOs with a strong associative relationship with the Aggregate.

Listing 6-7 shows the main listing of the ***Cargo Aggregate Object***:

Listing 6-7. Cargo Aggregate implementation

```
package com.practicalddd.cargotracker.bookingms.domain.model;
import java.lang.invoke.MethodHandles;
import org.axonframework.modelling.command.AggregateIdentifier;
import org.axonframework.spring.stereotype.Aggregate;
import org.slf4j.Logger;
import org.slf4j.LoggerFactory;
@Aggregate
public class Cargo {
    private final static Logger logger = LoggerFactory.
    getLogger(MethodHandles.lookup().lookupClass());
    @AggregateIdentifier
    private String bookingId; // Aggregate Identifier
    private BookingAmount bookingAmount; //Booking Amount of the Cargo
```

317

```
    private Location origin; //Origin Location of the Cargo
    private RouteSpecification routeSpecification; //Route Specification of
                                                    the Cargo
    private Itinerary itinerary; //Itinerary Assigned to the Cargo
    protected Cargo() { logger.info("Empty Cargo created);}
}
```

Listing 6-8 shows the ***Booking Amount Business Object***:

Listing 6-8. Booking Amount Business Object

```
package com.practicalddd.cargotracker.bookingms.domain.model;
/**
 * Booking Amount Implementation of the Cargo
 */

public class BookingAmount {
    private int bookingAmount;
    public BookingAmount() {}
    public BookingAmount(int bookingAmount) {
        this.bookingAmount = bookingAmount;
    }
}
```

Listing 6-9 shows the ***Location Business Object***:

Listing 6-9. Location Business Object

```
 package com.practicalddd.cargotracker.bookingms.domain.model;
/**
 * Location class represented by a unique 5-digit UN Location code.
 */
public class Location {
    private String unLocCode; //UN location code
    public Location(String unLocCode){this.unLocCode = unLocCode;}
    public void setUnLocCode(String unLocCode){this.unLocCode = unLocCode;}
    public String getUnLocCode(){return this.unLocCode;}
}
```

Listing 6-10 shows the *Route Specification Business Object*:

Listing 6-10. Route Specification Business Object

```
package com.practicalddd.cargotracker.bookingms.domain.model;
import java.util.Date;
/**
 * Route specification of the Cargo - Origin/Destination and the Arrival
   Deadline
 */
public class RouteSpecification {
    private Location origin;
    private Location destination;
    private Date arrivalDeadline;
    public RouteSpecification(Location origin, Location destination, Date
    arrivalDeadline) {
        this.setOrigin(origin);
        this.setDestination(destination);
        this.setArrivalDeadline((Date) arrivalDeadline.clone());
    }
    public Location getOrigin() { return origin; }
    public void setOrigin(Location origin) { this.origin = origin; }
    public Location getDestination() { return destination; }
    public void setDestination(Location destination) { this.destination =
    destination; }
    public Date getArrivalDeadline() { return arrivalDeadline; }
    public void setArrivalDeadline(Date arrivalDeadline) { this.
    arrivalDeadline = arrivalDeadline; }
}
```

Listing 6-11 shows the *Itinerary Business Object of the cargo*:

Listing 6-11. Itinerary Business Object

```
package com.practicalddd.cargotracker.bookingms.domain.model;
import java.util.Collections;
import java.util.List;
```

```
/**
 * Itinerary assigned to the Cargo. Consists of a set of Legs that the
   Cargo will go through as part of its journey
 */
public class Itinerary {
    private List<Leg> legs = Collections.emptyList();
    public Itinerary() {}
    public Itinerary(List<Leg> legs) {
        this.legs = legs;
    }
    public List<Leg> getLegs() {
        return Collections.unmodifiableList(legs);
    }
}
```

Listing 6-12 shows the **Leg Business Object of the cargo:**

Listing 6-12. Leg Business Object

```
package com.practicalddd.cargotracker.bookingms.domain.model;
/**
 * Leg of the Itinerary that the Cargo is currently on
 */
public class Leg {
    private  String voyageNumber;
    private  String fromUnLocode;
    private  String toUnLocode;
    private  String loadTime;
    private  String unloadTime;

    public Leg(
            String voyageNumber,
            String fromUnLocode,
            String toUnLocode,
            String loadTime,
            String unloadTime) {
        this.voyageNumber = voyageNumber;
        this.fromUnLocode = fromUnLocode;
```

```java
        this.toUnLocode = toUnLocode;
        this.loadTime = loadTime;
        this.unloadTime = unloadTime;
    }

    public String getVoyageNumber() {
        return voyageNumber;
    }

    public String getFromUnLocode() {
        return fromUnLocode;
    }
    public String getToUnLocode() {
        return toUnLocode;
    }

    public String getLoadTime() { return loadTime; }

    public String getUnloadTime() {
        return unloadTime;
    }

    public void setVoyageNumber(String voyageNumber)
    { this.voyageNumber =  voyageNumber; }
    public void setFromUnLocode(String fromUnLocode)
    { this.fromUnLocode = fromUnLocode; }
    public void setToUnLocode(String toUnLocode)
    { this.toUnLocode =  toUnLocode; }
    public void setLoadTime(String loadTime) { this.loadTime = loadTime; }
    public void setUnloadTime(String unloadTime)
    { this.unloadTime = unloadTime; }
    @Override
    public String toString() {
        return "Leg{" + "voyageNumber=" + voyageNumber + ", from=" +
        fromUnLocode + ", to=" + toUnLocode + ", loadTime=" + loadTime + ",
        unloadTime=" + unloadTime + '}';
    }
}
```

Aggregate state implementation is depicted in Figure 6-34. The next step is to *Handle Commands*.

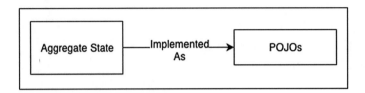

Figure 6-34. *Aggregate State implementation*

Command Handling

Commands instruct the Bounded Context to change its state, specifically the Aggregate (or any other identified Entities), within the Bounded Context. Implementing Command Processing involves the following:

- Identification/implementation of Commands

- Identification/implementation of Command Handlers to process Commands

Identification of Commands

Identification of Commands revolves around any operation that affects the state of the Aggregate. For example, the Booking Command Bounded Context has the following operations or commands:

- Book a Cargo

- Route a Cargo

- Change Destination of a Cargo

All three commands result in a change of state of the Cargo Aggregate within the Bounded Context.

Implementation of Commands

Implementing the identified Commands within Axon is done using regular POJOs. The only requirement for an Axon Command object is that while processing the Command, the Axon Framework needs to know which instance of an Aggregate does this particular

Command needs to be processed on. This is done by utilizing an Axon Annotation @TargetAggregateIdentifier. As the name suggests, while processing a Command, the Axon Framework knows the target Aggregate Instance on which the Command needs to be processed.

Let's look at an example. Listing 6-13 shows the BookCargoCommand class which is the implementation of the Book Cargo Command:

Listing 6-13. BookCargoCommand implementation

```
package com.practicalddd.cargotracker.bookingms.domain.commands;
import org.axonframework.modelling.command.TargetAggregateIdentifier;
import java.util.Date;
/**
 * Implementation Class for the Book Cargo Command
 */
public class BookCargoCommand {
    @TargetAggregateIdentifier //Identifier to indicate on which Aggregate
                                 does the Command needs to be processed on
    private String bookingId; //Booking Id which is the unique key of the
                               Aggregate
    private int bookingAmount;
    private String originLocation;
    private String destLocation;
    private Date destArrivalDeadline;
    public BookCargoCommand(String bookingId, int bookingAmount,
                            String originLocation, String destLocation,
                            Date destArrivalDeadline){
        this.bookingId = bookingId;
        this.bookingAmount = bookingAmount;
        this.originLocation = originLocation;
        this.destLocation = destLocation;
        this.destArrivalDeadline = destArrivalDeadline;
    }
    public void setBookingId(String bookingId){this.bookingId = bookingId;
}
```

```
public void setBookingAmount(int bookingAmount){this.bookingAmount =
bookingAmount;}
public String getBookingId(){return this.bookingId;}
public int getBookingAmount(){return this.bookingAmount;}
public String getOriginLocation() {return originLocation; }
public void setOriginLocation(String originLocation)
{this.originLocation = originLocation; }
public String getDestLocation() { return destLocation; }
public void setDestLocation(String destLocation)
{ this.destLocation = destLocation; }
public Date getDestArrivalDeadline() { return destArrivalDeadline; }
public void setDestArrivalDeadline(Date destArrivalDeadline)
{ this.destArrivalDeadline = destArrivalDeadline; }
}
```

The BookCargoCommand Class is a regular POJO which has all the necessary attributes required for processing of the booking of the cargo (Booking ID, Booking Amount, Origin and Destination Locations, and finally the Arrival Deadline).

The Booking Id represents the uniqueness of the Cargo Aggregate, that is, the Aggregate Identifier. We annotate the Booking Id field with the Target Aggregate Identifier Annotation. So every time a Command is sent to the Booking Command Bounded Context, it will process the Command on the Aggregate Instance identified by the Booking ID.

It is mandatory for the Aggregate Identifier to be set before the execution of any Command within Axon as without it, the Axon Framework will not know which Aggregate instance it needs to deal with.

Identification of Command Handlers

Every Command will have a corresponding Command Handler which needs to *process the Command*. The BookCargoCommand will have a corresponding handler which will take in the BookCargoCommand as an input parameter and process it. The handlers are typically placed on routines within Aggregates; however, Axon also allows to place Command Handlers outside of the Aggregates within the Application Services layer.

Implementation of Command Handlers

Implementation of Command Handlers as stated before involves identifying the routines within Aggregates that can process the Commands. Axon provides an aptly named Annotation "**@CommandHandler**" which is placed on Aggregate routines identified as the Command Handlers.

Let's walk through an example of the Booking Command Handler for the CargoBookingCommand. Listing 6-14 shows the @CommandHandler annotations placed on the Aggregate Constructors/Regular Routines:

Listing 6-14. Command handlers within the Cargo aggregate

```
package com.practicalddd.cargotracker.bookingms.domain.model;
import java.lang.invoke.MethodHandles;
import com.practicalddd.cargotracker.bookingms.domain.commands.
AssignRouteToCargoCommand;
import com.practicalddd.cargotracker.bookingms.domain.commands.
BookCargoCommand;
import com.practicalddd.cargotracker.bookingms.domain.commands.
ChangeDestinationCommand;
import org.axonframework.commandhandling.CommandHandler;
import org.axonframework.modelling.command.AggregateIdentifier;
import org.axonframework.spring.stereotype.Aggregate;
import org.slf4j.Logger;
import org.slf4j.LoggerFactory;
@Aggregate
public class Cargo {
    private final static Logger logger = LoggerFactory.
    getLogger(MethodHandles.lookup().lookupClass());
    @AggregateIdentifier
    private String bookingId; // Aggregate Identifier
    private BookingAmount bookingAmount; //Booking Amount
    private Location origin; //Origin Location of the Cargo
    private RouteSpecification routeSpecification; //Route Specification of
    the Cargo
    private Itinerary itinerary; //Itinerary Assigned to the Cargo
    protected Cargo() {
```

```
    logger.info("Empty Cargo created.");
  }
  @CommandHandler //Command Handler for the BookCargoCommand. The first
Command sent to an Aggregate is placed on the Aggregate Constructor
  public Cargo(BookCargoCommand bookCargoCommand) {
    //Process the Command
  }
  @CommandHandler //Command Handler for the Route Cargo Command
  public void handle(AssignRouteToCargoCommand assignRouteToCargoCommand)
{
    //Process the Command
}
  @CommandHandler //CommandHandler for the Change Destination Command
  public void handle(ChangeDestinationCommand changeDestinationCommand){
    //Process the Command
}
}
```

Typically, the first Command sent to an Aggregate is for the creation of the Aggregate and is placed on the Aggregate Constructor (or known as Command Handling Constructor).

Subsequent Commands are placed on regular routines within the Aggregate. RouteCargoCommand and ChangeCargoDestinationCommand are placed on regular routines within the Cargo Aggregate.

Command Handlers have the Business Logic/Decision making (e.g., validation of the Command Data that is being processed) to allow subsequent processing and generation of Events. This is the only responsibility of the Command Handlers: *it should not modify the state of the Aggregate*.

Listing 6-15 shows an example within the BookCargoCommand where we validate the Booking Amount:

Listing 6-15. Business Logic/Decision making within the Aggregate commands

```
@CommandHandler
public Cargo(BookCargoCommand bookCargoCommand) {
    //Validation of the Booking Amount. Throws an exception if it is
    negative
```

```
    if(bookCargoCommand.getBookingAmount() < 0){
            throw new IllegalArgumentException("Booking Amount
            cannot be negative");
}
 }
```

Figure 6-35 depicts the class diagram for the Cargo Aggregate with the corresponding Commands/Command Handlers.

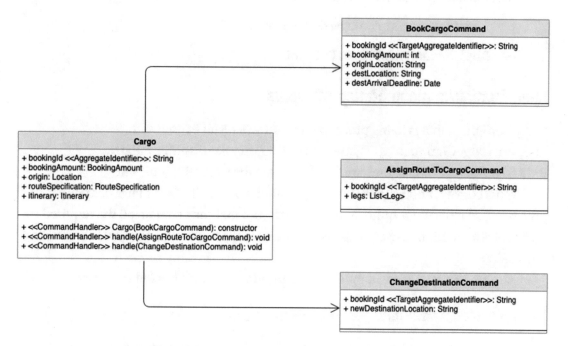

Figure 6-35. *Cargo Aggregate class diagram*

The Command Handler implementation is depicted in Figure 6-36.

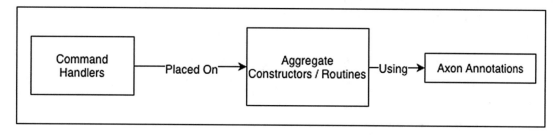

Figure 6-36. *Command Handler implementation*

The next step is to **Publish Events**.

Event Publishing

Once the Command is processed and we have completed all the Business/Decision Logic, we need to publish the Event that the Command has been processed, for example, BookCargoCommand results in the CargoBookedEvent which we need to publish. Events are always mentioned in the past tense as it indicates that something has occurred within the Bounded Context.

Event Publishing involves the following steps:

- Identification/implementation of Events

- Implementation of Event Publishing

Identification/Implementation of Events

Every Command that is being processed will always result in an Event. The BookCargoCommand will generate the CargoBookedEvent; similarly, the AssignRouteToCargoCommand will generate the CargoRoutedEvent.

Events convey the state of the Aggregate after a particular Command has been processed, so it becomes quite important to ensure that they contain all the required data. Implementation of Event classes is done as POJOs with no stereotype annotations required.

Listing 6-16 shows the example of the CargoBookedEvent implementation:

Listing 6-16. CargoBookedEvent implementation

```
package com.practicalddd.cargotracker.bookingms.domain.events;
import com.practicalddd.cargotracker.bookingms.domain.model.BookingAmount;
import com.practicalddd.cargotracker.bookingms.domain.model.Location;
import com.practicalddd.cargotracker.bookingms.domain.model.
RouteSpecification;
/**
 * Event resulting from the Cargo Booking Command
 */
public class CargoBookedEvent {
    private String bookingId;
    private BookingAmount bookingamount;
    private Location originLocation;
```

```
    private RouteSpecification routeSpecification;
    public CargoBookedEvent(String bookingId,
 BookingAmount bookingAmount,
Location originLocation,
RouteSpecification routeSpecification){
        this.bookingId = bookingId;
        this.bookingamount = bookingAmount;
        this.originLocation = originLocation;
        this.routeSpecification = routeSpecification;
    }
    public String getBookingId(){ return this.bookingId; }
    public BookingAmount getBookingAmount(){ return this.bookingamount; }
    public Location getOriginLocation(){return this.originLocation;}
    public RouteSpecification getRouteSpecification(){return this.
    routeSpecification;}
}
```

Implementation of Event Publishing

So where do we publish these events? **The place where it gets generated, that is, *in
the Command Handler.*** Going back to our implementation in the previous sections,
Command Handlers process the Commands; and once the processing is complete, they
are responsible for publishing the Event of the Command being processed.

The processing of a Command is part of the lifecycle of an Aggregate instance.
The Axon Framework provides the ***AggregateLifeCycle*** class which helps in performing
operations during the lifecycle of an Aggregate. This class provides a static function
"***apply()***" which helps in publishing generated events.

Listing 6-17 shows the snippet of code within the Command Handler for the
BookCargoCommand. After the completion of processing of the Command, the apply()
method is invoked to publish the Cargo Booked Event with the CargoBookedEvent class
the Event payload:

Listing 6-17. Publishing of the Cargo Booked Event

```
@CommandHandler
public Cargo(BookCargoCommand bookCargoCommand) {
                logger.info("Handling {}", bookCargoCommand);
```

```
                    if(bookCargoCommand.getBookingAmount() < 0){
                        throw new IllegalArgumentException("Booking Amount
                        cannot be negative");
                    }
//Publish the Generated Event using the apply method
        apply(new CargoBookedEvent(bookCargoCommand.getBookingId(),
                                new BookingAmount(bookCargoCommand.
                                getBookingAmount()),
                                new Location(bookCargoCommand.
                                getOriginLocation()),
                                new RouteSpecification(
                                        new Location(bookCargoCommand.
                                        getOriginLocation()),
                                        new Location(bookCargoCommand.
                                        getDestLocation()),
                                        bookCargoCommand.
                                        getDestArrivalDeadline()))));
}
```

The Event publishing is depicted in Figure 6-37. The next step is to *Maintain State*.

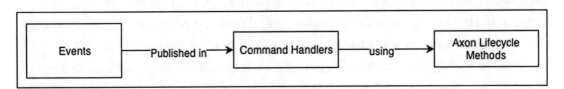

Figure 6-37. *Event Publishing implementation*

State Maintenance

The most important and critical part during the Event Sourcing process is to understand how state is maintained and utilized. This section contains some critical concepts related to state consistency, so we will explain it through examples instead of just plain literature.

We will again rely on the Cargo Booking Example within the Cargo Booking Bounded Context. To quickly recap until now, we have identified our Aggregate (Cargo), given it an Identity, processed Commands, and published Events.

To explain the concept of state maintenance, we will add an attribute to our Cargo Aggregate.

RoutingStatus – This determines the Routing Status of a booked cargo:

- A newly booked cargo will not have a route assigned to it yet as the cargo company decides the best optimal route (Routing Status – NOT_ROUTED).

- The cargo company decides on the route and assigns the cargo to that route (Routing Status – ROUTED).

Listing 6-18 depicts the implementation of the RoutingStatus as an Enum:

Listing 6-18. Routing Status enum implementation

```
package com.practicalddd.cargotracker.bookingms.domain.model;
/**
 * Enum class for the Routing Status of the Cargo
 */
public enum RoutingStatus {
    NOT_ROUTED, ROUTED, MISROUTED;
    public boolean sameValueAs(RoutingStatus other) {
        return this.equals(other);
    }
}
```

Event Handling within Aggregates

When an event is published from an Aggregate, the Axon Framework makes that ***Event first available to the Aggregate itself***. Since an Aggregate is Event Sourced, it relies on the Events to help maintain its state. This concept is a bit difficult to grasp at first since we are used to the traditional way of retrieving and maintaining Aggregate state. Simply put, an Aggregate depends upon an Event Source instead of a traditional source (e.g., Database) to maintain its state.

To process an Event that is supplied to it, an Aggregate utilizes an Axon Framework–provided annotation "***@EventSourcingHandler***". This annotation indicates that an Aggregate is an Event-sourced aggregate and it relies on the supplied event to maintain its state.

The mechanism of retrieving and maintaining Aggregate state is different for the first command received by an Aggregate vis-a-vis the subsequent commands it receives. We will walk through both of these in the example that follows.

State Maintenance: The First Command

When an Aggregate receives its first command, the Axon Framework recognizes the same and does not recreate state as the state of that particular Aggregate does not exist. Commands placed on the constructor (Command Constructors) indicate that this is the first Command received by the Aggregate.

Let us see how state is maintained in this case.

Listing 6-19 shows all the attributes representing the state of the Cargo Aggregate:

Listing 6-19. Aggregate Identifier implementation using Axon annotations

```
@AggregateIdentifier
private String bookingId; // Aggregate Identifier
private BookingAmount bookingAmount; //Booking Amount
private Location origin; //Origin Location of the Cargo
private RouteSpecification routeSpecification;
//Route Specification of the Cargo
 private Itinerary itinerary; //Itinerary Assigned to the Cargo
 private RoutingStatus routingStatus; //Routing Status of the Cargo
```

After the CargoBookedEvent is published in the BookCargoCommandHandler, the state attributes need to be set. The Axon Framework provides the CargoBookedEvent to the Cargo Aggregate first. The Cargo Aggregate processes the event to set and maintain the state attributes.

Listing 6-20 depicts the Cargo Aggregate processing the CargoBookedEvent supplied to it using the *"@EventSourcingHandler"* annotation and setting the corresponding state attributes. It is a hard requirement to set the Aggregate Identifier value (in this case Booking Id) in the first event that is processed by the Aggregate:

Listing 6-20. EventSourcing Handler implementation

```
@EventSourcingHandler //Annotation indicating that the Aggregate is Event
                      Sourced and is interested in the Cargo Booked Event
                      raised by the Book Cargo Command
public void on(CargoBookedEvent cargoBookedEvent) {
      logger.info("Applying {}", cargoBookedEvent);
```

//State Maintenance
```
        bookingId = cargoBookedEvent.getBookingId();
```
//Hard Requirement to be set
```
        bookingAmount = cargoBookedEvent.getBookingAmount();
        origin = cargoBookedEvent.getOriginLocation();
        routeSpecification = cargoBookedEvent.getRouteSpecification();
routingStatus = RoutingStatus.NOT_ROUTED;
}
```

The complete implementation is shown in Listing 6-21:

Listing 6-21. CommandHandler/EventSourcingHandler within the Cargo Aggregate

```
package com.practicalddd.cargotracker.bookingms.domain.model;
import java.lang.invoke.MethodHandles;
import com.practicalddd.cargotracker.bookingms.domain.commands.BookCargoCommand;
import com.practicalddd.cargotracker.bookingms.domain.events.
CargoBookedEvent;
import org.axonframework.commandhandling.CommandHandler;
import org.axonframework.eventsourcing.EventSourcingHandler;
import org.axonframework.modelling.command.AggregateIdentifier;
import org.axonframework.spring.stereotype.Aggregate;
import org.slf4j.Logger;
import org.slf4j.LoggerFactory;
import static org.axonframework.modelling.command.AggregateLifecycle.apply;;
@Aggregate
public class Cargo {
    private final static Logger logger = LoggerFactory.
getLogger(MethodHandles.lookup().lookupClass());

    @AggregateIdentifier
    private String bookingId; // Aggregate Identifier
    private BookingAmount bookingAmount; //Booking Amount
    private Location origin; //Origin Location of the Cargo
    private RouteSpecification routeSpecification;
    //Route Specification of the Cargo
    private Itinerary itinerary; //Itinerary Assigned to the Cargo
    private RoutingStatus routingStatus; //Routing Status of the Cargo
```

```
protected Cargo() { logger.info("Empty Cargo created."); }
@CommandHandler //First Command to the Aggregate
public Cargo(BookCargoCommand bookCargoCommand) {
    logger.info("Handling {}", bookCargoCommand);
    if(bookCargoCommand.getBookingAmount() < 0){
        throw new IllegalArgumentException("Booking Amount cannot be
        negative");
    }
    apply(new CargoBookedEvent(bookCargoCommand.getBookingId(),
                            new BookingAmount(bookCargoCommand.
                            getBookingAmount()),
                            new Location(bookCargoCommand.
                            getOriginLocation()),
                            new RouteSpecification(
                                    new Location(bookCargoCommand.
                                    getOriginLocation()),
                                    new Location(bookCargoCommand.
                                    getDestLocation()),
                                    bookCargoCommand.
                                    getDestArrivalDeadline()))));
}
@EventSourcingHandler //Event handler for the BookCargoCommand. Also sets
the various state attributes
            public void on(CargoBookedEvent cargoBookedEvent) {
    logger.info("Applying {}", cargoBookedEvent);
    // State being maintained
    bookingId = cargoBookedEvent.getBookingId();
    bookingAmount = cargoBookedEvent.getBookingAmount();
    origin = cargoBookedEvent.getOriginLocation();
    routeSpecification = cargoBookedEvent.getRouteSpecification();
    routingStatus = RoutingStatus.NOT_ROUTED;
        }
                }
```

A pictorial representation of the flow is shown in Figure 6-38.

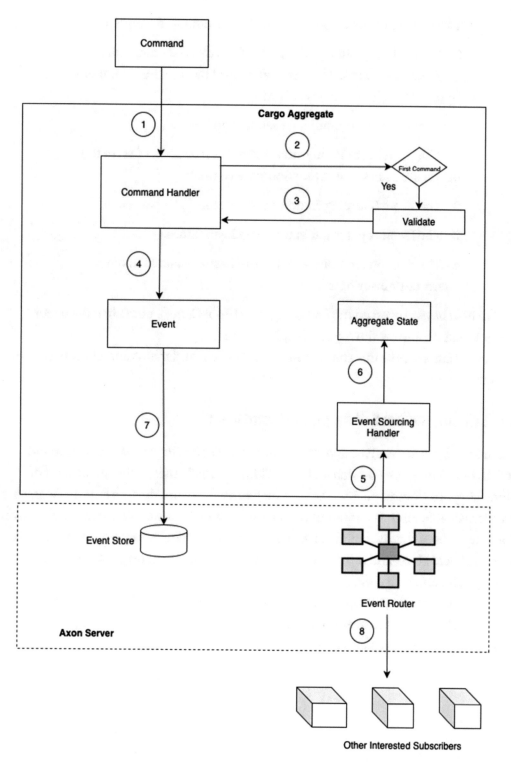

Figure 6-38. *State Maintenance – the first Command*

1 – The Command is routed to its Cargo Command Handler.

2 /3 – The Axon Framework checks if it is the first command on the Aggregate. If yes, it hands over control back to the Command Handler to do the Business Checks.

4 – The Command Handler generates the Event.

5 – The Axon Event Router makes the Event available first to the Aggregate itself via an Event Sourcing Handler.

6 – The Event Sourcing Handler updates the Aggregate state.

7 – The Event is persisted in the Axon Event Store.

8 – The Axon Event Router makes the Event available to other interested subscribers.

We now have processed the first command (BookCargo), published the event (CargoBooked), and set the Aggregate (Cargo) state.

Let us now see how this state is retrieved, utilized, and maintained in subsequent Commands.

State Maintenance: Subsequent Commands

When an Aggregate receives another Command, it needs to process the command with the current Aggregate state in hand. This essentially means that at the start of processing of a Command, the Axon Framework will ensure that the current Aggregate state is available for the Command Handler to do any Business Logic checks. The Axon Framework does this by loading an empty aggregate instance, sourcing all the events from the Event store, and replaying all the events that have occurred on that specific Aggregate instance till date.

Let us walk through this explanation by looking at the two additional Commands that the Cargo Aggregate needs to handle apart from the Cargo Booking Command, that is, Route a Booked Cargo and Change Destination of Cargo.

Listing 6-22 depicts the Command Handlers for the two Commands:

Listing 6-22. CommandHandler implementation within the Cargo aggregate

```
/**

    * Command Handler for Assigning the Route to a Cargo
    * @param assignRouteToCargoCommand
    */
    @CommandHandler
    public Cargo(AssignRouteToCargoCommand assignRouteToCargoCommand) {
                if(routingStatus.equals(RoutingStatus.ROUTED)){
                    throw new IllegalArgumentException("Cargo already
                    routed");
                }
            apply( new CargoRoutedEvent(assignRouteToCargoCommand.
            getBookingId(),
                                    new Itinerary(assignRouteToCargo
                                    Command.getLegs())));
        }
/**
* Cargo Handler for changing the Destination of a Cargo
* @param changeDestinationCommand
*/
        @CommandHandler
        public Cargo(ChangeDestinationCommand changeDestinationCommand){
            if(routingStatus.equals(RoutingStatus.ROUTED)){
            throw new IllegalArgumentException("Cannot change
            destination of a Routed Cargo");
        }
        apply(new CargoDestinationChangedEvent(changeDestinationCommand.
            getBookingId(),
                            new RouteSpecification(origin,
            new Location(changeDestinationCommand.getNewDestination
            Location())), routeSpecification.getArrivalDeadline())));
        }
```

Let's look at the "*AssignRouteToCommandHandler*" first. This command handler is responsible for processing the command to allocate the route of the cargo. The handler makes a check to see if the cargo has already been routed. It makes this check by examining the current routing status of the cargo which is represented by the Cargo Aggregate's "*routingStatus*" attribute. The Axon Framework is responsible for providing the latest "*routingStatus*" value to the "*AssignRouteToCommandHandler*", that is, it is responsible for providing the latest Cargo Aggregate status to the Command Handler.

Let us step through the process on how the Axon Framework does it:

- Axon recognizes that this is not the first Command on the Aggregate. Accordingly, it loads an empty instance of the Aggregate by invoking the protected constructor present on the Aggregate.

  Listing 6-23 shows the protected constructor in the Cargo Aggregate:

Listing 6-23. Cargo aggregate protected constructor as required by Axon

```
protected Cargo() {
        logger.info("Empty Cargo created.");
    }
```

- Axon then queries the Event source for all the events that have occurred on that Aggregate instance based on the Target Aggregate Identifier Id which we pass in the Command.

  Figure 6-39 depicts the general process that the Axon Framework follows to arrive at the current Aggregate state.

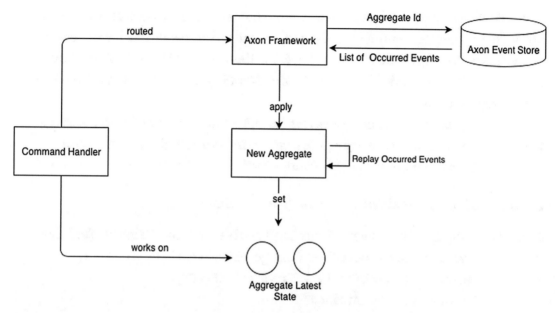

Figure 6-39. *Axon state retrieval/maintenance process*

Figure 6-40 depicts the process that the Axon Framework follows to arrive at the current Cargo Aggregate state after processing the Route Cargo Command Handler.

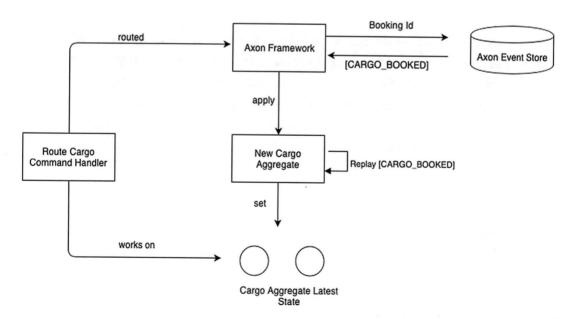

Figure 6-40. *Axon state retrieval/maintenance process – Assign Route to Cargo Command*

As depicted, when the Assign Route Command is received, the Axon Framework utilizes the Aggregate Identifier (Booking Id) to load all the events that have occurred on that particular Aggregate instance till date, in this case CARGO_BOOKED. Axon instantiates a new Aggregate instance with this Identifier and replays all the Events on this Aggregate Instance.

Replaying an event essentially means invoking the individual Event Sourcing Handler methods within the Aggregate that set the individual state attributes.

Let's go back to our Event Sourcing Handler for the Cargo Booked Event. See Listing 6-24.

Listing 6-24. Event replays within the EventSourcing handler

```
@EventSourcingHandler //Event Sourcing Handler for the Cargo Booked Event
    public void on(CargoBookedEvent cargoBookedEvent) {
        logger.info("Applying {}", cargoBookedEvent);
        // State being maintained
        bookingId = cargoBookedEvent.getBookingId();
        bookingAmount = cargoBookedEvent.getBookingAmount();
        origin = cargoBookedEvent.getOriginLocation();
        routeSpecification = cargoBookedEvent.getRouteSpecification();
        routingStatus = RoutingStatus.NOT_ROUTED;
    }
```

The aggregate state is set out here including the attribute "*routingStatus*". When this Event is replayed during the building of the Aggregate state, this attribute is set to the value of NOT_ROUTED. This attribute is made available as part of the entire aggregate state to the Command Handler of the AssignRouteToCargoCommand. Since its latest value is NOT_ROUTED, all the Command Handler checks are passed, and the processing continues with the itinerary of the Cargo set and the new value of the "*routingStatus*" attribute as ROUTED.

Let us now look at the next Command that is sent, the ChangeDestinationCommand. Listing 6-25 shows the Command Handler for the Change Destination Command. This Command intends to change the final destination of the cargo. We implement a business check within its Command Handler that if the cargo has already been routed, we do not allow the change of destination. Again, check is done against the "routingStatus" Aggregate Attribute which needs to be made available to the Command Handler of the Change Destination Command.

Figure 6-41 depicts the flow for the Change Destination Command.

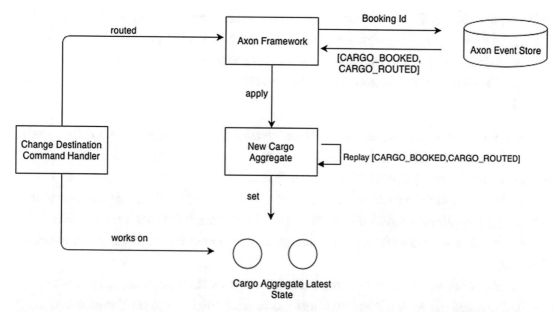

Figure 6-41. *Axon state retrieval/maintenance process – Change Destination Command after Route Cargo Command*

In this case, the Axon Framework retrieves two events from the Event store [CARGO_BOOKED and CARGO_ROUTED] which it replays. Again, the Event replays essentially mean invoking the Event Sourcing Handlers within the Aggregate for that particular Event.

Let's go back to our Event Sourcing Handlers for the Cargo Booked Event and the Cargo Routed Event:

Listing 6-25. EventSourcing Handlers within the Cargo Aggregate

```
@EventSourcingHandler //Event Sourcing Handler for the Cargo Booked Event
    public void on(CargoBookedEvent cargoBookedEvent) {
        logger.info("Applying {}", cargoBookedEvent);
        // State being maintained
        bookingId = cargoBookedEvent.getBookingId();
        bookingAmount = cargoBookedEvent.getBookingAmount();
        origin = cargoBookedEvent.getOriginLocation();
        routeSpecification = cargoBookedEvent.getRouteSpecification();
        routingStatus = RoutingStatus.NOT_ROUTED;
        transportStatus =
    }
```

```
@EventSourcingHandler //Event Sourcing Handler for the Cargo Routed Event
    public void on(CargoRoutedEvent cargoRoutedEvent) {
        itinerary = cargoRoutedEvent.getItinerary();
        routingStatus = RoutingStatus.ROUTED;
    }
```

Just focusing on the Aggregate attribute "**routingStatus**". At the end of the first event replay (CARGO_BOOKED), the value is set as NOT_ROUTED. At the end of the second event replay (CARGO_ROUTED), the value is set as ROUTED. This is the latest and current value of this attribute and is supplied as part of the overall Aggregate state to the Change Destination Command Handler. Since the Command Handler checks that the Cargo should not be ROUTED, it does not allow the processing to continue and raises an Exception.

On the other hand, if we had invoked the Change Destination Command before we had invoked the Assign Route to Cargo Command, the Command Handler would have allowed the processing to continue, since we would have only one Event replayed against the Cargo Aggregate instance (CARGO_BOOKED Event). Figure 6-42 depicts the scenario when we invoke the Change Destination Command after the Book Cargo Command and before the Assign Route to Cargo Command.

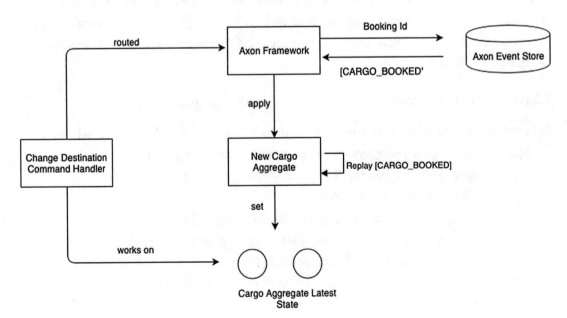

Figure 6-42. *Axon state retrieval/maintenance process – Change Destination Command before Route Cargo Command*

A complete pictorial representation of the flows is depicted in Figure 6-43.

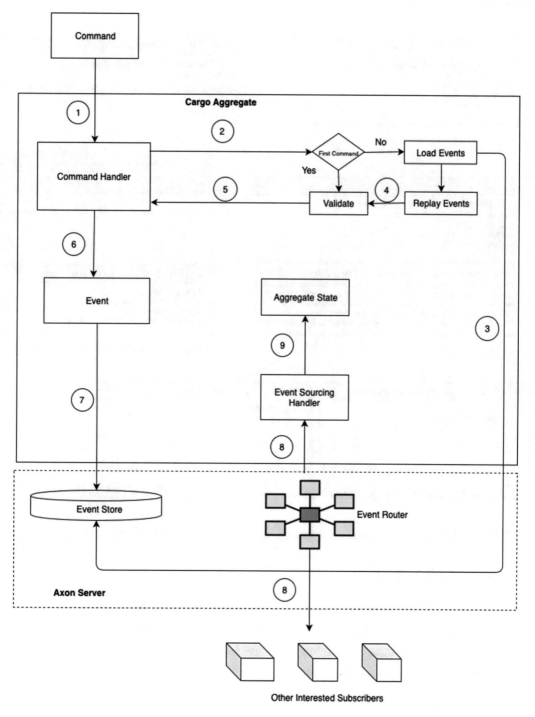

Figure 6-43. *Axon State Retrieval Process – first/subsequent Commands*

Figure 6-44 depicts the class diagram for the Cargo Aggregate with the corresponding Events/Event Handlers.

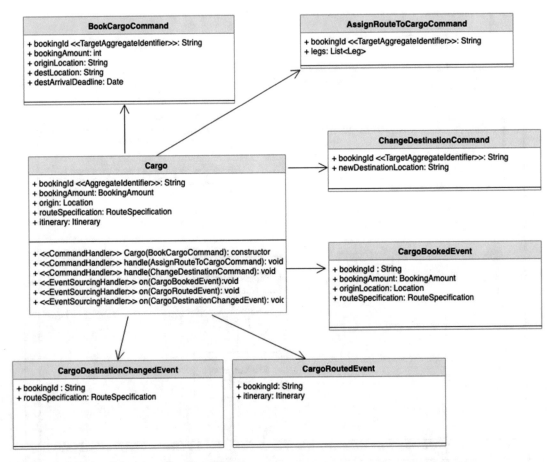

Figure 6-44. *Cargo Aggregate class diagram with Events/Event Handlers*

This completes the implementation of ***Aggregates*** for the Booking Bounded Context.

Aggregate Projections

We have seen a complete implementation of the Aggregate on the Command Side of the Bounded Context. As we have demonstrated and seen, we do not store the Aggregate state directly in a Database, but we just store the Events that have occurred on the Aggregate within a purpose-built event store.

Commands are not the only operations within a Bounded Context. We are going to have Query operations too which would intend to get to the. We are bound to have requirements where we would like to query the Aggregate state, for example, a web screen which shows the Cargo Summary for the operator. Querying the event store and trying to replay the events to get to the current state is not optimal and is definitely not recommended. Imagine an Aggregate which has undergone multiple Events as part of its lifecycle. Replaying each and every event on this Aggregate to get to the current state would be prohibitively expensive. We need another mechanism to be able to get the Aggregate state optimally and directly.

We use "***Aggregate Projections***" to help us achieve this. Simply put, an Aggregate Projection is a representation or view of the Aggregate state in various forms, that is, ***a Read Model*** of the Aggregate state. We could have multiple Aggregate Projections for an Aggregate depending upon the type of use case that the Projection needs to accomplish. An Aggregate Projection is always backed by a Datastore which contains the Projection Data. This Datastore could be a traditional relational database (e.g., MySql), a NoSQL Database (e.g., MongoDB), or even an in-memory store (e.g., Elastic). The Datastore is also dependent upon the type of use case that the Projection needs to accomplish.

The Projection's Datastore is always kept up to date by subscribing to the Events that the Command side generates and accordingly updates itself (see Event Handler Interfaces in the following). The Projection offers a Query layer which can be used by external consumers to get the Projection Data.

A summary of the projection flow is depicted in Figure 6-45.

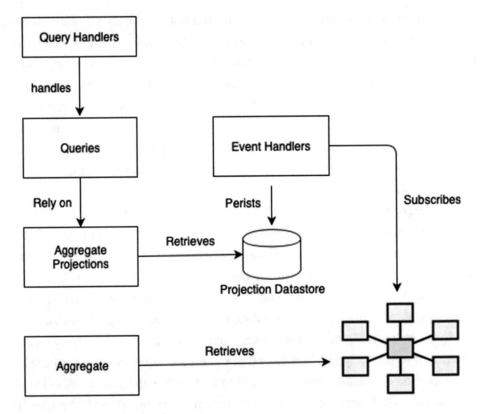

Figure 6-45. *Axon Projections*

Implementation of an Aggregate Projection covers the following aspects:

- Aggregate Projection Class Implementation

- Query Handler

- Projection State Maintenance

The implementation of the Aggregate Projection Class depends upon the type of Datastore that we decide to implement to store the Projection state. In our Cargo Tracking application, we have decided to store the Projection state in a traditional SQL Database, that is, MySQL.

Each of our Bounded Contexts will have a *Projection Datastore* which is based on *MySQL*. Each database could have multiple tables which contain various types of *Projection Data* depending upon the use case we need to satisfy. We build the Aggregate Projection classes on top of this projection data.

This is depicted in Figure 6-46.

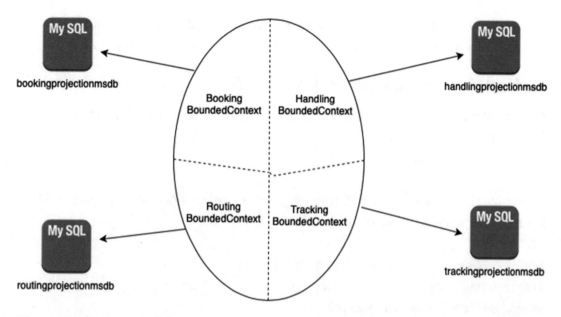

Figure 6-46. *Bounded Contexts – Projection Database on top of a MySQL Database*

Since our Datastore is going to be a SQL Database, our implementation for the Aggregate Projection Class would be based on JPA (Java Persistence API).

Let us walk through an implementation of an Aggregate Projection Class, the "*Cargo Summary*" projection. This projection uses the "*cargo_summary_projection*" table which is maintained in a MySql Database named "*bookingprojectiondb*".

The Projection needs to provide the following details of a booked cargo:

- Booking ID

- Routing Status (whether the cargo has been routed or not)

- Transport Status (whether the cargo is at port or on a vessel)

- Origin Location

- Destination Location

- Arrival Deadline

Again, the projection needs can differ based on the use case. The Cargo Summary projection is used by external consumers to get a quick snapshot of what is going on with a cargo.

Listing 6-26 depicts the Cargo Summary Projection implemented as a regular JPA Entity. We keep it within the domain model within the *"**projections**"* package:

Listing 6-26. Cargo Aggregate JPA Entity

```
package com.practicalddd.cargotracker.bookingms.domain.projections;
import javax.persistence.*;
import java.util.Date;
/**
 * Projection class for the Cargo Aggregate implemented as a regular JPA
Entity. Contains a summary of the Cargo Aggregate
 */
@Entity //Annotation to mark as a JPA Entity
@Table(name="cargo_summary_projection") //Table Name Mapping
@NamedQueries({ //Named Queries
        @NamedQuery(name = "CargoSummary.findAll",
                query = "Select c from CargoSummary c"),
        @NamedQuery(name = "CargoSummary.findByBookingId",
                query = "Select c from CargoSummary c where c.booking_id =
:bookingId"),
        @NamedQuery(name = "Cargo.getAllBookingIds",
                query = "Select c.booking_id from CargoSummary c") })
public class CargoSummary {
    @Id
    private String booking_id;
    @Column
    private String transport_status;
    @Column
    private String routing_status;
    @Column
    private String spec_origin_id;
    @Column
    private String spec_destination_id;
    @Temporal(TemporalType.DATE)
    private Date deadline;
    protected CargoSummary(){
```

```java
        this.setBooking_id(null);
    }
    public CargoSummary(String booking_id,
                        String transport_status,
                        String routing_status,
                        String spec_origin_id,
                        String spec_destination_id,
                        Date deadline){
        this.setBooking_id(booking_id);
        this.setTransport_status(transport_status);
        this.setRouting_status(routing_status);
        this.setSpec_origin_id(spec_origin_id);
        this.setSpec_destination_id(spec_destination_id);
        this.setDeadline(new Date());
    }
    public String getBooking_id() {    return booking_id;}
    public void setBooking_id(String booking_id) {this.booking_id =
    booking_id;}
    public String getTransport_status() {return transport_status; }
    public void setTransport_status(String transport_status) { this.
    transport_status = transport_status;}
    public String getRouting_status() {return routing_status;}
    public void setRouting_status(String routing_status) {this.routing_
    status = routing_status; }
    public String getSpec_origin_id() { return spec_origin_id;   }
    public void setSpec_origin_id(String spec_origin_id) {this.spec_origin_
    id = spec_origin_id; }
    public String getSpec_destination_id() {return spec_destination_id;}
    public void setSpec_destination_id(String spec_destination_id) {this.
    spec_destination_id = spec_destination_id; }
    public Date getDeadline() { return deadline;}
    public void setDeadline(Date deadline) {this.deadline = deadline;}
}
```

Figure 6-47 depicts the UML diagram for the Cargo Summary Aggregate Projection Class.

CargoSummary
+ booking_Id : String + routing_status: RoutingStatus + spec_origin_id: String + spec_destination_id: String + deadline: Date

Figure 6-47. *Class diagram for the Cargo Summary Aggregate Projection class*

With the Projection class mapped to a JPA Entity and a corresponding table, let us move to the Query layer.

Query Handlers

Queries are sent to a Bounded Context to retrieve the Aggregate state of the Bounded Context via Aggregate Projections. Implementing Query Handling involves the following:

Identification/implementation of Queries

Identification/implementation of Query Handlers to process Commands

Identification of Queries

To recap, Aggregate Projections represent the state of an Aggregate. An Aggregate Projection needs a Query Layer to enable external parties to consume the Projection Data. Identification of Queries revolves around any operations that are interested in the Aggregate Projection Data.

For example, the Booking Bounded Context has the following requirements from external consumers via the Cargo Summary Projection which has the required data to satisfy these requirements:

- Summary for an individual cargo

- List of summaries for all cargos

- List of Booking Identifiers for all cargos

Implementation of Queries

Implementing the identified Queries within Axon is done using regular POJOs. For every identified query, we would need to implement a *Query class* and a *Query Result class*. The Query class is the actual query that needs to be executed along with the criteria of execution, while the Query Result class is the result of the execution of the query.

Let us look at examples to explain this further. Consider the query that we have identified for getting the summary for an individual cargo. We will name it as "CargoSummaryQuery" and the result of the Query Execution class "CargoSummaryResult".

Listing 6-27 depicts the CargoSummaryQuery class. The name of the class conveys the intent, and it has a single constructor which takes in the Booking Id, that is, the criteria for executing the query:

Listing 6-27. CargoSummaryQuery implementation

```
package com.practicalddd.cargotracker.bookingms.domain.queries;

/**
 * Implementation of Cargo Summary Query class. It takes in a Booking Id
   which is the criteria for the query
 */
public class CargoSummaryQuery {
    private String bookingId; //Criteria of the Query
    public CargoSummaryQuery(String bookingId){
        this.bookingId = bookingId;
    }
    @Override
    public String toString() { return "Cargo Summary for Booking Id" +
    bookingId; }
}
```

There are no complications here – simple POJO which carries the intent and the criteria of the Query.

We then implement the "CargoSummaryResult" class which contains the result of the execution, in this case the CargoSummaryProjection.

Listing 6-28 depicts the same:

Listing 6-28. CargoSummaryResult implementation

```
package com.practicalddd.cargotracker.bookingms.domain.queries;
import com.practicalddd.cargotracker.bookingms.domain.projections.CargoSummary;
/**
 * Implementation of the Cargo Summary Result class which contains the
```

```
 * results of the execution of the CargoSummaryQuery. The result contains
 * data from the CargoSummary Projection
 */
public class CargoSummaryResult {
    private final CargoSummary cargoSummary;
    public CargoSummaryResult(CargoSummary cargoSummary) { this.
    cargoSummary = cargoSummary; }
    public CargoSummary getCargoSummary() { return cargoSummary;}
}
```

We now have implemented the **Query Class** (Cargo Summary) which has the **Query Intent** (Get the Cargo Summary) along with the **Query Criteria** (The Cargo's Booking Id).

Let us look at how to implement the handling of the Query.

Implementation of Query Handlers

As we had Command Handlers to handle Commands, similarly we have Query Handlers to handle Query instructions. Implementation of Query Handlers involves identifying Components which can handle Queries. Unlike Commands which were placed on the Aggregates itself, Query Handlers are placed on routines within regular Spring Boot components. Axon provides an aptly named Annotation "**@QueryHandler**" to help annotate routines within components marked as Query handlers.

Listing 6-29 depicts the "**CargoAggregateQueryHandler**" which handles all the queries against the Cargo Summary Projection for the Cargo Aggregate. We have two Query Handlers within this component, one for handling the *CargoSummaryQuery* and the other for the *ListCargoSummariesQuery*.

The query handlers

- Take the Queries (*CargoSummaryQuery, ListCargoSummariesQuery*) as input

- Execute named JPA queries against the CargoSummaryProjection JPA Entity

- Return back the results (*CargoSummaryResult, ListCargoSummaryResult)*

Listing 6-29 demonstrates the implementation of the Cargo Aggregate Query Handler:

Listing 6-29. CargoAggregateQueryHandler implementation

```
package com.practicalddd.cargotracker.bookingms.domain.queryhandlers;
import com.practicalddd.cargotracker.bookingms.domain.projections.
CargoSummary;
import com.practicalddd.cargotracker.bookingms.domain.queries.
CargoSummaryQuery;
import com.practicalddd.cargotracker.bookingms.domain.queries.
CargoSummaryResult;
import com.practicalddd.cargotracker.bookingms.domain.queries.
ListCargoSummariesQuery;
import com.practicalddd.cargotracker.bookingms.domain.queries.
ListCargoSummaryResult;
import org.axonframework.queryhandling.QueryHandler;
import org.slf4j.Logger;
import org.slf4j.LoggerFactory;
import org.springframework.stereotype.Component;
import javax.persistence.EntityManager;
import javax.persistence.Query;
import java.lang.invoke.MethodHandles;

/**
 * Class which acts as the Query Handler for all queries related to the
   Cargo Summary Projection
 */
@Component
public class CargoAggregateQueryHandler {

    private final static Logger logger = LoggerFactory.
    getLogger(MethodHandles.lookup().lookupClass());
    private final EntityManager entityManager;

    public CargoAggregateQueryHandler(EntityManager entityManager){
        this.entityManager = entityManager;
    }

    /**
     * Query Handler Query which returns the Cargo Summary for a Specific Query
```

```
 * @param cargoSummaryQuery
 * @return CargoSummaryResult
 */
@QueryHandler
public CargoSummaryResult handle(CargoSummaryQuery cargoSummaryQuery) {
    logger.info("Handling {}", cargoSummaryQuery);

    Query jpaQuery = entityManager.createNamedQuery("CargoSummary.
    findByBookingId", CargoSummary.class).setParameter("bookingId",
    cargoSummaryQuery.getBookingId());

    CargoSummaryResult result = new CargoSummaryResult((CargoSummary)
    jpaQuery.getSingleResult());
    logger.info("Returning {}", result);
    return result;
}
/**
 * Query Handler for the Query which returns all Cargo summaries
 * @param listCargoSummariesQuery
 * @return CargoSummaryResult
 */
@QueryHandler
public ListCargoSummaryResult handle(ListCargoSummariesQuery
listCargoSummariesQuery) {
    logger.info("Handling {}", listCargoSummariesQuery);

    Query jpaQuery = entityManager.createNamedQuery("CardSummary.
    findAll", CargoSummary.class);
    jpaQuery.setFirstResult(listCargoSummariesQuery.getOffset());
    jpaQuery.setMaxResults(listCargoSummariesQuery.getLimit());
    ListCargoSummaryResult result = new
    ListCargoSummaryResult(jpaQuery.getResultList());

    return result;
}
}
```

Figure 6-48 depicts the UML diagram for the Cargo Aggregate Query Handler Class.

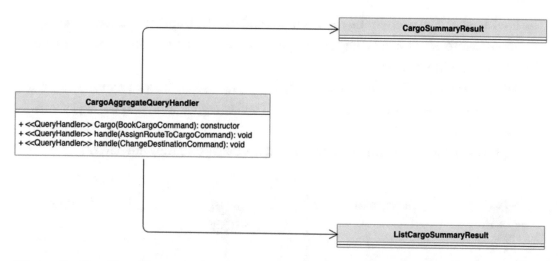

Figure 6-48. *Class diagram for the Cargo Aggregate Query Handler class*

Here is a short note about queries before we round up the implementation of Aggregate projections.

Axon provides three types of Query implementations:

- ***Point to Point*** – Our examples above have been based on Point-to-Point queries where each query has a corresponding Query Handler. The result classes are actually wrapped into a CompletableFuture<T> by Axon, but it is abstracted from the developer.

- ***Scatter Gather Queries*** - In this type, the query is sent to all the handlers subscribed to this query, and a Stream of results is returned which is then composed and sent to the client.

- ***Subscription Queries*** - This is an advanced query handling option provided by the Axon Framework. It enables the client to get the initial state of the Aggregate Projection it wants to query and stay up to date with the changes the projection data undergoes over a period of time.

This rounds up the implementation of Aggregate Projections.

Sagas

The final aspect of implementing the Domain Model is the implementation of Sagas. As explained before, Sagas can be implemented in two ways – via Choreography of Events or via Orchestration of Events.

Before we step into the implementation details, let us look back at a simplistic view of the various business flows within the Cargo Tracker Application and the Sagas that they fall within.

Figure 6-49 depicts the Business Flows and the Sagas that they are part of.

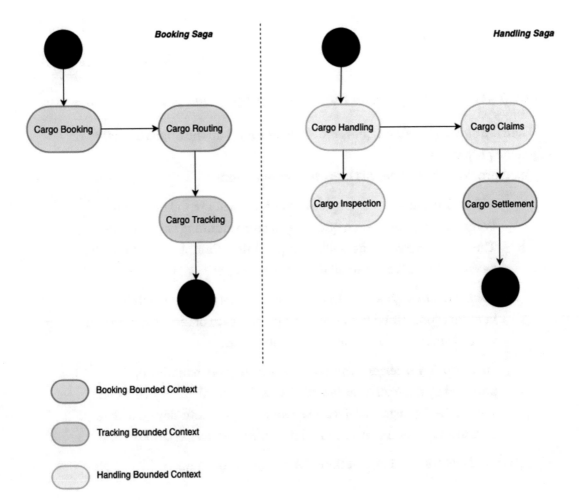

Figure 6-49. *Business Flows and the Sagas they are part of*

The Booking Saga involves the business operations within Cargo Booking, Cargo Routing, and Cargo Tracking. It starts with the cargo being booked and its subsequent routing and finally ends with the Tracking Identifier allocated to the booked cargo. This Tracking Identifier is used by the customers to track the progress of the cargo.

The Handling Saga involves the business operations within Cargo Handling, Inspection, Claims, and Final Settlement. It starts with the cargo being handled at the ports where it undergoes a voyage and claimed by the customer at the final destination and ends with the final settlement of the cargo (e.g., penalty for late delivery).

Both these sagas can be implemented either via Choreography or Orchestration. We will implement the Booking Saga which by example can be used to implement the Handling Saga too with the focus on the orchestration implementation using the Axon Framework's built-in support.

Before we step into the implementation, let us detail out the various Commands, Events, and Event Handlers of the Booking Saga.

Figure 6-50 depicts this.

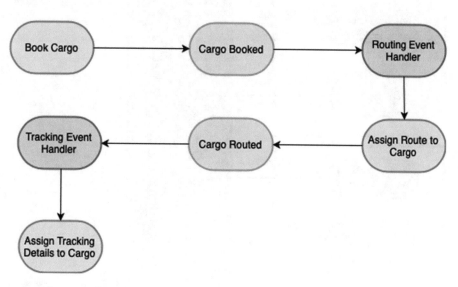

Figure 6-50. *The Booking Saga*

This is essentially a representation of the implementation using a choreography approach wherein we have Commands being Invoked, Events being raised, and Event Handlers processing events in a chain until the final event is handled.

The implementation of the Orchestration approach differs significantly wherein we have a central component that handles the events and subsequent invocation of Commands. In other words, we move the responsibility of handling events and invoking commands away from individual event handlers to a central component which performs the same.

Figure 6-51 depicts the orchestration approach.

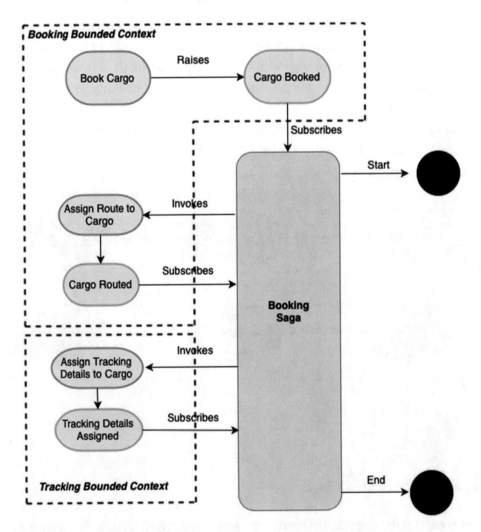

Figure 6-51. *The orchestration approach*

Let us walk through the implementation steps followed by the code:

- We denote the name of our Saga, that is, in this case, we denote our Saga as the Booking Saga.

- After the processing of the **Book Cargo Command**, the **Cargo Booked Event** is raised.

- The **Booking Saga** subscribes to the **Cargo Booked Event** and kick-starts the Saga process.

- The **Booking Saga** sends an instruction to process the **Assign Route to Cargo Command.** This command raises the **Cargo Routed Event.**

- The **Booking Saga** subscribes to the **Cargo Routed Event** and then sends an instruction to process the **Assign Tracking Details to Cargo Command.** This command raises the **Tracking Details Assigned Event.**

- The Booking Saga subscribes to the **Tracking Details Assigned Event** and since there are **no more Commands** to be processed decides to **end the saga.**

As seen, the centralized Saga component now takes over the responsibility of the entire coordination and sequencing of Commands and Events across multiple Bounded Contexts. None of the Domain Model Objects within the Bounded Contexts are aware that they are participating in a Saga process. In addition, they do not need to subscribe to events from other Bounded Contexts to participate in a transaction. They rely on the Saga to do so centrally.

The orchestration-based saga is a very powerful way of implementing distributed transactions in a microservices architecture due to its inherent delinked nature which helps in

- Isolating Distributed Transactions to a dedicated component

- Monitoring and tracing the flow of Distributed Transactions

- Fine-tuning and improving the flow of Distributed Transactions

The code for a Saga is implemented through the various annotations that Axon provides. The steps are outlined as follows:

- We take a regular POJO and mark it with a Stereotype annotation (*@Saga*) which denotes that this class acts as a Saga component.

- As stated, the Saga responds to Events and invokes Commands. The Axon Framework provides a saga-specific event handler annotation to handle events (*@SagaEventHandler*). Just like regular event handlers, these are placed on routines within the Saga class. Every Saga Event Handler needs to be provided with an **association property**. This property helps the Axon Framework to map the Saga to a particular instance of the Aggregate which is participating in the Saga.

- Invoking of Commands is done the standard Axon way, that is, utilizing the Command Gateway to invoke the Command.

- The final part is to implement the lifecycle methods to the Saga component (Start Saga, Stop Saga). The Axon Framework provides the "*@StartSaga*" annotation to denote the start of the Saga and "*SagaLifecycle.end()*" to end the Saga.

Listing 6-30 depicts the implementation of the Booking Saga:

Listing 6-30. Booking Saga implementation

```
package com.practicalddd.cargotracker.booking.application.internal.
sagaparticipants;
import com.practicalddd.cargotracker.booking.application.internal.
commandgateways.CargoBookingService;
import com.practicalddd.cargotracker.booking.domain.commands.
AssignRouteToCargoCommand;
import com.practicalddd.cargotracker.booking.domain.commands.
AssignTrackingDetailsToCargoCommand;
import com.practicalddd.cargotracker.booking.domain.events.
CargoBookedEvent;
import com.practicalddd.cargotracker.booking.domain.events.
CargoRoutedEvent;
```

```
import com.practicalddd.cargotracker.booking.domain.events.
CargoTrackedEvent;
import org.axonframework.commandhandling.gateway.CommandGateway;
import org.axonframework.modelling.saga.SagaEventHandler;
import org.axonframework.modelling.saga.SagaLifecycle;
import org.axonframework.modelling.saga.StartSaga;
import org.axonframework.spring.stereotype.Saga;
import org.slf4j.Logger;
import org.slf4j.LoggerFactory;

import java.lang.invoke.MethodHandles;
import java.util.UUID;

/**
 * The Booking Saga Manager is the implementation of the Booking saga.
 * The Saga starts when the Cargo Booked Event is raised
 * The Saga ends when the Tracking Details have been assigned to the Cargo
 */
@Saga //Stereotype Annotation depicting this as a Saga
public class BookingSagaManager {

    private final static Logger logger = LoggerFactory.
getLogger(MethodHandles.lookup().lookupClass());
    private CommandGateway commandGateway;
    private CargoBookingService cargoBookingService;
    /**
     * Dependencies for the Saga Manager
     * @param commandGateway
     */
    public BookingSagaManager(CommandGateway commandGateway,CargoBooking
Service cargoBookingService){
        this.commandGateway = commandGateway;
        this.cargoBookingService = cargoBookingService;
    }
```

```
/**
 * Handle the Cargo Booked Event, Start the Saga and invoke the Assign
 Route to Cargo Command
 * @param cargoBookedEvent
 */
@StartSaga //Annotation indicating the Start of the Saga
@SagaEventHandler(associationProperty = "bookingId")
// Saga specific annotation to handle an Event
public void handle(CargoBookedEvent cargoBookedEvent){

    logger.info("Handling the Cargo Booked Event within the Saga");

    //Send the Command to assign a route to the Cargo
    commandGateway.send(new AssignRouteToCargoCommand(cargoBookedEvent.
                        getBookingId(),
                                    cargoBookingService.getLegs
                                    ForRoute(cargoBookedEvent.
                                    getRouteSpecification())));

}
/**
 * Handle the Cargo Routed Event and invoke the Assign Tracking Details
 to Cargo Command
 * @param cargoRoutedEvent
 */
@SagaEventHandler(associationProperty = "bookingId")
public void handle(CargoRoutedEvent cargoRoutedEvent){
    logger.info("Handling the Cargo Routed Event within the Saga");
    String trackingId = UUID.randomUUID().toString();
    // Generate a random tracking identifier
    SagaLifecycle.associateWith("trackingId",trackingId);
    //Send the COmmand to assign tracking details to the Cargo
    commandGateway.send(new AssignTrackingDetailsToCargoCommand(
        cargoRoutedEvent.getBookingId(),trackingId));
}
```

```
/**
 * Handle the Cargo Tracked Event and end the Saga
 * @param cargoTrackedEvent
 */
@SagaEventHandler(associationProperty = "trackingId")
public void handle(CargoTrackedEvent cargoTrackedEvent) {
    SagaLifecycle.end(); // End the Saga as this is the last Event to
                         be handled
}
}
```

Implementation Summary

This completes the implementation of the Domain Model with the Axon Framework.
Figure 6-52 depicts the summary of the implementation.

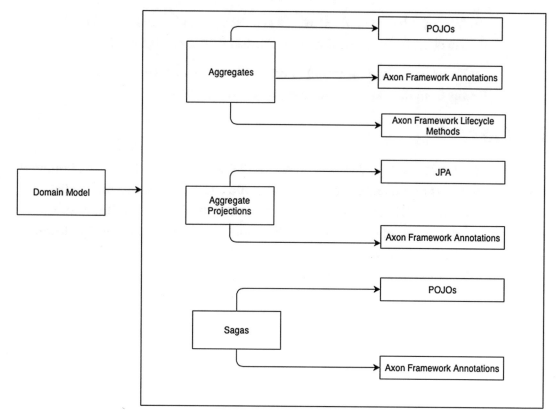

Figure 6-52. *Domain Model implementation summary*

Implementing Domain Model Services with Axon

To recap, Domain Model services provide supporting services to the Domain Model (e.g., to facilitate external parties to consume the Domain Model, to help the Domain Model to communicate to External Repositories). The implementations are done using a combination of the capabilities provided by Spring Boot and what the Axon Framework provides. We need to implement the following types of Domain Model Services:

- Inbound Services

- Application Services

Inbound Services

Inbound services (or Inbound Adaptors as denoted in the Hexagonal Architectural Pattern) act as the outermost gateway for our core Domain Model.

Within our Cargo Tracker application, we provide the following inbound services:

- An API Layer based on REST which is used by external consumers to invoke operations on the Bounded Context (Commands/Queries)

- An Event Handling Layer implemented by Axon which consumes Events from the Event Bus and processes them

REST API

The responsibility of the REST API is to receive HTTP requests on behalf of the Bounded Context from external consumers. This request could be for Commands or Queries. The responsibility of the REST API layer is to translate it into the Command/Query Model recognized by the Bounded Context's Domain Model and delegate it to the Application Services Layer to further process it.

Figure 6-53 depicts the REST API flows/responsibilities.

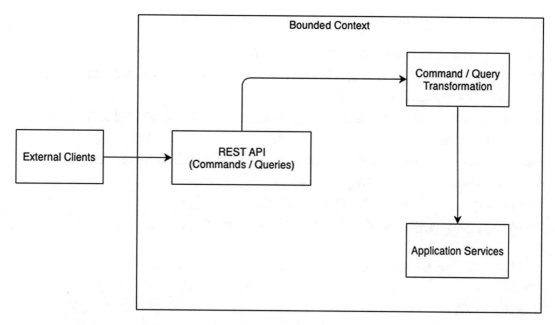

Figure 6-53. *REST API flows/responsibilities*

Implementation of the REST API is utilizing the REST capabilities provided by Spring Web. To recap earlier in the chapter, we added this dependency for our Spring Boot applications.

Let us walk through an example of a REST API. Listing 6-31 depicts the REST API/ Controller for our Cargo Booking Command:

- It has a single POST method that accepts a BookCargoResource which is the input payload to the API.

- It has a dependency on the CargoBookingService which is an Application services (see later).

- It transforms the Resource Data (BookCargoResource) to the Command Model (BookCargoCommand) using an Assembler utility class (BookCargoCommandDTOAssembler).

- After transforming, it delegates the process to the CargoBookingService for further processing.

Listing 6-31. CargoBookingController implementation

```
package com.practicalddd.cargotracker.bookingms.interfaces.rest;
import com.practicalddd.cargotracker.bookingms.interfaces.rest.transform.
assembler.BookCargoCommandDTOAssembler;
import com.practicalddd.cargotracker.bookingms.interfaces.rest.transform.
dto.BookCargoResource;
import com.practicalddd.cargotracker.bookingms.application.internal.
commandgateways.CargoBookingService;
import org.springframework.http.HttpStatus;
import org.springframework.web.bind.annotation.*;
/**
 * REST API for the Book Cargo Command
 */
@RestController
@RequestMapping("/cargobooking")
public class CargoBookingController {
    private final CargoBookingService cargoBookingService;
// Application Service Dependency
    /**
     * Provide the dependencies
     * @param cargoBookingService
     */
    public CargoBookingController(CargoBookingService cargoBookingService){
        this.cargoBookingService = cargoBookingService;
    }
    /**
     * POST method to book a cargo
     * @param bookCargoCommandResource
     */
    @PostMapping
    @ResponseStatus(HttpStatus.CREATED)
    public void bookCargo(@RequestBody final BookCargoResource
    bookCargoCommandResource){
```

```
    cargoBookingService.bookCargo(BookCargoCommandDTOAssembler.toComman
    dFromDTO(bookCargoCommandResource));
  }
}
```

This rounds up the implementation of the REST API Inbound Services.

Event Handler

Event Handlers within a Bounded Context are responsible for handling Events that are subscribed by that Bounded Context. Event Handlers are responsible for transforming the Event Data to a model recognizable for further processing. Event Handlers generally delegate to an Application Services to process the event post-transformation.

Figure 6-54 depicts the Event Handler flows/responsibilities.

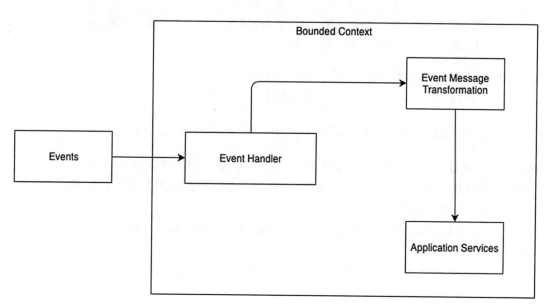

Figure 6-54. *Event Handler flows/responsibilities*

Implementation of Event Handlers is done by utilizing the Axon Framework Stereotype annotations (**@EventHandler**). These annotations are placed on routines within Regular Spring Services and contain the specific Event that the Event Handler is going to handle.

Let us walk through an example of an Event Handler. Listing 6-32 depicts the
Event Handler CargoProjectionsEventHandler. This Event Handler subscribes to state
change events from the Cargo Aggregate and accordingly updates the Cargo Aggregate
Projections (e.g., CargoSummary):

- The Event Handler class is annotated with a @Service annotation.

- It has a dependency on the CargoProjectionService which is an
  Application services (see later).

- It handles the CargoBookedEvent by marking the
  handleCargoBookedEvent() method within the handler class with
  the @EventHandler annotation.

- The handleCargoBookedEvent() uses the CargoBookedEvent as the
  Event payload.

- It transforms the Event Data (CargoBookedEvent) to the Aggregate
  Projection Model (CargoSummary).

- After transforming, it delegates the process to the
  CargoProjectionService for further processing.

Listing 6-32. CargoProjectionsEventHandler implementation

```
package com.practicalddd.cargotracker.bookingms.interfaces.events;
import com.practicalddd.cargotracker.bookingms.application.internal.
CargoProjectionService;
import com.practicalddd.cargotracker.bookingms.domain.events.
CargoBookedEvent;
import com.practicalddd.cargotracker.bookingms.domain.projections.
CargoSummary;
import org.axonframework.eventhandling.EventHandler;
import org.axonframework.eventhandling.Timestamp;
import org.slf4j.Logger;
import org.slf4j.LoggerFactory;
import org.springframework.stereotype.Service;

import javax.persistence.EntityManager;
import java.lang.invoke.MethodHandles;
import java.time.Instant;
```

```java
/**
 * Event Handlers for all events raised by the Cargo Aggregate
 */
@Service
public class CargoProjectionsEventHandler {
    private final static Logger logger = LoggerFactory.
    getLogger(MethodHandles.lookup().lookupClass());

    private CargoProjectionService cargoProjectionService; //Dependencies

    public CargoProjectionsEventHandler(CargoProjectionService
    cargoProjectionService) {
        this.cargoProjectionService = cargoProjectionService;
    }
    /**
     * EVent Handler for the Cargo Booked Event. Converts the Event Data to
     * the corresponding Aggregate Projection Model and delegates to the
     * Application Service to process it further
     * @param cargoBookedEvent
     * @param eventTimestamp
     */
    @EventHandler
    public void cargoBookedEventHandler(CargoBookedEvent cargoBookedEvent,
    @Timestamp Instant eventTimestamp) {
        logger.info("Applying {}", cargoBookedEvent.getBookingId());

        CargoSummary cargoSummary = new CargoSummary(cargoBookedEvent.
        getBookingId(),"","",
                "","",new java.util.Date());
        cargoProjectionService.storeCargoSummary(cargoSummary);
    }
}
```

This rounds up the implementation of the Inbound Services.

Application Services

Application Services act as a façade or a port between the Inbound Services and the Core Domain Model. Within an Axon Framework application, Application services within a Bounded Context are responsible for receiving requests from the Inbound Services and delegating them to the corresponding Gateways, that is, Commands are delegated to the Command Gateway, while Queries are delegated to the Query Gateway. Events are processed, and the results are persisted depending upon the output desired (e.g., Projections are persisted into a datastore).

Figure 6-55 depicts the responsibilities of the Application Services.

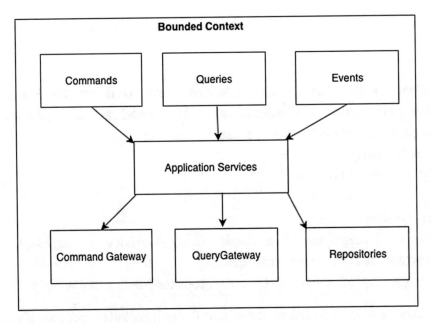

Figure 6-55. *The responsibilities of the Application services*

Listing 6-33 depicts the Cargo Booking Service class which is responsible for handling all Commands sent to the Booking Bounded Context:

Listing 6-33. Cargo Booking Service implementation

```
package com.practicalddd.cargotracker.bookingms.application.internal.
commandgateways;
import com.practicalddd.cargotracker.bookingms.domain.commands.
AssignRouteToCargoCommand;
```

```java
import com.practicalddd.cargotracker.bookingms.domain.commands.
BookCargoCommand;
import com.practicalddd.cargotracker.bookingms.domain.commands.
ChangeDestinationCommand;
import org.axonframework.commandhandling.gateway.CommandGateway;
import org.springframework.stereotype.Service;
/**
 * Application Service Class to Book a Cargo, Route a Cargo and Change the
 * Destination of a Cargo All Commands to the Cargo Aggregate are grouped
 * into this sevice class
 */
@Service
public class CargoBookingService {
    private final CommandGateway commandGateway;
    public CargoBookingService(CommandGateway commandGateway){
        this.commandGateway = commandGateway;
    }

    /**
     * Book a Cargo
     * @param bookCargoCommand
     */
    public void bookCargo(BookCargoCommand bookCargoCommand){
        commandGateway.send(bookCargoCommand); //Invocation of the Command
                                            gateway
    }
    /**
     * Change the Destination of a Cargo
     * @param changeDestinationCommand
     */
    public void changeDestinationOfCargo(ChangeDestinationCommand
    changeDestinationCommand) {
        commandGateway.send(changeDestinationCommand); //Invocation of the
                                            Command gateway
    }
```

```
/**
 * Assigns a Route to a Cargo
 * @param assignRouteToCargoCommand
 */
public void assignRouteToCargo(AssignRouteToCargoCommand
assignRouteToCargoCommand){
    commandGateway.send(assignRouteToCargoCommand); //Invocation of the
                                                    Command gateway

}
}
```

This rounds up the implementation of our Application Services and our Domain Model Services.

Summary

Summarizing our chapter

- We started by establishing the details about the Axon Platform including the Axon Framework and Axon Server.

- We did a deep dive into the development of the various DDD artifacts – first the domain model including Aggregates, Commands, and Queries using Spring Boot and the Axon Framework.

- We dove into details of the Event Sourcing pattern adopted by Axon.

- We rounded off by implementing the Domain Model Services using the capabilities provided by the Axon Framework.

Index

Q

@QueryHandler annotation, 289

Query handlers, domain model with Axon

@QueryHandler, 352

Cargo Aggregate, 352, 354, 355

queries

Aggregate projections, 350

Bounded Context, 350

CargoSummaryQuery class, 351

CargoSummaryResult class, 351, 352

point-to-point, 355

POJOs, 350

scatter gather queries, 355

subscription queries, 355

R

Retail banking services, 4

S

SagaManager, 294

Sagas, 13, 15, 30–32

Sagas, domain model with Axon

Booking Saga, 357, 360, 361, 363

business flows, 356

choreography approach, 357

code, implementation, 360

handling, 357

orchestration approach, 358, 359

Separate Bounded Contexts, 7, 8

@Service annotation, 272

@Service marker annotation, 255

Single bounded context, 7

@SpringBootApplication annotation, 199

Spring Cloud, 194

Spring platform

capabilities, 193

cloud, 194, 195

components, 194

contexts (*see* Bounded context)

core domain (*see* Domain model)

project portfolio, 190, 191

requirements, 192

State maintenance, Axon domain model

Aggregate, 331

Assign Route Command, 340

AssignRouteToCommandHandler, 338

Cargo Aggregate, 332, 339, 344

ChangeDestinationCommand, 340–342

command handlers, 337

@EventSourcingHandler, 331, 332, 341

first command, 333–336

process, Axon framework, 338, 339

RoutingStatus, 331, 338

state retrieval process, 343

@StreamListener annotation, 245

Sub-Domains/bounded contexts, 4

billing, 6

claims, 6

collections, 5

originations, 5

products, 6

servicing, 5

T, U

@TargetAggregateIdentifier, 323

Technology compatibility kits (TCKs), 40

Tracking activity class diagram, 28

@TransactionalEventListener
    annotation, 272

Transform package, 112

V, W, X, Y, Z

Value Objects, 10, 24

Voyage aggregate class diagram, 28